LINCOLN'S COUNSEL

LESSONS FROM AMERICA'S MOST PERSUASIVE SPEAKER

ARTHUR L. RIZER, III

LINCOLN'S COUNSEL

LESSONS FROM AMERICA'S MOST PERSUASIVE SPEAKER

**Defending Liberty
Pursuing Justice**

Printed in the United States of America.

14 13 12 11 10 5 4 3 2 1

Library of Congress Cataloging-in-Publication Data
Rizer, Arthur L.
Lincoln's counsel : lessons from American's most persuasive speaker / by Arthur L. Rizer III.
   p. cm.
   Includes bibliographical references and index.
   ISBN 978-1-61632-040-9
   1. Lincoln, Abraham, 1809–1865—Career in law. 2. Lincoln, Abraham, 1809–1865—Oratory. 3. Forensic oratory. 4. Lawyers—Illinois—Biography. I. Title.

   KF368.L52R59 2010
   352.23'80973—dc22

2010043428

To my Mother, Ann Rizer—you were my greatest cheerleader.

Contents

❧ CHAPTER 6
EVEN THE GREAT MAKE MISTAKES   165

ACKNOWLEDGMENTS

A majority of this book was drafted while I was deployed to Iraq as a Captain in the United States Army. Despite the horrors of war, I was always encouraged by the outstanding quality of our men and women in uniform—they truly are our country's greatest treasure. This book is dedicated to our soldiers, marines, sailors, and airmen, and a portion of the proceeds from this book will be donated to "Our Military Kids," a charity that sponsors military children while a parent is deployed.

I would like to thank my agent, E.J. McCarthy, and my editor, Erin Nevius, from ABA Book Publishing, for their help in getting this book published. I would also like to thank my friend, Pastor Tim Fisher, and his daughter Laura, and most importantly my father and my mentor, Arthur L. Rizer Jr., and my wife and best friend, Monique Rizer, for their input and help in editing this book.

PROLOGUE

Many books have been written about Lincoln; almost all of them about his presidency. However, for lawyers and persuasive speakers of all stripes, his years as a lawyer may offer more "lessons." This book attempts to analyze and extract some of those lessons, so that we might be able to improve our own careers by examining Lincoln's successes and failures. This is not a history book, but every attempt has been made to be historically accurate. Even if not proven to be true, some anecdotes are included if they illustrate the greater "truth" of Lincoln's style and personality.

Before Abraham Lincoln was called "Mr. President," he was called "counselor" and "esquire." Some consider him to be one of the nation's greatest attorneys and an enormously persuasive speaker. He spent more years practicing law than any other president, and his years in the legal profession were essential to his eventual election to the presidency.[1]

This book does not attempt to replace those books that describe his presidency, or that laud his tremendous achievements as president. Most Americans recognize President Abraham Lincoln as one of the greatest—perhaps *the* greatest—president the Unites States has had. His careful leadership during a war that claimed more American lives than any other probably preserved this nation. His title as "the Great Emancipator" is deserved (even though his role is more nuanced than most people understand), because as president, Lincoln acted honorably because it was the right thing to do. He built those skills and a sense of honor while serving as a lawyer.

Herbert Stern, a renowned trial attorney and former federal judge, once asked a rhetorical question: "would you rather (1) be head counsel in a case where you had mastered the facts, (2) try a case in an area wherein you have mastered the law, or (3) hire Abraham Lincoln to try the case for you?" The point was that a lawyer who can emulate Lincoln's skills of persuasion holds the key to legal greatness.

Many great lawyers come to be called "great" because of a single case—a pinnacle they never again achieve. Although he did not win every case he tried or participated in, Lincoln was widely recognized as one of the nation's foremost trial lawyers. He did not earn this reputation because of a single dramatic event. It was earned through consistent smart practice of the law in virtually every case he took on; sheer brilliance can be seen in several of his cases for which we have records.

During more than twenty-three years of practice in both state and federal courts, Lincoln handled more than five thousand cases. It is impossible to determine his win/loss record with precision because many case files were lost in the Great Chicago Fire of 1871, and others have succumbed to the ravages of time. However, what is known about his intact record suggests he did *not* have a remarkably impressive win rate. Of the eighty-seven cases argued before a judge without a jury for which there are extant records, verdicts were entered against Lincoln's clients 45 percent of the time. His numbers are slightly better with a jury present, winning forty-three of the eighty-two cases for which we have uncontaminated trial records.

These numbers do not seem to indicate that Lincoln was a powerhouse in the courtroom. However, this is an admittedly small sampling of his trial record, and it is not reasonable to equate his prowess for trial work from the 169 cases where court records exist—a mere .3 percent of the total five thousand cases he handled.

In order to see Lincoln's capacity for oral arguments and his capability to persuade, we must look past simple numbers. One Lincoln commentator said, "[d]efeats and victories in legal contests, depending as they do upon other antecedent facts and circumstances, are those ultimate results that may or may not prove anything in so far as the respective abilities of the contesting lawyers are concerned."[2] Any lawyer or persuasive speaker who has lost a slam-dunk case or an easy sale knows how true this statement is. Perhaps the best indicator of Lincoln's excellence in law is demonstrated by looking at his reputation in the legal community. In an era before multimedia, the single most important factor to the success of an attorney's practice was his standing in the community. Thus, Lincoln's client list is a powerful indicator of Lincoln's prowess.

Daniel Webster, one of the greatest attorneys of his time, hired Lincoln to represent him in a land dispute in Illinois. The Illinois Central Railroad also used Lincoln consistently for many years. Lincoln would not have gained Mr. Webster or the Illinois Central Railroad as clients if he were only batting .500. Indeed, Lincoln may have been the busiest lawyer of his time, arguing at least 172 cases in front of the Illinois Supreme Court and at least 1 in front of the United States Supreme Court, suggesting that he was extremely successful. Consuming such a heavy caseload also meant that Lincoln's less-talented colleagues struggled to make legal careers for themselves.

Other evidence suggests Lincoln was much more effective than indicated in the intact legal records. For instance, Stephen Logan, a prominent member of the bar, lost at least three appeals to Lincoln and was so impressed with Lincoln's capabilities in court that he asked him to join his firm as a junior partner—even with Lincoln's abilities in court, Logan would not have done this if Lincoln had had a mediocre win/loss record.

Above all, it was his presence in front of the jury, his mastery of facts, and his passion for the law that gave him the reputation of a great lawyer. All attorneys and persuasive speakers today, including salespeople, pastors, lobbyists, parents, teachers, and anybody else who spends their days convincing others they are right, can learn something from the greatest trial attorney of all time.

In addition to telling Lincoln's stories, this book takes "time-outs" to explicitly describe **lessons** (noted in bold face) we can glean from his life. Additionally, key lessons are collected at the end of chapters under "**Lessons Learned**." By examining Lincoln's triumphs, blunders, and God-given skills, this book attempts to help us learn from the best so that we can become better persuaders ourselves.

The idea for this book took root after I read the Gettysburg Address for what felt like the thousandth time. I was "forced" to memorize the Address in eighth grade by my history teacher, and it has stuck with me ever since. Since then I'd made it a point to read it a few times a year to make sure I could still sound smart at cocktail parties if the subject of Lincoln or great speeches ever came up (at which time, I would of course rattle it off). It was not until I started law school and was learning how to deliver a persuasive opening and closing statement that I realized how amazing a speech it really is. I was struck at how many rules on "how to write a persuasive closing argument" the Gettysburg Address follows.

This book was originally written as a short article to be published in a law journal; the article argued that students of persuasive speaking should look to the Gettysburg Address for learning points. While doing research for this paper, I became more and more aware of how powerful Lincoln was as a persuader, not only in the legal realm but also as a salesman, a politician, and even in his very brief stint as a soldier. As a young, aspiring trial lawyer, I was hooked—I read everything I could about Lincoln, making a journal about how I could become a better persuader and attorney by emulating his life and career. Those notes eventually became this book. While Lincoln's example was not the primary reason I entered into the practice of law, I'm sure that learning from him has made me a better trial attorney and a better persuader.

ॐ ॐ ॐ

Notes

1. AMERICA'S LAWYER-PRESIDENTS: FROM LAW OFFICE TO OVAL OFFICE 128 (Norman Gross ed., Northwestern Univ. Press 2004).

2. ALBERT A. WOLDMAN, LAWYER LINCOLN 247 (Carroll & Graf 2001) (1936).

CHAPTER 1

EDUCATING A GENIUS

To understand Lincoln's skill as a persuader, it is important to understand his education, and to understand his education, one must first understand his background and family.

In today's legal community, great credence is placed on formal education—the more elite, the better. This is a bit ironic considering many of our most revered lawyers were educated at relatively inconspicuous schools. In Lincoln's case, the road he took to become a lawyer was the most humble of all—self-education.

ॐ ॐ ॐ

Learning to Learn

The Lincoln family pedigree is one of pioneers and farmers who emigrated from Hingham, England, to Hingham, Massachusetts, and later to Kentucky. Lincoln's father, Thomas Lincoln, was a frontiersman who enjoyed the hard life of the wilderness. On June 12, 1806, Thomas Lincoln married Nancy Hanks. Regrettably, almost nothing is known about Lincoln's mother. She came from an impoverished family in Virginia and is said to have been thin, tall, and dark-haired—all three attributes which she obviously passed on to her son. Soon after their marriage, the newlyweds moved from Hardin County, Kentucky, to Elizabethtown, Kentucky. In Elizabethtown, Thomas Lincoln made a living as a handyman and part-time carpenter.

In 1807, the Lincoln family grew to include a daughter, Sarah. The small family then moved to the south fork of Nolin Creek, what is now known as Hodgenville, Kentucky, where Thomas built a small cabin. It was there on February 12, 1809, that Nancy bore a son they named Abraham. Abraham was named after his grandfather, who was killed by a Native American while he was building a farm near Louisville, Kentucky. (Lincoln's brother, Thomas Lincoln, was later born in this same little log cabin but died in infancy.)

When Lincoln was two years old, the family moved to another farm in Kentucky, on Knob Creek. Five years later, the future president and his family moved to Pigeon Creek, in what is now known as Gentryville, Indiana. In all, the family moved four times during Lincoln's childhood.

Lincoln's parents lacked a formal education. His father, Thomas Lincoln, was, in his son's words, a "wandering labor boy, [who] grew up literally without education. He never did more in the way of writing than to bunglingly sign his own name." Lincoln's mother was wholly illiterate, to the point that she signed her name with an "X."

Lincoln's parents' lack of schooling aside, they taught their son the values that molded him into the man he was. As Baptists, they were abolitionists, which is likely where Lincoln's disdain of slavery was born. In fact, it was partly because of Thomas Lincoln's absolute opposition to slavery and not wanting to live in a slave state that the family moved to Indiana from Kentucky.

The move did more than influence Abraham's opinion on slavery; it also was one of the early events that fashioned his views on the law. Another reason Thomas was anxious to move out of Kentucky was his constant legal disputes over his claims to land, which he ultimately lost.[1]

Perhaps this issue impressed on the young Lincoln the understanding that knowledge is power, especially knowledge of the law.

On October 5, 1818, Lincoln's mother died from "milk sick," an illness that spread throughout the frontier. Milk sick was caused by drinking poisoned milk from cows that had eaten the snakeroot plant. Her death was a huge blow to Abraham, who suffered from bouts of depression throughout the remainder of his life.

In 1819, Thomas Lincoln left his family in Indiana and traveled to Elizabethtown, Kentucky, in search of a wife. He found and married Sarah Bush Johnston, a widow with three children, and took the family, old and new, back to the farm at Pigeon Creek. Abraham called his new mother Aunt Sarah and described her as his "angel mother." It was Sarah who spurred his quest for an education; she was continuously encouraging him to seek knowledge, because she understood that it was an escape from their harsh surroundings to a better life.

When Lincoln was not clearing the forest of his father's farm with an ax or splitting rails (the origin of his first presidential campaign nickname, "Rail Splitter"), he attended "ABC schools," which were frontier schools that taught basic reading, writing, and arithmetic. These schools were substandard by any stretch of the imagination. The job of "teacher" was given to someone in the community who could read and write. Because paper currency was somewhat rare, teachers were often paid by the parents of schoolchildren with produce, meat, and animal skins. Class was held in a one-room log cabin; there was no fixed school year, as students went to school whenever there was an available teacher.

Lincoln first attended school in the winter of 1815 at the age of six. Much frontier schooling was conducted in the winter, when students were not needed for farm chores. Lincoln walked four miles to school, where his fellow classmates were of all ages. He attended a formal school in Kentucky and Illinois when he was 6, 7, 11, 13, and 15; however, the entire amount of schooling he received did not total more than one full year. Among Lincoln's teachers were Andrew Crawford, Azel W. Dorsey, and a man named Mr. Sweeney.

People who knew Lincoln during this time have attested that his minimal time in school had more to do with the primitive education system than his ability or desire to attend. It is said that it was not long before Lincoln was ahead of his masters, as is evidenced by his later writing that there was "absolutely nothing to excite ambition for education." Thus, when Lincoln's teachers could teach him no more, he attended classes no more. From this experience, Lincoln learned the critical **lesson** that a person must have the ability to recognize that he has learned everything of value from a place or event and it is time to move on. **This concept can**

**also be applied to a single speech: a successful persuader must
recognize when his or her point is made and move on**. Needlessly
dwelling on an issue drowns your argument.

Early in life Lincoln could read and do arithmetic. Books and other
printed materials that made it to the western frontier were of importance
and were highly valued. He became intimately familiar with the Lincoln
family Bible because it was the most readily accessible book. He read plays
when he could, particularly the Greek tragedies and Shakespeare. He also
read the nineteenth-century equivalent of "self-help books" about the
human moral compass, along with any history books he could get his
hands on. Specifically, we know that Lincoln read two books by M. L.
Weems: *The Life of George Washington; With Curious Anecdotes, Equally
Honorable To Himself, and Exemplary To His Young Countrymen* (1837)
and *The Life and Memorable Actions of George Washington* (1800). These
books became Lincoln's favorites and filled his mind with the grandeur
of George Washington and the Founding Fathers; it was from this that
he gained his immense reverence for the first president and established his
own principles about what the United States was and what it could be.

While living in Indiana, Lincoln borrowed a copy of the *Revised Statutes of Indiana* from David Turnham, a prosperous farmer and constable
who was connected with his local township's justice of the peace. As an
officer of the law, Turnham kept a copy of the revised code and gener-
ously lent the book, which was more than four hundred pages long, to
the young and ambitious Lincoln. Here, Lincoln found not only Indiana's
statutory law but also the Declaration of Independence and the Constitution of the United States.

With his stepmother's encouragement, Lincoln's ambition for learning on his own grew. He would pore over books, and collect and read
any newspapers he could obtain. But Lincoln did more than just read; his
stepmother noted his systematic consumption of any information with
which he came into contact. Interestingly, Lincoln did not keep a formal
diary of his life's experiences; however, when he would come across a
verse that he particularly enjoyed, he would write it down in a pseudo
journal called his "copy book" and repeat the passage until he had it
memorized. There is a **subtle lesson learned here: good ideas and
passages are reusable**. By committing an inspiring quote or a good idea
to memory, you will be able to use it when you least expect it and most
need it. This is an acceptable version of intellectual plagiarism.

Those who knew Lincoln would first describe him as an insatiable
reader. Mr. John Hanks, who lived with the Lincoln family, remembered
Abraham as "a constant and voracious reader." David Turnham said that
he read everything in the small community, "never forgetting what he

read." He considered books precious and would walk miles to borrow a piece of literature; it was rumored that once he walked twenty miles to borrow a book. Lincoln once said that his "best friend is the man who will give me a book I haven't read."

As Lincoln developed his mind, he also developed a formidable physique, standing at six feet four inches by his nineteenth birthday. Despite his abilities with an ax and notable strength, he loathed farm work. Often his father mistook his preference for intellectual rather than physical labor as laziness, making his zealous reading a point of friction between them. Lincoln's cousin, Dennis Hanks, described him as a "stubborn reader, his father having sometimes to slash him for neglecting his work by reading." His cousin went on to say that, "I never saw Abe after he was 12, that he didn't have a book in his hand or in his pocket. It just didn't seem natural to see a guy read like that." His father once said that his son was fooling himself with getting an education, but once something got into his son's head "it can't be got out."

It is important to note that it is not totally clear how much truth to attribute to the accounts that Thomas frowned on Abraham's efforts to obtain an education. Specifically, Sarah Lincoln said that her husband would not prevent or stop Abraham from reading if at all possible. More interesting, she said that because of his obvious lack of an education, Thomas wanted his son to possess the power an education wielded and actually encouraged him in the simple ways he could.

Lincoln's sister taught and encouraged him to write, in addition to reading. He would often write poems after he tired of reading or arithmetic. He became such an accomplished writer with agreeable handwriting that he was often asked by his neighbors to compose letters for them.

His public speaking education started when, at the age of 15, Lincoln would stand on a tree stump after Sunday worship and, in jest, repeat the sermon almost word for word, in addition to performing some of this own skits. Later in life, Lincoln joined a literary and debating club that met weekly, where he practiced formulating and presenting an argument quickly. In these practices he gained the reputation of a strong debater and public speaker.

Despite rumors of punishment by his father and being labeled by some friends, family, and employers as "lazy," Lincoln continued to be an assiduous learner. In a time when a son usually followed in his father's footsteps, Lincoln decided at an early age that he would rather not be a farmer and instead started walking his own path.

ε❧ ε❧ ε❧

On-the-Job Education

The Lincolns' Pigeon Creek farm was near the Ohio River, which afforded Abraham opportunities to work on the water. When Lincoln was 19, he took a job from James Gentry, a local merchant, to pilot a cargo ferry flatboat down the Mississippi River on journeys as far as New Orleans. These trips to the South were Lincoln's introduction to both big city life and the horrors of slavery. On one trip, after witnessing slavery first hand, he said that he would "do what he could to stop it"—a foreshadowing statement if ever there was one.

Lincoln also got a taste for being an advocate while working on the river. He launched a small enterprise near the farm, ferrying passengers to riverboats waiting in midstream. A local business owned and operated by the Dill brothers had a similar business, which carried travelers across the river and saw Lincoln's business as a threat. Claiming that they had the exclusive right to transport passengers, they tricked Lincoln into accompanying them to the home of Squire Samuel Pate, the Justice of the Peace. At Pate's home the brothers swore a warrant against Lincoln for violating the "Act Respecting the Establishment of Ferries."

The Dills testified that they had witnessed Lincoln carrying commuters from the Indiana shore to steamboats that had stopped in the river, thus violating the Act. The young Lincoln was to some extent intimidated by the case against him, but gained his wits quickly. He admitted that he did indeed take customers to awaiting steamboats and admitted he had no idea it was against the law. But, never defeated, he asked a question: even if the Dill brothers held a monopoly on ferrying passengers *across* the river—did they also hold a monopoly for carrying passengers *midstream*? The brothers contended that this was a mere technicality of the law and that Lincoln had clearly violated the act, but the Justice of the Peace was not convinced—he reread the statute in question and determined that indeed it concerned trans-river boats exclusively, and prohibited individuals without licenses to carry a fare over a river where there were public ferries available. "This was not an offense within the contemplation of the statute, Squire Pate reasoned; and despite the angry protests of the Kentucky ferryman, he dismissed the warrant."[2]

Pate was impressed with Lincoln's on-the-spot legal argument and promoted the idea that the young Lincoln should study the law. While this was not the culminating event that sparked his aspiration to become a lawyer, the encounter did encourage Lincoln's love of learning and he began to absorb any legal material he could get his hands on. Lincoln said that the more he read, "the more intensely interested I became. Never in my whole life was my mind so thoroughly absorbed."

In 1830, the Lincoln family, in the frontiersmen spirit, moved to the Illinois countryside. They settled in an area near what is now Decatur, Illinois, on the Sangamon River. It was there that Lincoln got his first taste of politics—giving a speech in response to a local candidate, John F. Posey.[3] As the story goes, in the summer of 1830, Lincoln, then only 21 years old, came to Decatur from a nearby farm where he was helping with the daily labor. Lincoln was persuaded to give the speech by the crowd who were disappointed because candidate Posey did not hand out booze during his speech, as was expected in the day. Lincoln stood barefoot on top of a box to respond to Posey's speech, beginning his speech with his usual modesty—pleading with his friends in the crowd not to laugh if he "broke down." After the opening remarks, Lincoln discussed questions of politics, specifically addressing the navigation of the Sangamon River. After the speech, Posey approached Lincoln and asked him where he had learned so much about politics. Lincoln told him his knowledge was from simple reading. Posey encouraged Lincoln to "persevere," likely referring to a future political career.

A year later, when Abraham Lincoln was 22, he set out on his own and settled in the small—but promising—village of New Salem, Illinois, where he lived from 1831 to 1837. The population of the city was one hundred souls, the biggest town he had ever lived in. When he arrived, he referred to himself as a "friendless, uneducated, penniless boy—a piece of floating drift wood."

While in New Salem, Lincoln put serious thought into entering an apprenticeship to learn the trade of blacksmithing. However, he took a job working as a store clerk for $15 a month plus accommodations. In 1833, Lincoln's ambition got the best of him, and he borrowed money to open a county store that went bankrupt by the end of the year. Lincoln spent the next seventeen years paying off the debt he incurred from the failed enterprise. Further, the venture forced him to learn the trade of land surveying to both pay off the debt of the country store and to make a living.

With his ability to self-teach, Lincoln became proficient in land surveying in six short weeks. He started this endeavor with nothing but a book on surveying, a chain, and a compass; his work involved laying out road plans and town sites, and marking property. As a surveyor, Lincoln acted as a witness in contract formations suits and in the settlement of land boundary disputes, and he composed correspondence for his clients—more interaction with the law.

Lincoln gained substantial experience in the law with this job, as he was named as a defendant in four lawsuits resulting from his surveys. Most important, the job enabled Lincoln to meet the electorate in his community; and because the vast majority of people who met Lincoln truly liked him, these contacts resulted in positive and widespread name recognition. Lincoln held other jobs in his early years, all with relatively high profiles, allowing his charm to be seen by many people. Among other things, he was postmaster, which gave him incredible access to his future constituents.

In 1832, a militia in Illinois was mustered and deployed to fight in the Black Hawk War, and Lincoln eagerly volunteered. He saw little actual combat and later remarked that he was only bloodied by a few mosquitoes in the course of his service. Still, his service in the militia served as another conduit for making friends. He became particularly popular because of his abilities as a wrestler, which ended up getting him elected captain of his company—his first election and a success that he would later declare gave him "more pleasure than any I have had since."[4]

Lincoln was not in New Salem for long before he ran for a seat in the 1832 Illinois General Assembly, announcing his candidacy one week before the election. He lost the election, but saw it as a small victory: 277 out of the 300 votes that came from New Salem and its surrounding areas were cast for him. It was after this defeat that Lincoln began to seriously contemplate a career in the legal field. For the time being, however, he continued working in his different professions and exercising his knack for making friends.

Lincoln made friends easily with men because of his physical abilities. He could beat almost anyone at a weightlifting or a wrestling contest and was said to be an accomplished horseshoe player. With women, Lincoln used his humor and charm. People would gather around him at the post office or general store to hear his stories and joke telling. Two years after his first political defeat, and with his increased popularity, he again ran for the Illinois General Assembly, and this time he won a seat as a state representative for Sangamon County. **The lesson here is simple and powerful: being a potent public speaker and persuader does not mean much if people don't like you**. We have all been approached by a salesperson who was technically proficient and had a good "spiel," but just rubbed us the wrong way—and probably didn't make the sale. Moreover, friends will be your best customers and supporters—the more friends you have, the more people you have already persuaded. Cultivate the ability to sell yourself.

By 1834, when he was elected to the Illinois General Assembly, politics had become Lincoln's life. The campaign and elected office taught him a valuable lesson about debating and public speaking: people appreciate "plain speak," rather than overindulgent politicians who sound self-important and overeducated. Lincoln's folksy way of speaking carried on into his legal practice and presidency. **This lesson is twofold: 1) figure out what works, and then 2) use it.** In this instance, plain speak (a lesson that is discussed in detail later).

Abraham Lincoln, the farmer's son, was moving up in the world. He had held three public offices: postmaster, assistant county surveyor, and now member of the Illinois General Assembly. However, despite this gain in public standing, he was still poor and had to borrow money to make simple purchases and buy clothes appropriate for the Assembly floor.

Being a state legislator was only a part-time job—to pay the bills, Lincoln started to think seriously about becoming a lawyer. He already had had various encounters with the local courts while living in New Salem through writing legal documents for Bowling Green, the local Justice of the Peace, and appearing as a witness in several lawsuits as well as sitting on juries. In addition, Lincoln gained experience through the lawsuits in which he was a defendant, particularly cases arising from his surveying job and when creditors sued him for debts from his failed general store venture. In fact, it was an event that took place while Lincoln was working at the general store that became his defining inspiration to become a lawyer. A man came in and offered to sell him an old barrel with unknown contents for the bargain price of fifty cents. On another occasion of telling this story, Lincoln recounted that the man contended that the barrel was filled with household goods, nothing of special value. The man was selling it because he was moving and had no room on his wagon for the heavy barrel. Lincoln had no particular use for the barrel, but out of kindness he helped the man by buying it. Lincoln put the barrel in storage without opening it. Some time later, he came across the barrel while cleaning. He dumped the contents on the floor, discovering mostly junk, save for something at the barrel's bottom that gave the young Lincoln great elation. What Lincoln discovered was a complete edition of Blackstone's Commentaries (the first methodical treatise on the common law), a prize not only worth a substantial amount of money, but also having inspirational value to Lincoln, who was already toying with the idea of studying law. Seeing the discovery as divine intervention, Lincoln decided that he would become a lawyer.

There are two lessons to learn from Lincoln here: sometimes helping somebody out with something small can provide huge dividends, and more important, sometimes you need to take a chance. This holds true in the field of persuasive speaking. While playing it safe is, well, safe, sometimes swinging for the fences is what changes the game. For example, in the 2008 presidential election President Barack Obama gave what has been referred to as his "Race Speech" in Philadelphia, across the street from Liberty Hall where the Constitution was signed. Many on his election team advised the then Senator Obama not to give the speech, that the country was not ready for such a straight-forward approach to race relations. Yet Mr. Obama swung for the fences and delivered what many believe is one of his greatest speeches, helping him secure the nomination and the presidency. Dare to persuade.

ᾧ ᾧ ᾧ

Lincoln's Law School

According to his 1860 campaign autobiography, Lincoln's original reason
for delaying his quest to become a lawyer was his belief that he needed
more education to succeed. Notwithstanding being a state representative
and being considered one of the most intelligent men in his community,
Lincoln was exceedingly self-conscious about his lack of education. It was
fellow legislator and practicing attorney John Todd Stuart, discussed in
detail later, who convinced him otherwise. Not only did Stuart encourage
him to become a lawyer, he also actively helped him to reach that goal.

At that time, an aspiring lawyer would usually attend law school or
would become an apprentice for an established attorney or judge, and
then apply for the bar. The farther west an individual was, the more sparse
law schools became. Thus, most "frontier" attorneys chose the second
path. In Lincoln's case, neither of these options was available. While his
academic training was far from formal, his legal education was even less
so. He borrowed law books from Stuart's law office in Springfield, bought
more at auctions, and studied intently when the State Assembly was not
in session. He pored over Blackstone's Commentaries, case law, and the
Illinois codified statutes to learn black letter law.[5] For more practice material, he read legal pleadings and practice treatises to understand the "art"
of being a lawyer. Neighbors would comment on him walking down the
streets or lying under a tree with his legs stretched up the trunk, reciting
what he had absorbed earlier in the day.

In addition to copious reading, Lincoln attended numerous court trials. One court that Lincoln frequently observed was the court held by
his friend JP Bowling Green. Because there was no resident attorney in
New Salem, Green would allow Lincoln, who by then had substantial
knowledge of the Revised Laws of Illinois, to act as a "next friend" (an
individual who acts on behalf of another individual who does not have
the legal capacity to act on his or her own behalf) and represent parties.
Green observed that Lincoln was not only a capable advocate in court,
but was also downright impressive in his ability to persuade on behalf of
his clients. Green continued to allow Lincoln to work in this capacity
in order to gain experience. Lincoln found this arrangement extremely
advantageous—even though he was not getting paid ("pettyfogging,"
as he referred to the practice), he viewed this "lawyering" as the only
apprenticeship he could afford.

Lincoln also intently studied lawyers in frontier courthouses, particularly their impassioned closing arguments to juries. He noted what

worked and what didn't, remembering everything he saw and heard. He also rehearsed cases by himself and for friends. He would analyze the legal points from a variety of angles to see which had the greatest impact on his collected mock judge or jury.

Lincoln studied three years before he had read all the required law books and felt ready to apply for bar membership. On March 24, 1836, the Sangamon County Circuit Court in Springfield certified that Lincoln was of good moral character. The certification was forwarded to the Illinois Supreme Court, who, on September 9, 1836, issued him a license to practice law. In addition to being issued a license, Illinois required the final step of appearing before the clerk of the Supreme Court for enrollment.

A month after his acceptance into the bar, Lincoln moved to Springfield. He sold his surveying compass, marking stakes, and Jacob's staff. This was a symbolic move for Lincoln—he was not only starting a new profession, but a new life as well.

ᘛ ᘛ ᘛ

Lessons Learned

Many things great and small can be learned from Lincoln's years as a student and his path to becoming a lawyer. But of all Lincoln's skills and attributes, in my opinion his greatest was his ability to educate himself. Lincoln was able to use books and observation to master almost any subject. New subject matter, techniques, and methods occur throughout any career, no matter if you are selling cars or practicing law. Therefore, the ability to self-educate and use this new knowledge is a powerful tool. It appears Lincoln perfected this trait better than almost anyone. If he was weak at contracts, he would quickly learn and become proficient in contract law. As president, he was weak at military tactics, so he taught himself to be a great "general."

This ability to self-teach was enhanced by his willingness to reach a goal by any possible method. When Lincoln could not afford to go to a formal law school or work as a law clerk, he found an alternative route to becoming a lawyer. If you cannot find a "traditional" apprentice/mentor relationship, find a nontraditional one. If you want to learn a subject but cannot afford school tuition, go to a library. Almost all of life's obstacles have a backdoor solution.

Another Lincoln trait to admire was his thirst for knowledge. One thing I have noticed when reading about history's geniuses was their love of reading and learning. Those who believe education stops with the presentation of a degree are often the ones who stop growing. It was Lincoln's love of education that spurred him into politics and gave him his great persuasive skills. While he obviously had natural talent, most of his greatness was learned.

A final lesson that can be learned from Lincoln's education was the variety of methods he used to teach himself. The majority of his schooling came from reading books, because it was virtually the only media outlet of the time. He also recited and recalled the information he would read, in addition to the "passive" reading itself. He used his natural storytelling skills to entertain (and inform) audiences, which also reinforced the knowledge in his own head. Lincoln learned persuasion by watching others in a courtroom, and learned public speaking by practicing it on a tree stump. Lincoln understood early on that most education in life comes from watching someone else try (as the way children learn to speak by mimicking their parents) or trying something new yourself—not from classroom lectures.

🐿️ 🐿️ 🐿️

Notes

1. In 1808, Thomas Lincoln purchased three hundred acres near the Sinking Spring in Kentucky (then part of Virginia). *See* U.S. Department of the Interior, National Park Services, Abraham Lincoln Birthplace National Historic Site, *available at* http://www.nps.gov/nr/travel/presidents/lincoln_birthplace.html. The land's soil was stony red and yellow clay, however, its natural spring provided an important source of water. *Id.* Thomas tried to work the land, but just two years after he purchased it, he was sued in a title dispute that he ultimately lost in 1816. *Id.* In 1811, while waiting for the title dispute to be settled, Thomas Lincoln leased thirty acres from a larger farm in Knob Creek Valley, Kentucky. *Id.* It was there that Lincoln attended an antislavery church and where his first views of slavery were likely formed. *See id.* In 1816, after the title dispute was final and because of his dislike of living in a slave state, Thomas moved his family across the Ohio River to Indiana. *See id.*

2. ALBERT A. WOLDMAN, LAWYER LINCOLN 9–10 (Carroll & Graf 2001) (1936).

3. The information here was prepared for the Heritage Committee, Inc. by Otto Kyle, author of "Abraham Lincoln in Decatur" for the occasion of the unveiling of the Lincoln Monument in Lincoln Square on October 12, 1968, *available at* http://genealogytrails.com/ill/lincolnspeech.html. The first reliable account of the speech is mentioned in William D. Howell's 1860 campaign biography of Lincoln. Howell's account did not have any sources for the information; however, because Lincoln read the account and did not make any corrections, it is generally considered authentic by historians. *See also, Mr. Lincoln and Friends, available at* http://www.mrlincolnandfriends.org/inside. asp?pageID=35&subjectID=2.

4. RICHARD CARWARDINE, LINCOLN: A LIFE OF PURPOSE AND POWER 7 (Alfred A. Knopf 2006) [hereinafter CARWARDINE].

5. The phrase "black-letter law" was used in the Pennsylvania Supreme Court case *Naglee v. Ingersoll*, 7 Pa. 185 (1847), and refers to basic legal principles.

CHAPTER 2

PRACTICING BEING A LAWYER

Considering Lincoln's great success as an attorney, it is interesting that in his early career he was so insecure about his ability to practice law. When he started practicing law, he said he was beginning "an experiment as a lawyer." Little did he know that his little experiment would prepare him for the daunting road ahead.

Shelby M. Cullom was a young attorney who sometimes served with Lincoln as his co-counsel. He described Lincoln as the greatest trial lawyer he ever witnessed. "He was a man of wonderful power before a court or jury. When he was sure he was right, his strength and resourcefulness were well-nigh irresistible. In the court-room he was at home."[1]

Lincoln had a profound reverence for the law. He demonstrated this respect during a speech when he said:

> Let reverence for the laws be breathed by every American mother to the lisping babe . . . ; let it be taught in schools, in seminaries, and in colleges; let it be written in . . . spelling-books, and in almanacs; let it be preached from the pulpit, proclaimed in legislative halls, and enforced in courts of justice.

This adherence to the law sometimes conflicted with his other convictions. For instance, when someone informed Lincoln that he had aided a runaway slave and was in fear of going to jail for violating the Fugitive Slave Act, Lincoln, although he felt the law was inhumane, replied "Oh, it is ungodly!, it is ungodly! No doubt it is ungodly. But it is the law of the land, and we must obey it as we find it!"

More than just a respect for the rule of law, Lincoln had a respect for his profession. He felt that the reputation of the legal community was critical for the public to have a healthy attitude toward the law itself. He was assiduous in representing his profession in a way that encouraged others to join him, but also to be fair and honest in their practices.

A tool he used in this promotion was giving lectures. Lincoln gave many law lectures. In one of his most famous, he said that anyone aspiring to become an attorney should reflect and ask themselves "[i]f, in your judgment, you cannot be an honest lawyer, resolve to be honest without being a lawyer. Choose some other occupation, rather than one in the choosing of which you do, in advance, consent to be a knave."

For nearly twenty-five years, Abraham Lincoln was one of the hardest-working lawyers in Illinois. In total he had three separate law practices with three different partners. From each he learned something different. He was a general practitioner who represented a broad assortment of clients in almost every type of case in every type of court.

⁊◗ ⁊◗ ⁊◗

Partnership with John Todd Stuart

John Todd Stuart, cousin to Lincoln's future wife Mary Todd, encouraged Lincoln to enter the law profession and gave him books to help him study for the bar. In the spring of 1837, Stuart gave him a job as the junior partner of his firm, which commenced on April 15, 1837. This was an enormous opportunity for the young Lincoln, one which he accepted enthusiastically. In addition, Stuart gave Lincoln a home, allowing him to live in the law office and sleep on the office's couch.

A major source of revenue of their partnership was debt collection and debt protection. However, the practice was a general one, which also handled various criminal, equity, and civil cases. Their case load was large, handling more cases in the Circuit Court of Sangamon County than any other partnership. However, despite being a busy firm, the practice was not very financially rewarding and never exceeded sixteen hundred dollars a year.

Stuart was a politician first and a lawyer second; thus, little mentoring was given to his new junior partner. As a result, Lincoln did what he did best—taught himself. His main method of learning, as it had been for many years, was reading about lawyers and trying cases. This baptism-by-fire approach was intensified after Stuart won a seat in the United States House of Representatives in November of 1838. When he left for Congress, Stuart left Lincoln to manage the partnership. This "sole partnership" went on until Stuart returned from Congress in 1843. During Stuart's lengthy time away from the firm, Lincoln had to be the junior and senior partner; this not only taught him the business aspects of a law practice but also how to think creatively on advanced legal problems that were normally handled by senior attorneys.

J.T. STUART AND A. LINCOLN,

A TTORNEYS and Counsellors at Law, will practice conjointly, in the Courts of this Judicial Circuit—Office No. 4 Hoffman's Row, upstairs.
Springfield, April 12, 1837.   4

PARTNERSHIP ADVERTISEMENT

While this sole partnership arrangement seemed to work, at least at first, not all of Stuart's clients were thrilled to have their experienced attorney replaced with a scruffy-looking novice. One client in particular, John Baddeley, refused Lincoln's assistance and took his business elsewhere. While Stuart was obviously not enthusiastic about the loss of his clients in this manner, it was to be expected. In Stuart's mind it was a fair trade, because it allowed him to focus the majority of his attention on his political career.

In 1839, The Illinois state capital moved from Vandalia to Springfield. This move benefited the Stuart and Lincoln practice, particularly because the federal and Illinois Supreme Court moved to Springfield as well, opening a whole new practice area for the partnership. Lincoln and Stuart rode the First Judicial Circuit (see "Riding the Circuit" on page XX of this chapter for more information on this practice) until 1839, when Sangamon County was moved into the Eighth Judicial Circuit. Because Lincoln and Stuart focused their practice in Sangamon, Tazewell, Logan, and McLean counties, they began to travel on the Eighth Judicial Circuit.

Despite gaining valuable experience, Lincoln was not advancing in his legal profession, primarily because both he and Stuart considered the practice of law merely a catalyst for their political careers. Stuart was either in Washington or campaigning to stay in Washington and paid little attention to the practice. In the courtroom, both Stuart and Lincoln relied more on their natural abilities than legal research. The lack of preparation was not a serious handicap on the circuit due to the nature of the work at the time. This is because the cases the partnership worked on "dealt mostly with such commonplace matters as damage to growing crops from marauding livestock, the ownership of hogs, horses, cows, and sheep, small debts, libel, slander, or assault and battery, with an occasional action for divorce. . . ."[2]

However, after Springfield became the hub of the state, the partnership soon found its most profitable cases were in the state appellate and federal district courts, where scrupulous preparation was necessary. "Many capable lawyers practiced in these courts, and as the state developed and litigation became more complex, sound legal learning was needed in order to cope with them. Even circuit work became more demanding as time went on."[3]

Soon after Stuart was reelected to Congress, Lincoln reassessed his position. He realized that his legal career was stagnating and that he was no longer learning from Stuart. Lincoln also determined that he was unable to maintain the partnership by himself. They reached an amicable agreement, and the Stuart-Lincoln partnership formally dissolved.

The lessons Lincoln learned from Stuart are twofold. First, **do not be afraid of a learning environment where you have to jump in with both feet**. While baptism by fire is not always the preferred method to learn a new profession, sometimes it is the most effective. Lincoln easily could have become overwhelmed when Stuart left for Washington; instead, he took advantage of the situation and gained experience that is usually reserved for senior partners.

The second lesson here is to **take away what you can out of each experience**. If you focus on the problems of being in your situation, you only will be resentful and will gain very little or nothing from the experience. However, if you focus on learning as much as you can, despite the hardships, you will learn not only the skills of the task you are completing but also how to complete those goals under trying circumstances.

&ə̃ &ə̃ &ə̃

Partnership with Stephen Trigg Logan

After the Stuart partnership was dissolved, in the spring of 1841, Lincoln formed a law partnership with Stephen T. Logan. It was from Logan that Lincoln learned to give critical attention to the details of a case. Logan also helped to expand Lincoln's legal career by introducing him to new areas of the law and helping him expand his appellate practice. In his 1952 biography, *Abraham Lincoln*, Benjamin P. Thomas says the "[a]ssociation with Logan became one of the most constructive influences in Lincoln's life, for Logan would not tolerate haphazard methods. Methodical, industrious, painstaking, and precise, he had not only grounded himself in precedents and method, but was a student of the philosophy of law as well."[4]

Logan was ten years older than Lincoln and one of the circuit's most accomplished and respected attorneys. By the time Logan moved to Springfield, he was already a veteran attorney with ten years of practice under his belt. He had served as a judge from 1835 to 1837 on the First Circuit and was the preeminent attorney in Sangamon County.

Logan was similar to Lincoln in many ways, yet was a polar opposite in others. Logan was small and wiry with a small voice. However, what he lacked in presence he made up for in "convincing power."[5] Like Lincoln, he was rumpled and usually looked a bit shabby. Both he and Lincoln had exceptional minds and a love for the law. Up to that point, Lincoln had a "shoot from the hip" style, emphasizing his personable nature and ability to work with the jury. Logan was methodical and emphasized the value of careful preparation.

In 1841, the United States Congress passed the Bankruptcy Act, which granted relief to debtors. Because the federal court had moved to Springfield, the Logan and Lincoln law firm handled many of these cases. In addition to focusing on bankruptcy, the Logan and Lincoln partnership

Logan & Lincoln,
A TTORNEYS and Counsellors at Law, Springfield, —Office opposite Hoffman's Row.

PARTNERSHIP ADVERTISEMENT

started to monopolize much of the docket on the Illinois Supreme Court. They were quickly becoming one of the leading firms in Illinois.

In addition to his law practice, Lincoln was starting his family. On November 4, 1842, he and Mary Todd exchanged vows and became husband and wife. Their first child, Robert Lincoln, was born on August 1, 1843.

Soon after Logan hired his younger partner, he stopped traveling the circuit and remained in Springfield. Lincoln rode the Eighth Circuit whenever the court traveled, usually in the spring and fall. In addition to the Eighth Circuit, Lincoln expanded the practice to Coles County, where his father lived. On occasion, he would travel as far as Clark County on the Indiana border and Madison County on the Missouri border. (See Chapter 3 for information on specific trials.)

Logan detested Lincoln's unmanageable ways of legal practice and put great pressure on his junior partner to grasp the finer points of practicing law. Logan obliged Lincoln to study the appropriate legal authorities before entering into a courtroom. In addition to augmenting Lincoln's knowledge of the practice of law, Logan also taught Lincoln the importance of attention to detail on the business side of law practice. It was here that Lincoln, under Logan's counsel, learned about legal fees, how to sue delinquent clients, and how to run a law office. Lincoln "appreciated the soundness of judgment, accuracy of learning, and brilliancy of legal conceptions of his senior associate."[6] Logan's emphasized "the value of exactitude and thorough preparation,"[7] which greatly increased Lincoln's effectiveness as a lawyer; no longer did Lincoln rely on "mere cleverness"[8] or try to cover up "deficiency in the knowledge of law with florid rhetoric and flighty appeal."[9] Indeed, "[t]he years spent as Logan's associate were . . . constructive [ones]. They were years of education, training, and discipline. The benefits were to last Lincoln all his days."[10] By combining Logan's philosophy of a strong work ethic with his own God-given talents, Lincoln steadily became a powerhouse in his profession.

Under Logan's tutelage, Lincoln was soon able to hold his own against the most capable attorneys of the Illinois bar. Most lawyers considered him a dangerous rival in any case and without peer before a jury.

The successful Logan and Lincoln partnership ended in 1844. Some evidence points to a clash of political ambitions between the two lawyers. It was also suggested that Lincoln eventually became dissatisfied with the one-third profits he received as the junior partner. Moreover, Logan was demanding and short-tempered. When Logan "expressed a wish to take his son as a partner, Lincoln willingly agreed to dissolve the firm."[11] As with most people who encountered Lincoln, Judge Logan and Lincoln remained friends after their partnership dissolved.

It is rumored that Judge Logan originally did not expect much out of Lincoln when the partnership began, besides gaining a junior partner who was well liked by juries. However, it was not long before Logan recognized Lincoln as a well-rounded, formidable attorney. After the partnership dissolved, Logan would face Lincoln in court several times—and lose.

Looking at history's greatest individuals, most have a mentor, someone who taught them the finer points of their field. Alexander had Aristotle, Hamilton had Washington, and Lincoln had Logan.

The best mentors never tell you what to do; they let you figure it out, realizing that the process of thought is usually more important than the solution itself. **Nobody becomes a master persuader without on some level learning from someone else who is better**. Often the most effective way to become better in any discipline is to learn from someone you respect and trust; this can be a formal mentor or just someone who has a skill you admire.[12]

While there is some evidence that Lincoln was often annoyed by Logan's moody disposition, Lincoln was astute enough to glean everything he could from Logan's wisdom. He was able to accept Logan's criticism, filter out what he felt was "true," and learn from it.

ン♪ ン♪ ン♪

Partnership with William H. Herndon

After the dissolution of the Logan-Lincoln law practice in 1844, Lincoln asked William H. Herndon, Lincoln's junior by nine years, to be his junior partner in his new law practice. Lincoln had known Herndon for years—he first met his future partner in 1832 when Herndon's cousin, Rowan Herndon, employed Lincoln to navigate a steamer on the Sangamon River. Later, William worked in the Speed Country store; Joshua F. Speed was Lincoln's best friend in his early days in Springfield. Speed said of his and Lincoln's meeting that Lincoln rode in on a borrowed horse, "with no earthly goods but a pair of saddle-bags, two or three law books, and some clothing which he had in the saddle-bags." Speed went on, "he came into my store, set his saddle-bags on the counter, and asked me 'what the furniture for a single bedstead would cost.'" Speed took his "slate and pencil, and made calculation, and found the sum for furniture complete, would amount to seventeen dollars in all." Lincoln agreed that "it is probably cheap enough; but I want to say that cheap as it is I have not money to pay. But if you will credit me until Christmas, and my experiment here as a lawyer is a success, I will pay you then. If I fail in that I will probably never be able to pay you at all." Speed recounted that "the tone of his voice was so melancholy that I felt for him. I looked up at him, and I thought then as I think now, that I never saw so gloomy, and melancholy a face." Speed loaned him the furniture.

WILLIAM H. HERNDON

Courtesy of The Lincoln Museum, Fort Wayne, Indiana

Herndon idolized Lincoln, saying "there was something in his tall and angular frame, his ill-fitting garments, honest face and lively humor that imprinted his individuality on my affection and regard." Lincoln also worked with Herndon's father, Archer G. Herndon, in the Illinois State Assembly.

During Lincoln's partnership with Logan, he offered Herndon a law clerk position while he studied for the bar. While Herndon was clerking for them, after an angry moment with Logan, Lincoln told Herndon "of his determination to leave Logan, and invited the young man to become his partner."[13] In December of 1844, the newly licensed attorney became Lincoln's junior partner.

"Springfield people were surprised when Lincoln chose Herndon for a partner—any number of experienced lawyers would have welcomed such an alliance. But Lincoln regarded Herndon as a promising young man."[14] Herndon himself was surprised at Lincoln's selection, saying, "I confess I was surprised when he invited me to become his partner. I was young in the practice and was painfully aware of my want of ability and experience." Lincoln reassured Herndon by telling him "Billy, I can trust you, if you can trust me." Herndon later said, "I felt relieved and accepted his generous proposal."

Another reason Lincoln chose Herndon is that he had spent eighteen years as a junior partner himself. Lincoln reasoned by hiring a young freshman attorney, he could have a more active role in training the attorney to his own methods and procedures and would no longer be dominated by an older, more experienced attorney.[15] This protégé relationship lasted through the partnership as evidenced by the fact that Lincoln called Herndon "Billy," and Herndon always called Lincoln, with much affection, "Mr. Lincoln" until the day he called him "Mr. President." Henry B. Rankin, in his book *Personal Recollections of Abraham Lincoln*, reflected on this relationship by stating, "no father or brother I ever knew exerted a more complete control over their kin than did this senior partner over his junior. It was a quaint peculiar power that Lincoln exerted; silent, steady, masterful."

More than simply looking for a protégé, Lincoln thought Herndon brought assets that he lacked. Lincoln thought that Herndon could organize the office and improve the practice's poor bookkeeping, but this assumption turned out to be an erroneous one; Herndon was no better at office management than his senior partner.

Herndon spent most of his first year with Lincoln doing clerk work. Herndon also worked several outside jobs while partnering with Lincoln. He was the deputy clerk for the Illinois Supreme Court and also the city attorney for Springfield. Lincoln handled the important litigation and drafted the necessary pleadings.

Initially, the new partners remained in the same office that Logan and Lincoln had occupied in the Tinsley building. They stayed there until 1847, when Lincoln was elected to the United States House of Representatives; when Lincoln left for Washington the practice moved to a smaller office in the same building. They worked out of this office until 1852, when they moved to an office next to the state capitol building, where they remained until Lincoln became president.

While Lincoln was in Congress for two years, Herndon kept the firm in business. When Lincoln returned from Congress he jumped back into his legal career with both feet. His reputation had grown to the point that he was offered a position at a prominent Chicago firm, with a very generous salary. Lincoln was apprehensive about being overwhelmed by a big-city practice and declined the offer. Riding the circuit was not as lucrative, but it provided the more footloose lifestyle that Lincoln loved.

For the purpose of simplicity, historians often divide Lincoln's legal career into three parts, correlating with these three partnerships. However, a more accurate division would be two parts: before and after Congress. He did a great deal of hard work before his election to Congress, but it was not until he returned from Congress that he built an empire of goodwill on the name "Lincoln." Lincoln believed that his political career was over, so when he returned to law, it was with every intention of building the practice into his permanent livelihood. The partners expanded the practice into one of the largest in Illinois. By 1850, Lincoln was earning the largest fees of his life. He made so much money one year from his booming practice that he added a second story onto his house, a significant event in the mid 1800s. He was one of the most sought after attorneys in the state, taking on cases ranging from runaway pigs to murder, with clients ranging from penniless widows to his premier client—the Illinois Central Railroad.

The myth that Lincoln was a public lawyer who did not want to get rich from helping others is simply that—a myth. Lincoln had no qualms about charging what he could to his clients, so long as the fee was fair. However, while he was happy about his financial success, it is true he was not fulfilled by getting rich—he knew he was destined for something bigger than wealth, but with his political career "dead," this "something bigger" was elusive.

Despite not placing fee collection at the top of his priorities, Lincoln was not afraid to sue for fees he felt he had earned. Indeed, Lincoln was forced to sue Illinois Central Railroad for five thousand dollars—and collected. Despite being sued, the railroad was so happy with his work that they continued to retain his services. Obviously, to sue a client and keep its business is very rare, if not unheard of—this clearly demonstrates Lincoln's legal *and* interpersonal skills.

As far as the nuts-and-bolts of the law practice, Lincoln traveled the circuit while Herndon did office work. This is not to say that Herndon did not handle cases. Rather, he focused on traveling to counties abutting Sangamon County. He also maintained a steady clientele in Menard County, which was outside the Eighth Circuit. As the junior partner, Herndon would sometimes check legal citations and proofread Lincoln's work. He would also conduct legal research for some of Lincoln's briefs. However, each man generally worked on his own cases, without interference from the other. "In some respects it was as though two lawyers worked in the same office independently of one another."[16]

Unlike Lincoln, Herndon was fine in his clothes and stood five feet nine inches, a good height for that time, although dwarfed by Lincoln's monstrous six feet four inches. Also, unlike Lincoln, Herndon "never acquired any fondness for the law; a temperance advocate, he frequently got drunk. Although he was an earnest student of philosophy, he never learned to systematize his thoughts." Herndon, despite his lack of enthusiasm for his profession, he was a good lawyer. He had a nervous energy that spilled into his lawyering. He was high-strung and humorless. He used every technicality to win and played to jurors' emotions by being overly dramatic. He once said that "when you get tears on the jury, you win your case." Herndon's arguments would "sometimes [become] so heated that he would break out with an oath or fling his coat on the floor."[17]

The partnership was not without some discord. It was said that Lincoln would tell a story over and over, which strained Herndon. Most annoying to Herndon was the presence of Lincoln's four children, who would accompany their father to work on Sundays. Lincoln could ignore his young children and work. Herndon, on the other hand, would be overwhelmed with their presence. He stated that they "'soon gutted the room—gutted the shelves of books—rifled the drawers and riddled boxes—battered the points . . . of gold pens against the stove—turned over the ink stand on the papers—scattered letters over the office and danced over them . . . .'"[18]

Herndon also took issue with Lincoln's office habits. Lincoln reached the office every day at nine o'clock, where he routinely picked up a newspaper, "spread himself out on an old sofa, one leg on a chair, and read aloud, much to my discomfort. Singularly enough Lincoln never read any other way but aloud." Also to the frustration of Herndon—despite not having great organization skills himself—was Lincoln's haphazard approach to office organization. Herndon observed that:

> Lincoln had always on the top of our desk a bundle of papers into which he slipped anything he wished to keep and afterwards refer to. It was a receptacle of general information. Some years ago, on removing the furniture from the office, I took down the bundle and blew from the top the liberal coat of dust that had accumulated thereon. Immediately underneath the string was a slip bearing this endorsement, in his hand: "When you can't find it anywhere else, look in this."

Herndon was not the only one to notice the untidiness of Lincoln's office. Gibson Harris, a law student who was hired by the Lincoln and Herndon partnership as a clerk, described the office in this way:

> The furniture, somewhat dilapidated, consisted of one small desk and a table, a sofa or lounge with a raised head at one end, and a half-dozen plain wooden chairs. The floor was never scrubbed. . . . Over the desk a few shelves had been enclosed; this was the office bookcase holding a set of Blackstone, Kent's Commentaries, Chitty's Pleadings, and a few other books. A fine law library was in the Capitol building across the street to which the attorneys of the place had access.

In addition, there was some friction between Herndon and Lincoln over the slavery issue that was hanging heavy over the country. Herndon was an ardent abolitionist and constantly urged Lincoln to use his pulpit, as a highly respected attorney, to speak out against slavery, both morally and legally. At the time Lincoln was against slavery, but his political and legal position had not come into full fruition; he remained fairly quiet on the issue, not wanting to damage his political prospects before they had even started by coming out strongly on one side of a contentious issue.

Despite a strong business partnership, there was not a social relationship between the two men. This was due to Mrs. Lincoln's contempt for Herndon. Herndon attributed Mary Todd's aversion to him to a comment he made when they first met. They were introduced at a ball, where "he became so fascinated by her pliant grace that he likened her to a serpent. Mrs. Lincoln took this intended compliment as an insult and never forgave him."[19]

Beyond their differences on these few matters, the partners got along very well. Benjamin Thomas states that "[a]s the years passed, their relationship became more than a mere business arrangement and took on something of the nature of that between father and son."[20] "And if, in time, Lincoln grew somewhat beyond his junior partner's comprehension, no diminution of trust, faithfulness, and affection showed on either side."[21] After Lincoln's death, Herndon said that "it has always been a matter of pride with me during our long partnership, continuing on until it was dissolved by the bullet of the assassin Booth, we never had any personal controversy or disagreement."

Lincoln is the only lawyer-president who practiced law up to the time he was elected as President of the United States of America. Indeed, Lincoln even handled cases after winning the Republican nomination. This "attention to his law practice reflects his commitment to the law as a profession. . . ."[22] Although the practice itself ended when Lincoln left for the White House in 1861, the partnership lasted until Lincoln's death in 1865. Indeed, when Lincoln left for Washington, he left Herndon with an eerie prophecy: "if I live I'm coming back some time, and then we'll go right on practicing law as if nothing had ever happened."

One lesson for persuasive speaking and for life that can be seen in the Lincoln-Herndon practice was Lincoln's resistance to selling out for more money. Specifically, when Lincoln was offered a prestigious job at a Chicago firm, he turned it down despite the sizable salary. The point is not to turn down high-paying jobs; rather, it is to **be driven by something bigger than money**. If you only care about money, all you will find in life is money, not happiness and certainly not satisfaction.

People do not lie on their deathbed and say, "I wish I had made more money." Rather, they often say "I wish I had spent more time with my family," or "I wish I had made a bigger difference." If Lincoln had cared only about money, he would have taken the job in Chicago or the one later offered by the New York Railroad in early 1860 as its General Counsel (lead attorney for one of the biggest companies in the United States at the time).[23] Instead, he cared about making a difference and made one of the biggest contributions in the history of this country.[24] And, as will be seen in later chapters, when Lincoln was arguing for something he really believed in, he was unbeatable.

Another lesson from this part of Lincoln's practice is to **focus your energies on one thing at a time**. Just as it is hard to learn both Spanish and Chinese simultaneously, Lincoln found it hard to press both his political and legal careers at the same time. Indeed, it was not until after he felt his political career was over and he returned from Congress that he truly put his heart into the legal profession and saw it flourish into a booming practice.

⋙ ⋙ ⋙

Riding the Circuit

The Eighth Circuit, which Lincoln traveled, consisted of over twelve thousand square miles and extended from Springfield to the eastern border of Illinois and included most of the Sangamon River Valley. Much of the circuit was sparsely populated, and the county seats were often not much more than a crossroad in a settlement. Moving from county to county, thirty-five miles a day, was considered hard riding and, depending on the condition of the roads, could be downright atrocious. Until the late 1850s, when railroads became more prevalent, the circuit members would travel by horse or horse-drawn buggy. When railroads came to Illinois, Lincoln was able to reach more county seats by rail and took advantage of the opportunity. Until then, it was all done by horses—it's funny to think of perhaps our greatest President riding around in a buggy.

Lincoln lost his very first case in the Eighth Circuit, only a month after becoming a member of the bar. He rode the circuit for nearly six months out of the year, three months in the fall and three in the spring. He continued traveling this circuit for more than twenty years and handled over five thousand cases with considerable success.

By 1849, the Eighth Circuit had fourteen counties. This made the Eighth the largest circuit in Illinois; the other circuits contained between four to ten counties. Most practicing attorneys worked only a few neighboring counties. Lincoln was the only attorney, besides the state's attorney and the circuit judge, who traveled the entire circuit. The judge would hold court from a few days to a few weeks before packing up and moving to the next county seat.

Lincoln was diligent about riding the circuit regardless of health or weather. In 1850, Lincoln was on the road for 175 days, and in 1852 for 155. After Lincoln's stint in Congress, his time on the circuit increased; he won clients from pure hustle, taking every case that came his way, no matter how small. He increased his travels further due in part to his wife's erratic behavior after their son Eddie died in 1850. Because Herndon only traveled with Lincoln on the circuit about one-fourth of the time, Lincoln would form quasi-partnerships while on the circuit if he thought a case needed more than one attorney.

While traveling the circuit, Lincoln stayed at local taverns because only the county seats on the rail line had large enough populations to support a hotel. Most of the time, the attorneys ate at common tables and shared beds because of the meager accommodations that were available. When the weather was particularly treacherous, attorneys would group together and stay at a rural farmhouse on the way to the next county seat. A fellow attorney, Elihu B. Washburne, noted that "[t]he lawyers of that day were brought much closer together than they ever have been since, and the 'esprit de corps' was much more marked. Coming from long distances and suffering great privations in their journeys, they usually remained a considerable time in attendance upon the court."

When Lincoln reached his destinations, local attorneys would ask for his help on a particular case, or litigants would seek his services when they heard he was in town. The cases Lincoln worked on while he rode the circuit were normally simple and required minimum preparation. Only the most intricate cases made use of memoranda or case notes; instead, Lincoln generally would absorb the necessary facts and work the case from his feet. Often Lincoln would only have a few minutes to confer with his client before going to trial. Long hours of trial preparation was not needed since the cases typically dealt with such trivial matters as crop damage by wandering livestock, ownership of farm animals, small debts, and assault and battery, with the occasional more complex divorce or murder cases.[25] Lincoln represented accused murders on at least twenty-seven occasions.[26] In addition to being trial lawyers, Lincoln and Herndon maintained a healthy clientele for writing deeds, registering land, and dispensing general legal and tax advice.

During the antebellum period, the majority of Lincoln's trials involved debt collection. He represented both the creditors and debtors in these cases, but saw more success as the plaintiffs' attorney due to many defendants defaulting. Defendants also lost more frequently because the justice system at the time strongly favored creditors.

After the Illinois legislature passed laws supporting railroads, cases arose all over the state involving the different railroad companies. Much of this litigation was over right of way, stock issues, and damage the railroads made to property while they underwent construction. Eventually, the Illinois Central Railroad secured Lincoln as their attorney because of his impressive win/loss record. Lincoln also represented six other railroads that operated tracks within his circuit. Although he worked hard for the railroad, handling fifty-seven cases in eight years, he was not under a permanent retainer and would occasionally be retained to oppose the Illinois Central and other railways; in fact, he did so sixty-two times.[27]

At the time Lincoln rode the circuit in Illinois, "[j]urisprudence was still in infancy, so that no intricate accumulation of precedent need[ed to] be mastered, and the issues were usually decided according to fundamental precepts of right and wrong."[28] Courtroom presentations were informal, and cases were won more often by the lawyer with the best oral advocacy skills rather than on the merits of the case.

The facts of each case were known to the local townspeople; thus the circuit court's sessions became a popular occasion for the townsfolk. Lincoln, the other traveling attorneys, and the judge were treated as celebrities. Lincoln was particularly popular in the courtroom because of his skillful storytelling.

Although Lincoln had a strong connection to politics, his political affiliation never played a role in the cases he took on. A political rival and Democrat, Joel Seth Post, sat with Lincoln as co-counsel for fifteen cases. For fifteen other cases, the two battled each other in court. Also, Lincoln teamed up with his friend Ward Hill Lamon on numerous occasions; in fact, the two advertised together in the Vermilion County local newspapers. However, this *de facto* partnership did not stop Lincoln from dominating Lamon in the few cases that they opposed each other in.

Beyond being a lawyer, Lincoln occasionally served as a *pro tem* judge in the Eighth Circuit. It is not completely clear where the authority for Lincoln to act as presiding judge came from; however, because of his reputation of not playing favorites and of being intently fair, litigants or their attorneys would rarely object to his holding court. Typically he would only serve as judge for a few cases a session. But he did serve as judge for an entire circuit session once. During that time he heard one case that was overturned because one attorney objected to the practice of having another attorney preside over the case. From that point on, he would only hear a case if both parties consented on the record to his presence.

Despite the hardship of circuit riding, living in dirty rooms, and consuming barely edible food, Lincoln truly liked the lifestyle. Not only did traveling the circuit give him the opportunity to meet people and gain votes for the future campaign (that was always on his mind), but Lincoln also liked the art of being a trial attorney. Lincoln enjoyed the occasion to play speechmaker and be sociable in the evenings; he also enjoyed the esteem the local people held for lawyers. Judge Davis[29] observed that "[i]n my opinion Lincoln was happy—as happy as he could be, when on this Circuit—and happy no other place. This was his place of enjoyment."

Lincoln liked to be around people, and he enjoyed the male camaraderie that the circuit provided. Lincoln's law partner Herndon wrote in his biography about Lincoln's legal career that, "I know that life on the circuit was a gay one. It was rich with incidents, and afforded the nomadic lawyers ample relaxation from all irksome toil that fell to their lot."[30] Lincoln stayed on the road even if it was not necessary. Many of the circuit attorneys, if they were within a reasonable distance, would travel home on weekends in order to get fresh supplies. Lincoln was an exception—he would spend Sundays in the county tavern with loungers and would typically only return home when that season of the circuit had finished.

LINCOLN'S MENTOR AND LATER
APPOINTEE TO THE SUPREME COURT,
JUSTICE DAVID DAVIS.

Indeed, Lincoln loved the circuit, and the circuit loved Lincoln. Lincoln's success as an attorney soon made him the shining star of the local bar. Judge Davis said that "[t]he meanest man in the [legal] bar would always pay great deference and respect to Lincoln." Another very successful attorney at the time, Usher Linder, wrote that "I don't know whether he was strongest before a judge or the jury. I certainly never like to have him against me."[31]

Not only did Lincoln's fellow lawyers hold him in high regard, so did the judges before whom he tried cases. In Frederick Trever Hill's book, *Lincoln the Lawyer*, colleagues of Lincoln's stated that Judge Davis "would brook no interruption of the conversation when Lincoln had the floor; and if his favorite happened to be absent, he took . . . little interest or enjoyment in the rest of the company. . . . 'Where's Lincoln?' he would inquire irritably. 'Here, somebody, go and tell Lincoln to come here.'"[32]

This favoritism also brought forth some resentment. Herndon wrote that as his partner grew into "public favor and achieved such marked success in the profession, half the bar of Springfield began to be envious of his growing popularity."[33] However, the evidence suggests that Lincoln did not gain any sort of favorable treatment in the courtroom from Judge Davis. In fact, out of the eighty-seven cases tried by Lincoln where Judge

Davis sat with no jury, Lincoln lost forty-seven—more than half of them. In addition, when Judge Davis ruled against Lincoln, Lincoln had no qualms appealing the decision and getting Judge Davis overturned.

Riding the circuit helped Lincoln hone his legal skills, make friends, and develop his character. The long trips provided an abundance of time for self-reflection and quiet thought. During this time, he would study mathematics, politics, and reread Shakespeare. However, despite the fact that Lincoln enjoyed riding the circuit, there were times when his colleagues saw him as withdrawn and blasé about his surroundings. At one point during the day, he could be seen surrounded by lawyers listening to him telling one of his stories with the usual animation. An hour later, he would be seen with his back against the wall and his hat tipped to cover his face. His eyes would no longer be sparkling; rather, they appeared sad and dejected. Absorbed within his thoughts, he would "sit for hours at a time defying the interruption of even his closest friends. No one ever thought of breaking the spell by speech; for by his moody silence no one dared to break through."[34]

LINCOLN WHILE A TRAVELING LAWYER, TAKEN
IN DANVILLE, ILLINOIS.

ᘒᖴ ᘒᖴ ᘒᖴ

Appellate Work

Beyond the booming practice Lincoln built riding the circuit, he was also frequently engaged in appellate work before the Illinois Supreme Court. The success of his appellate practice can be attributed to his detailed thinking, a format perfect for this type of work. In fact, the Lincoln and Herndon partnership maintained one of the largest appellate practices in the state. William Herndon claimed that when it came to appellate work, Lincoln was at his best because he had time to ponder the facts of a case and thoroughly prepare his arguments.

The supreme court held court exclusively in Springfield until 1849, when it began to hear cases in Ottawa and Mt. Vernon as well. Lincoln would occasionally travel to Ottawa to argue a case before the supreme court, but primarily worked only on those to be heard in Springfield; this diminished the total number of appellate cases he handled in his career. Still, over the course of the partnership, Lincoln and Herndon handled 411 cases in front of the Illinois Supreme Court, with Lincoln handling the vast majority of those.

In whole, work before the Illinois high court represented 10 percent of Lincoln's legal work. Because of his residence in the state capital and his reputation as the state's foremost appellate practitioner, Lincoln received most of his appellate cases by referrals from far reaches of the state.

Working on appellate cases carried several benefits over circuit practice. First, appeals tend to be more complex and better honed Lincoln's legal reasoning abilities. Appellate cases also carried higher fees, so Lincoln's wallet increased as well. However, more than the exercising of his brain or the padding of his bank account, Lincoln enjoyed working on appellate cases because of their social impact. The heart of Illinois' social and professional life for lawyers was the Supreme Court Library. This was the rendezvous for the attorneys. After a long day's work, attorneys, including Lincoln, and often judges would sit in the library late into the night—talking about cases and politics or just swapping stories. Most of the legal work coming from the Eighth Circuit was entrusted to Springfield lawyers because of their familiarity with the high court, particularly Lincoln and Herndon, Stuart, or Logan.

ᕽᕽ ᕽᕽ ᕽᕽ

Federal Work

Appellate cases were not the only cases that carried extra status and money. Cases heard in front of the federal courts also claimed higher fees and prestige. In fact, Lincoln's federal practice supplied a healthy portion of his overall income. A federal suit based on diversity (meaning disputes between citizens of different states) could not be brought unless the case in controversy exceeded five hundred dollars. Thus, Lincoln could charge higher fees when in federal court because the clients were almost always wealthier.

The typical federal case dealt with diversity. Out-of-state residents would attempt to collect debts in federal court from Illinois residents. Lincoln would represent either side in these disputes—as his reputation as a competent attorney reached other states, debtors from New York, St. Louis, or Philadelphia would retain Lincoln to represent them in federal court with regularity.

Lincoln had a reputation of having considerable knowledge concerning federal law. Because of this, attorneys from all over Illinois referred cases to him or asked him for legal advice. Overall, the Lincoln-Herndon partnership worked more than three hundred cases in district and circuit courts, with the exact number impossible to determine because records were destroyed in the Great Chicago Fire of 1871. Lincoln was also the attorney of record for at least six cases that were before the United States Supreme Court. One such case he argued in 1849 while he was a congressman.[35]

෧ ෧ ෧

Lincoln's Colleagues

The day that Lincoln was admitted to the bar in Illinois was the day he joined an extended family that would play a vital role in his personal, professional, and political life for the next twenty-nine years. The Eighth Circuit was especially conducive to his political and professional development. Here, the most gifted litigators in the state gathered, each bringing a different perspective and something to teach. Lincoln absorbed it all. William Herndon wrote:

> The very best minds in the State, if not in the great West, met here, the capital of the State, and energetically struggled for wealth or fame. . . . These men were, taken them as a whole, great men, full of energy and of great natural capacities, and were very ambitious and struggled to rise in the world; they were giants and fought like giants.

This elite group was a positive environment for Lincoln's legal education and political career. Judge Davis said that it was in this elite group that Lincoln found his fraternal core and where Lincoln was "loved by his brethren of the bar. His presence on the circuit was watched for with interest, and never failed to produce joy or hilarity. When [Mr. Lincoln was] casually absent the spirits of both bar and people were depressed."

To appreciate the prowess of the Eighth Circuit, one must consider the influence that flowed from this particular area. Lincoln's community and its surrounding areas bore a president of the United States, a candidate for the presidency, six senators, eight congressman, and a cabinet secretary[36]—not to mention the "other men who distinguished themselves professionally in later years. Almost without exception, these men were lawyers, and Lincoln met and practised against them during the . . . years of his professional life."[37]

The friends that Lincoln made in his fellow Illinois lawyers later turned into political allies. Albert A. Woldman wrote in *Lawyer Lincoln* that, "these circuit associates became in time bulwarks of strength during his political struggles. They became his loyal, devoted district leaders, upon whom he could rely at all times to promote his local interests among the voters of their respective regions."[38]

Lincoln gained these political allies because of his universal popularity. Elihu Washburne, a political ally of Lincoln's, said Lincoln "never used the arts of the demagogue to ingratiate himself with any person. Beneath his ungainly exterior he wore a gold heart. He was ever ready to do an act of kindness whenever in his power, particularly to the poor and lowly." After gaining a friend, Lincoln would remain loyal to that individual in the most trying of circumstances. One example of this can be seen when Usher Linder, a legal colleague, had his son captured while he was fighting for the Confederate Army. Lincoln sent a presidential order that stated: "Please administer the oath of allegiance to him, discharge him, and send him to his father."

In addition to his fellow attorneys, Lincoln's clients and the court clerks enjoyed working with him. William H. Somers, who was a clerk in Champaign, said that he "became warmly attached to [Lincoln] because of his genial disposition and the kindness shown to me as [a] clerk." Young attorneys especially liked to work with Lincoln due to his skills and encouraging words. In fact, many young men chose the law as a career because they were so enamored with him. One of those young attorneys, Lawrence Weldon, had this to say about Lincoln:

> He was particularly kind to young lawyers, . . . and I remember with what confidence I always went to him, because I was certain he knew all about the matter, and would most cheerfully tell me. I can see him now through the decaying memories of thirty years, standing in the corner of the old courtroom, and as I approached him with a paper I did not understand, he said: "Wait until I fix this plug for my 'gallis,' and I will pitch into that like a dog at a root."[39]

୧ ୧ ୧

Practicing Law as a Business

When Lincoln was partnered with Stuart, his legal fees ranged from five to ten dollars. However, in the murder case of *People v. Truett*, the small firm earned five hundred dollars for their representation. Stuart and Lincoln would normally divide the incoming fees equally, despite Stuart's being the senior partner.

When Lincoln started his partnership with Logan, Lincoln was earning twelve hundred dollars to fifteen hundred dollars a year from his practice. This was considered a good salary in 1842. However, to earn such a salary required diligent work; fees ranged from two dollars and fifty cents to fifty dollars for each case, with an average of about five dollars. In addition to cash, Lincoln would also be paid with produce, meat, or clothes.

By the time the Lincoln and Herndon firm was established, Lincoln had built some goodwill and was charging a typical client between five and twenty dollars. However, it is impossible to pin down Lincoln's fees with any certainty because the partnership only kept its fee journal current for a handful of years. What is clear, however, is that Lincoln was often imprudent with how he handled the business side of his practice. There are numerous recorded instances where Lincoln was careless in obtaining money owed to his firm. This is not to say that he would not sue clients if they refused to pay their legal bills—he did so on a regular basis. Other times, Lincoln would charge next to nothing for his rendered services; conversely, there are other recorded instances of the firm charging what could be described as exorbitant fees.

During Lincoln's time as an attorney in the 1850s, there were over twenty-seven hundred licensed attorneys in Illinois. Despite the glut of lawyers, there was plenty of work due to the rapid settlement the state was experiencing. Most of the "growing pains" cases dealt with land disputes and contract cases, as well as cases dealing with transportation growth, like those involving the railroad.

Throughout the country there was a professional stratification within the lawyer ranks. At the top was a small elite group, principally located in the commercially heavy cities on the east coast. In this environment, the legal family dynasty an attorney came from was just as important as the skills an attorney had in the courtroom.

In the 1850s, Illinois was growing its own legal elites with the majority of them concentrated in Chicago. Illinois also had the 1850s version of "ambulance chasers"—these lawyers scrambled to catch the table scraps of legal cases and often worked an additional job to make ends meet.

Between these two classes of attorneys were the skilled trial attorneys who were not from "noble blood," but were too talented to work for scraps. Because of their skill, they attracted the most profitable clients in their areas of operation.

Despite benefiting from Stuart's existing clientele, Lincoln started his legal career as an "ambulance chaser" who had to scramble for clients. However, he steadily built a reputation as a skilled and conscientious attorney, and quickly rose through the attorney ranks in the first ten years of his career.

By the time Lincoln joined with Herndon in 1844, he had a commanding and desirable caseload filled with prestigious appellate and federal cases. His typical debtor client was largely replaced by the more lucrative creditor client.

By the time Lincoln left the legal field to run for the presidency, he was at the apex of the legal community in Illinois and was held in great esteem by the east coast elites because of his dominating trial record. There is ample evidence that if he had not become the sixteenth President of the United States, he would have eventually been recognized as one of the foremost attorneys in America, a peer of Clarence Darrow.

ằ ằ ằ

Balancing Two Careers

During Lincoln's legal career, he suspended his practice on numerous occasions to focus on politics. During the 1840s, for example, he traveled throughout Illinois to campaign for the Whig party. Lincoln would also combine his legal and political careers by traveling to a county to argue a case, and after representing the client, he would then give a political speech on the courthouse steps.

While it appears from Lincoln's written record that he was easily able to balance both his political and legal careers, Lincoln would not agree. In 1854, after Lincoln lost his Senate bid, he wrote to some of his clients that his "experiment" in politics had caused him to neglect some of his cases. While Lincoln ran against Douglas for the United States Senate seat, he stopped practicing almost completely, only to return to his caseload after he lost the election.

After Lincoln was nominated as the Republican candidate for president of the United States, he continued to work on a few cases in federal court. After his election, he settled his business affairs with Herndon before leaving for Washington, but asked Herndon to leave their law shingle advertising their practice for when he returned to continue their partnership.

Lincoln's legal friends played a critical role in his nomination as the Republican candidate as well as his eventual election to the presidency. Despite this intensive work from his lawyer friends in Illinois, many of his former colleagues felt forsaken by the new president. Many who had supported Lincoln anticipated executive appointments upon Lincoln's election. One congressman wrote to Lincoln's old mentor and friend, Judge Davis, commenting on this perceived political betrayal, stating that "an Administration that you breathed into power is now passing away without your valuable aid and comfort."

What many of his friends did not know was that Lincoln was trying to bring his allies and supporters into the administration, but having only moderate success. For instance, Lincoln attempted to appoint Judge Davis to Commissary General of the army, only to have the appointment defeated by General Winfield Scott, who insisted on an army officer being awarded the position. While some of Lincoln's friends never received appointments, Lincoln did nominate Judge Davis to the United States Supreme Court after Justice John McLean died in April of 1861.

Lincoln's dual careers were intertwined beyond separation. His political career served as advertising for his legal career, and his legal career gave him the standing for a national political career. Without both, he would have never become president of the United States.

❧ ❧ ❧

Notes

1. Shelby M. Cullom, Fifty Years of Public Service 84–85 (A. C. McClurg & Co. 1911).

2. Benjamin P. Thomas, Abraham Lincoln: A Biography 92 (Barnes & Noble 1994) (1952) [hereinafter Thomas].

3. Thomas, supra note 2, at 95.

4. Id.

5. Id.

6. Albert A. Woldman, Lawyer Lincoln 41 (Carroll & Graf 2001) (1936) [hereinafter Woldman].

7. Thomas, supra note 2, at 95.

8. Id.

9. Woldman, supra note 6, at 47.

10. Id.

11. Thomas, supra note 2, at 96.

12. I personally have had a half dozen such people in my life, individuals who through my life and professional career made me say: "I wish I could do that." When I make that statement, I know I have something to learn.

13. Woldman, supra note 6, at 49.

14. Thomas, supra note 2, at 97.

15. Id.

16. Thomas, supra note 2, at 98.

17. Id. at 98.

18. Id. at 100.

19. Thomas, supra note 2, at 100.

20. Id.

21. Id.

22. America's Lawyer-Presidents: From Law Office to Oval Office 130 (Norman Gross ed., Northwestern Univ. Press 2004) [hereinafter Gross].

23. In early 1860, Lincoln encountered Erastus Corning, then president of the New York Central Railroad. Corning asked Lincoln: "I understand that in Illinois you win all your lawsuits." Lincoln, in his usual humility responded, "Oh, no, Mr. Corning, that is not true, but I do make it a rule to refuse unless I am convinced the litigant's cause is just." It was then that Corning offered Lincoln the job of New York Railroad's General Counsel. Specifically, Corning asked: "would you entertain an offer from the New York Central Railroad, Mr. Lincoln to become its General Counsel at a salary of $10,000 a year?" Lincoln gently declined the generous offer, saying, "Mr. Corning, what could I do with $10,000 a year? It would ruin my family to have so much income. I don't believe I had better consider it."

24. While there are fabulous persuaders who work only for money, I have found that the ones who work for "the cause" (I call them "believers") were always the ones that were fighting for something bigger.

25. THOMAS, *supra* note 2, at 92.

26. GROSS, *supra* note 22, at 131–32.

27. *Id.* at 132.

28. THOMAS, *supra* note 2, at 92.

29. In 1848, Judge Davis was elected to the bench for the Eighth Circuit. As discussed, the Eighth Circuit was Lincoln's circuit, and Judge Davis was very fond of Lincoln (although he was scrupulously impartial in his legal decisions). After Lincoln returned from Congress and picked up his circuit practice, many said that Davis and Lincoln "parented" the circuit together, with Judge Davis being the head but Lincoln being the heart. Trevor Hill wrote in *Lincoln the Lawyer* that "the lawyers of the Eighth Circuit were practically a big family of which Davis was the official head, and over which he exerted a really parental influence. Not only did his Honor's ample girth and other physical proportions suggest a paterfamilias, but his mental attitude toward the bar was at once domineering and fatherly, with the domineering element always prominent." In 1862, President Lincoln appointed Judge Davis to the U.S. Supreme Court.

30. WILLIAM H. HERNDON & JESSE W. WEIK, HERNDON'S LIFE OF ABRAHAM LINCOLN 248–49 (Da Capo Press 1889) (1983) [hereinafter HERNDON & WEIK].

31. CHARLES H. COLEMAN, ABRAHAM LINCOLN AND COLES COUNTY, ILLINOIS 123 (Scarecrow Press 1955).

32. FREDERICK TREVOR HILL, LINCOLN THE LAWYER 183 (Fred B. Rothman & Co. 1986) [hereinafter HILL].

33. HERNDON & WEIK, *supra* note 30, at 287.

34. HILL, *supra* note 32, at 175–76.

35. Lincoln commented that arguing in front of the highest court of the land brought great pride and satisfaction to him; it was then that he himself recognized that he was a leading attorney in his state.

36. HILL, *supra* note 32, at 90–91.

37. *Id.*

38. WOLDMAN, *supra* note 6, at 100–01.

39. *Id.* at 106.

CHAPTER 3

LINCOLN'S TRIALS

Some historians claim that Lincoln was the greatest attorney who ever lived, while others maintain that his overall legal abilities have been slightly exaggerated because of his status as a martyr. Lincoln's long time partner, William Herndon, praised his partner's ability to think critically, prepare a case, and persuade a decision maker. However, Herndon was also quick to criticize certain aspects of Lincoln's practice. For instance, Herndon once wrote that Lincoln was "strikingly deficient in the technical rules of law."

Despite the discrepancies in Lincoln's reputation as a lawyer, there is one point that almost everyone agrees on: Lincoln was a fabulous persuasive speaker, and this helped his trial practice (maybe almost even carried his trial practice). He had the uncanny ability to win over a jury, a judge, and the audience in a courtroom. A Lincoln observer once stated that "his illustrations were often quaint and homely, but always clear and apt, and generally conclusive. . . . His wit and humor and inexhaustible [collection] of anecdotes, always to the point, added immensely to his powers as a jury advocate."

Lincoln tried thousands of cases, having varied success. However, three cases in particular stand out as examples of Lincoln's skill in the art of wooing a jury: the Almanac Trial, the Effie Afton Case, and the Chicken Bone Case.

ﻌﻉ ﻌﻉ ﻌﻉ

The Almanac Trial

Lincoln's most celebrated criminal case is undoubtedly the Almanac Trial, where he effectively defended William Armstrong from a murder conviction. Indeed, this case has been so popular that a film called *Young Mr. Lincoln,* starring Henry Fonda, was loosely based on it.

Interestingly enough, this case started with a wrestling match that took place more than twenty-five years before the crime was committed. During Lincoln's early days in New Salem, he was challenged to a match by William's father, Jack Armstrong, who was the leader of a local gang called Clary's Grove Boys. This match became famous in the Lincoln mythology, with many different accounts claiming who the winner of the match actually was. Douglas L. Wilson examines the match in detail in his book, *Honor's Voice,* and convincingly argues that it was in fact Armstrong who narrowly won the match. As fights often end with young men, Lincoln and Armstrong became close friends.

After Lincoln was elected captain and commander of his militia company in 1832 during the Black Hawk war (interestingly he was elected

LINCOLN, ON THE DAY OF THE
ALMANAC TRIAL.

captain because of his wrestling abilities), Armstrong served as a sergeant in his company. This companionship during Lincoln's campaign created an even closer friendship between Lincoln and Armstrong. It was this friendship that drew Lincoln into the most famous criminal trial of his legal career.

On the evening of August 29, 1857, James Metzker was beaten to death by two assailants. The attack seems to have stemmed from a drunken brawl that got out of control. Metzker died from his injuries two days after the attack. Two individuals were arrested and charged with Metzker's murder, James Norris and William Armstrong, who was nicknamed "Duff." Norris was accused of bludgeoning Metzker from behind with a piece of wood from a wagon frame. Duff Armstrong was said to have hit the victim from the front or side with a slung shot, which was a kinetic energy weapon with a leather pouch attached to a string with a lead ball or other material inside the pouch to give it weight.

After the two defendants were indicted, Duff Armstrong's first lawyer made a motion for a change of venue, which was granted, and his case moved from Mason to Cass County. Norris never made a motion to change venue and his case was tried in Mason County, where he was convicted of manslaughter. Norris's trial lasted only one day; four eyewitnesses took the stand, placed the attack at 11:00 p.m., and testified that they saw the defendant attack the victim under bright moonlight. In addition to the eyewitnesses, there was expert medical testimony that gave the opinion that Norris's blow to the back of the victim's head was the fatal injury.

Jack Armstrong died before his son was brought to trial, but his dying wish to his wife Hannah was that she save his son from the criminal charge—including selling the family farm if necessary. Hannah Armstrong wrote to her husband's longtime friend, Abraham, who was now a leading attorney in Springfield, asking him to represent her son at trial. Lincoln immediately took the case pro bono, refusing any offer for payment as a symbolic gesture to his deceased friend.

The trial was held in Beardstown, a town forty-five miles northwest of Springfield in the heart of Illinois farm country. Even today, a sign is posted on the edge of town reading "Home of Lincoln's Famous Almanac Trial." Lincoln made his first appearance as legal counsel for Duff Armstrong in the Beardstown courtroom sometime in late 1857. But the prosecution quickly moved for a continuance, which was granted. This pushed the trial to May of 1858, thirteen months after the crime occurred—a relatively long delay and usually to the disadvantage of the prosecution, considering it has the burden to prove guilt.

Before the trial started, Lincoln thoroughly researched the case, starting with Norris's case, to determine the prosecution's strategy and evidence that would likely be produced. He acquired an expert medical witness who could testify that the blows given by Norris to the back of the head could have been the victim's only serious injuries. Lincoln also tracked down the owner of the slung shot, a man named Watkins, and discovered that Watkins had the weapon in his possession when the murder took place. Moreover, he convinced Watkins to testify to this fact. Watkins also testified that the reason the weapon was found near the murder scene is because he had thrown it away in the area the day following the murder (the reason he discarded the weapon is not totally clear). In addition, Lincoln found an eyewitness to contradict the allegations that Duff Armstrong used a weapon; rather the witness was prepared to testify that Duff had only used his hands during the assault.

Bizarrely, before the trial began, Lincoln headed off a conspiracy to kidnap Charles Allen, a key witness for the prosecution. Days before the trial began, Armstrong's brothers conspired to hide Allen to prevent his testimony. When Lincoln learned of the plot he personally promised the government that Allen would be present at trial.

At trial, the prosecution presented expert medical testimony to support its version of how Metzker had received his injuries. The testimony implicated Lincoln's client in the crime as a contributing factor to the cause of death. Allen testified that he clearly saw Norris and Armstrong attack the victim, with Armstrong striking him from the front with a slung shot. Furthermore, Allen testified that he had a perfect view of the fight because of the moon's position at moon-high, giving him plenty of illumination to witness the crime. As Allen was testifying Lincoln sat in his chair looking absolutely unconcerned despite the damaging testimony taking place. The prosecution rested its case after Allen gave his dramatic recreation of the gruesome crime for the jury.

Lincoln began by presenting his expert and eye witnesses to refute the case presented by the prosecution. Lincoln's principal expert was Dr. Charles Parker, who testified to a string of hypothetical questions. Lincoln ignored Norris's conviction and aimed the crux of Dr. Parker's testimony at showing that Metzker's falling from a horse could have caused the injury that the prosecution called the "fatal blow." He testified that the injury to the front of Metzker's head caused damage, but that it was the injury in the back of the skull that killed him. After the trial, the presiding judge "said that Parker's testimony was the most persuasive on the defendant's behalf."[1]

However, it was Lincoln's unconventional calling of the prosecution's key witness, Allen, back to the stand to conclude his case that transformed this from a typical murder trial with a very skilled attorney into legal lore. Lincoln's examination of Allen was planned well before the jury was sworn in, and was completed in a systematic manner. First Lincoln had Allen re-testify as to what he saw that night, which is normally taboo for lawyers. After Allen rehashed the facts, Lincoln focused on his distance from the assault:

Q: Did you actually see the fight?
A: Yes.
Q: And you stood very near to them?
A: No, it was one hundred and fifty feet or more.
Q: In open field?
A: No, in the timber.
Q: What kind of timber?
A: Beech timber.
Q: Leafs on it rather thick in August?
A: It looks like it.

After he established the distance was one hundred fifty to one hundred sixty feet and slightly obscured by beech leafs, Lincoln methodically questioned him as to his ability to see the attack and the location of the "bright full moon," as Allen called it in his earlier testimony:

Q: What time did all this take place?
A: Eleven o'clock at night.
Q: Did you have a candle there?
A: No. What would I want a candle for?
Q: How could you see from a distance of one hundred fifty feet or more, without a candle, at eleven o'clock at night?
A: The moon was shining real bright.
Q: Full moon?
A: Yes, a full moon, and as high in the heavens as the sun would be at ten o'clock in the morning.

After Allen persistently claimed that the moon was at its highest point and very bright, thus giving him more than enough light to observe the crime, Lincoln felt Allen had sufficiently dug himself into the hole Lincoln had designed. Lincoln calmly walked back to his briefcase and produced an almanac where he turned to the page with the information for August 29, 1857. After obtaining judicial notice that the almanac was in fact accurate, Lincoln casually showed Allen the page that documented that the moon was in fact set in its highest position at 12:03 a.m., a full hour after Allen had testified that the moon had set:

Q: Does not the almanac say that on August 29th the moon was barely past the first quarter of being full?
A: [Inaudible answer]

Q: Does not the almanac also say that the moon had disappeared by eleven o'clock? If the moon was at its highest position at 12:03 a.m. it would have been at low in the West at 11 p.m.
A: [Inaudible answer]
Q: Is it not a fact that it was too dark to see anything from so far away, let alone one hundred fifty feet?
A: [Inaudible answer]

This line of questioning proved that the illumination was poor at the time of the crime, which impeached Allen's entire testimony. Since the government had made Allen its star witness, the prosecution's case fell apart with this simple flip of an almanac's page. After Lincoln discredited Allen on the stand, the courtroom's audience burst out laughing. Lincoln published the almanac to the jury and calmly walked back and sat down.

In summations, Lincoln described with authentic emotion his friendship with Duff's father with tears trickling down his face, which essentially amounted to a personal plea for a verdict of not guilty. He told the jury of "the motherly kindness of Mrs. Armstrong towards him when he was a penniless young man, struggling to fit himself for some useful employment in life."[2] Lincoln's co-counsel in the case, William Walker, said of the summation: "I have never seen such mastery exhibited over the feeling and emotions of men as on that occasion. His genuine passion roused the same emotion in the jury, evidenced by several jurors wiping tears from their eyes when Lincoln sat down."

In addition to his compelling closing argument, Lincoln fought hard to have jury instructions selected that most benefited his client, specifically to shift blame to Norris and dispel reasonable doubt. The court instructed:

> The Court instructs the jury that if they have any reasonable doubt on the eye, or the blow on the back of the head, they are to find the defendant *Not Guilty,* unless they further believe from the evidence, beyond all reasonable doubt, that *Armstrong and Norris acted by concert,* against Metzker, and that Norris struck the blow on the back of the head. That if they believe from the evidence that Norris killed Metzker, they are to acquit Armstrong, unless they also believe from the evidence, beyond a reasonable doubt, that Armstrong acted in concert with Norris in the killing, or purpose to kill or hurt Metzker.

The jury took only one hour of deliberations to acquit Duff Armstrong. The acquittal represented a great triumph for Lincoln on a personal and professional level. He fulfilled a promise to an old friend and demonstrated his dominance as a trial attorney.

There are several lessons to be learned from Lincoln's conduct in the Almanac Trial. The first dates back to the foundation of his friendship with Jack Armstrong. All business people and lawyers know that **networking is a key to success**. It can never be foreseen when a simple friendship will turn out to be a life-changing relationship. Lincoln was renowned for making friends. Even more important and impressive was his ability to keep his friends. His written archives demonstrate this ability, with scores of letters to friends he had made as a store owner, lawyer, and later as president of the United States.

In the 1800s, court trials were the equivalent of blockbuster Hollywood movies. Everybody who was anybody waited for news about the hot trials and took note of clever attorneys. Displays of brilliancy such as Lincoln's in the Almanac Trial pushed lawyers onto the national stage. As a candidate for president, when an opponent would accuse him of being a country bumpkin, it was cases like the Almanac Trial that proved them wrong.

Another critical lesson that is brought up in this trial: the importance of having a back-up plan. **Never place all your eggs in one basket**. Lincoln knew that re-calling Allen to the stand put his client in a precarious position—if the strategy failed and if there were no back-up plan, it could have been disastrous for Duff Armstrong. You can never absolutely account for all the variables and emotions that will arise in a trial and sway the outcome. Here we see that Lincoln undoubtedly had two major plans: The first and foremost was to impeach Allen and discredit the government's case. The second was to demonstrate that even if the witnesses were believable and Duff Armstrong was there that night, he did not inflict the deadly blows that killed James Metzker.

Lincoln's expert witness rebutted the government's medical testimony and opined that the blows delivered by Norris to the back of Metzker's head could easily have been the only significant injuries. This statement alone could have supported reasonable doubt for the jury by suggesting that even if Duff Armstrong was present at the time in question, and even if he was involved with the attack, his actions were merely negligible.

However, in case this medical testimony were not enough, Lincoln, through extensive detective work, found the owner of the slung shot and had him testify that he was in possession of the device during the time of the murder. Another witness testified that Duff Armstrong never had a weapon at all. Again, all of these witnesses supported the notion that even if his client was there, he was not the cause of death. The easiest way to show reasonable doubt is to give the jury an alternative theory for the case. Asking a jury to acquit a defendant without another possibility is difficult. Jurors need answers, and if you do not provide them, they will go with the persuader that provides the most plausible story, choosing the path of least resistance.[3]

It is important to note that sometimes proffering an alternative theory at trial (or in an argument) can be harmful. It may show a jury a "divided front' or give them the feeling that a slick attorney is trying to bamboozle them. This is where good judgment must come in: you must find a balance between the benefits of having two arguments on the table with the benefit of putting everything into one theory and hitting it hard. If one argument is strong and the other is tenuous, it is probably wise to stick with the strong argument. A compromise strategy is to develop two theories for a case. In this strategy, play the strongest hand and keep the alternate argument in your back pocket; use it only if large holes appear in your primary theory. Holes always appear; there is never a perfect case. The critical question to ask is "how big are the holes."

In this case, Lincoln appears to play both theories at the same time, an arduous task. One theory was argued vicariously through Allen: that there was definitely not enough evidence to say that Duff was there beyond any reasonable doubt. The other theory was that maybe Duff was there, but even if he was, his actions were not the causation of the victim's death. Lincoln had to play both arguments at the same time, because it was impossible to know what Allen was going to say on the stand. Allen could have had a very reasonable explanation for the discrepancy between the almanac and his former testimony. If that had happened and if Lincoln had counted on the impeachment of Allen for his entire case, Duff Armstrong would likely have been convicted.[4]

Another lesson learned from the Allen impeachment is the need for thorough research. An experienced persuasive speaker or lawyer will never undermine the value of mastering the facts of your case or product; rhetoric is not often enough. Lincoln thoroughly researched Armstrong's case. He would have known that the prosecution would probably rely on the Allen testimony from researching Norris's criminal trial. Armed with what Allen would probably say at Armstrong's trial, Lincoln researched all sources that would enable him to discredit Allen—hence the almanac.

Typically, there will not be such a clear-cut outline of your opponent's strategy as there was for Lincoln, coming after the Norris trial. However, by brainstorming and putting yourself in your opponent's shoes, you should be able to deduce at least 80 percent of your opponent's case. Once the logical strategy is discovered, the remainder of research can be focused to find an Achilles' heel that can be exposed, such as Lincoln's Almanac.

One of the most ingenious aspects of the Allen testimony is that Lincoln turned the government's star witness into the government's greatest impediment. Using legal jujitsu to turn a witness against its own side through shrewd cross-examination is not always possible. However, when it is available, it should be exploited to its fullest—it's one of the surest paths to a courtroom victory. Nothing is more of an encumbrance to opponents than when their own weapons are used against them. They almost always do not know what to do.[5]

Another lesson from the Allen testimony is the ability to keep your opponent off-balance at all times. By calling Allen back to the stand as a defense witness, Lincoln probably caused the prosecution to have a panic attack as they desperately tried to figure out what he was up to. If your opponent is constantly trying to figure out what you will pull out of your hat next, they will have less time to plan a systematic defense to your strategy. In addition to throwing off the prosecutor, Lincoln also successfully threw Allen off-balance. Specifically, if the witness is confused and distracted trying to size you up, attempt to keep him that way and gain as much ground as possible until he gets back on his feet.

An impressive lesson that can be learned from Lincoln's use of the Allen testimony is driving a witness into a corner, allowing him no room to wiggle free before impeaching his entire testimony. Lincoln set up Allen with dozens of questions, all with the intent to lock up his testimony so he would have no wiggle room after he was shown to have been lying (or badly mistaken). Lincoln had Allen go over virtually his entire direct testimony again and then made him state once again that the moon was very bright the night he witnessed the crime. It was at this point Lincoln produced the almanac, which in effect showed that Allen's entire testimony was untrustworthy and possibly perjurious. Because Lincoln had "cornered" Allen's examination before he pulled out his trump card, Allen had nowhere to run and no lies to save him.

This brings up another point, one that shows Lincoln's skill as an attorney. The great law professor Irving Younger said only a true maestro of cross-examination can break its basic rules—and one such rule is that, "if the jury hears a fact once they may believe it, hears it twice they will believe it, and if heard a third time Jesus Christ himself will have to tell them otherwise." Allen told the jury once on his direct, and Lincoln allowed him to tell his story two more times during his cross-examination. He allowed Allen to do this because his plan of attack required Allen to paint himself in a corner by convincing the jury he was right so that Lincoln could then prove him wrong, leaving huge doubt in the jury's mind.

Another reason to allow a witness to re-testify during cross might be to show the witness as the opposing attorney's mouthpiece. By allowing the witness to tell his story again and again, the jury can hear how perfect it is, how memorized it is, and how coached it is. Lincoln knew that one of the worst things that could happen would be for the jury to disbelieve a witness because they are convinced they were fed their testimony from lawyers.

In 1911, there was a famous trial concerning the New York Triangle Shirtwaist Factory fire on March 25th of that year. The fire killed 146 workers, almost all of them very young, poor women who died from the fire itself or when they jumped from the building trying to escape the inferno. The disaster resulted in a prosecution for manslaughter of the owners Isaac Harris and Max Blanck; they had locked the doors and stairwells to prevent workers from taking breaks, which trapped the women in the fire. Max Steuer, an exceptionally famous and accomplished trial attorney of his day, represented the defense. When Steuer cross-examined Kate Alterman, one of the workers in the factory, he used an atypical approach. Specifically, he asked Alterman to repeat the testimony she gave on direct examination—usually an unwise decision. After she finished, he then asked her to repeat it again and then again. Steuer noticed that as she repeated her account of the fire, it was verbatim each time, and he suggested that she had been coached to deliver the lawyer's testimony and not her own. This line of questioning damaged Alterman's credibility and the credibility of the prosecution's case—the defendants were acquitted.

Another lesson we can learn from Lincoln in this case is from his use of expert witnesses. An expert witness is an immensely valuable tool in a trial or setting where one is trying to convince another of a certain set of facts. In the legal field, an expert can testify to his or her opinion based on facts given or a hypothetical fact pattern. Experts are not mandated to have personal knowledge about the case or the parties involved in order to give their testimony, unlike lay witnesses. An additional advantage is the weight expert opinions carry. For example, when a doctor gives an opinion about medical matters to a non-medically trained person, he is typically trusted and given credibility based on his position; with a normal witness, you have to prove a history of reliability. This is particularly important at trial where "credibility" has to be established in a matter of minutes.

An additional lesson to be observed from this case is the importance of jury instructions. You can put on the most persuasive case, with a great story and great facts, but if the jury instructions do not leave room for your theory, your hard work was for nothing. Today, because most judges follow "model jury instructions," you can usually predict the jury instructions before the case starts and certainly before closing arguments.

Therefore, you must consider jury instructions in the development of your case.

Judicial notice can be another wonderful tool for attorneys. In essence, judicial notice is when an attorney asks the judge to deem something trustworthy and admissible in court. It is useful for many of the same reasons expert testimony is—it adds instant credibility to the facts one intends to tender. Before Lincoln showed the almanac to Allen, he asked for judicial notice of it, which the judge granted. In effect, he got the judge to affirm that the almanac was true as printed, which puts the court's weight behind the evidence.

A critical lesson can be seen in the closing argument, where Lincoln showed how emotion can be an extremely positive influence. Although Lincoln's reference to his friendship with Duff's father and his personal plea for his acquittal is wholly inappropriate in today's courtrooms, one can see how a display of authentic emotion from counsel can go a long way in the eyes of a decision maker. Juries and other decision makers are people who want to do their duty as well as help other people; they can sense when somebody vests himself or herself in a cause. When they see this, it not only adds reliability to what you say but it also adds a human touch to your argument, invoking the instinct to help that resides in almost every human. However, just as people can sense authentic emotion, they can usually detect when it is artificial. A persuader does much more damage to a cause with an obvious synthetic display of emotion than by playing it dry.

The last lesson that can be learned from Lincoln in the Almanac Trial is his participation in getting Armstrong's brothers to release Allen so he could testify in the case. Lincoln was renowned for being honest and playing hard but fair in his law practice. This kind of reputation is hard-earned and easily lost. The damage is far reaching if one gains the reputation of playing fast and loose with the rules, not to mention the possibility that doing so can result in professional discipline or jail time if the offense is egregious enough. There is another more calculated reason for Lincoln's actions with regard to his obtaining the release of Allen. Lincoln knew one of his strategies was to impeach Allen, and if the Armstrong brothers detained Allen, he would have no one to impeach. Thus, his goodwill was also good business.

❧ ❧ ❧

The Effie Afton Case

In April of 1856, a two-part, 1,585-foot iron and timber bridge was completed in Illinois, spanning between Rock Island and Davenport. The
bridge allowed trains to cross the Mississippi River and bring crops from
the Iowa farms directly to Chicago and the East Coast cities for the first
time.

The construction of the bridge caused turmoil in the local area and
the entire shipping community—many people (especially those in the
steamboat industry) viewed the bridge as a hazard to river navigation.
However, the real controversy was between the railroad and steamboat
industries over how goods should move throughout the country: across
the prairies by rail, or by steamboats using the river networks.

On May 6, 1856, only one month after the bridge was completed and
just fifteen days after the first train used it to cross the Mississippi River,
a steamer packed with cattle named the Effie Afton crashed into one of
the bridge's piers. The Effie Afton was traveling from St. Louis to St. Paul
when one of its side wheels stopped. The boat twisted around a pier and
either a kerosene lamp or a stove onboard the boat tipped over and set the
boat and the bridge on fire. The Effie Afton sank, but luckily the crew and
the three hundred cattle survived. The bridge suffered extensive damage
due to the impact and the fire that resulted. In addition to the damaged
pier, the bridge's draw pivot was jammed, further obstructing water traffic.
Eight days after the crash, a portion of the bridge span fell into the water.

Immediately after the crash, there was speculation that it may have
been an intentional arson rather than a simple accident. The arson charge
was never admitted nor proven, but the rumors of foul play persisted.
These theories were primarily based on the fact that the steamboat owners
wanted the bridge gone because the railroads were stealing their customers. Local newspapers reported "delight" on behalf of the steamboat owners, which further fueled the rumors, with one report stating: "Mississippi
Bridge Destroyed—Let All Rejoice."

The event was what the steamboat owners were waiting for in order
to launch into legal action against the railroad. Soon after the crash, the
owners of the Effie Afton sued the Railroad Bridge Company. The suit
claimed that the bridge was a public nuisance and injurious to navigators
of steamboats. Furthermore, the suit asked for an injunction order from
the court to prohibit all future bridges over the river.

The Railroad Bridge Company hired three attorneys to protect their
interests in the case; one of those lawyers was Abraham Lincoln. By that

time, Lincoln was known as a highly skilled railroad litigation attorney. When the Effie Afton case was filed, he had already handled several cases for the Illinois Central Railroad; of course, he had also argued numerous cases against the railroads.

Although this case was specifically about the Effie Afton and the Rock Island Bridge, every party involved understood the far-reaching implications of the case's outcome—it was really about the future of transportation and shipping in the United States. In addition, the case was shaping the significance of two cities. St. Louis was the steamboat capital, while Chicago was the railroad center. Both cities had a significant amount of their prosperity riding on the outcome.

One of Lincoln's great attributes was the way he prepared for a trial; when time permitted he examined every detail of a case. In the case at hand, he scrutinized a survey of the rapids near the bridge, which had been completed in 1837 by the U.S. Army Corps of Engineers. Not content to simply read books and surveys, Lincoln went to the crash site to see the damage firsthand. He even took his own measurements and examined the way the water flowed between the piers. Lincoln talked to Benjamin Brayton, who engineered the bridge, and he talked to captains who sailed the river about its navigation. Through this research he learned that less than 1 percent of all the boats that navigated the bridge had any problems. This personal examination of every fact of a case was typical of the way Lincoln prepared for trial. Herndon said of Lincoln's research that if he "had occasion to learn or investigate any subject he was thorough and indefatigable in his search. He not only went to the root of the question, but dug up the root, and separated and analyzed every fiber of it."

The trial began on September 8, 1857, in the Chicago federal courthouse. The plaintiff claimed a case of nuisance and took ten days to present its case in chief. When the defense took the stand, Lincoln's course of examinations and arguments astonished the jury and the courtroom audience. He admitted that the bridge was indeed dangerous to river navigation, but argued that it was an unavoidable risk. This admission was not a confession of his client's guilt; rather, it was presented to lay a weak point of his case on the table and take the sting out of the topic so his opponent could not exploit it during the cross-examination of his witnesses.

Lincoln also made convincing arguments that while the bridge was an obstacle, the boat was ultimately at fault. Moreover, he argued that the river was wide enough to support both the railroads and the steamboats.

In his closing argument, Lincoln argued two key points. The first was how rail was the future of America. He said, "it is growing larger and larger, building up new countries with a rapidity never before seen in the history of the world." The second point has been coined as the

"American Doctrine of Bridges," in which Lincoln stated that "one man has as much right to cross a river as another man has to sail up or down it." The trial ended in a hung jury, which was not the all-out victory Lincoln had hoped for, but it was definitely not a loss. The case went up to the United States Supreme Court, where attorneys used many of Lincoln's arguments to hold that building bridges over rivers was legitimate and legal. On a professional level, the case was a tremendous success for Lincoln. Because the trial's outcome had such a considerable impact, he received national attention as a leading attorney.

Lincoln recognized the case as being a nation-changing event. He was also well aware that when two business industries collide over issues involving fortunes, and those parties start a battle in court, there are huge sums of money to be made by the lawyers. It is not clear exactly what Lincoln's fees were in the Effie Afton trial, but they were substantial.[6] However, more important to Lincoln was that the case gave him national name recognition, putting him in a position to run for the presidency.

Lincoln's preparedness in the Effie Afton case won the day. Despite his reputation of being sloppily dressed, having poor organizational skills, and even Herndon's claim that he was deficient in his knowledge of technical legal rules, he was nothing but meticulous when he was working on a case. Not only does thorough research give you confidence in your position, it also helps ensures that all possible arguments are available.

In addition to scrupulous research, Lincoln knew there was never a substitute for firsthand knowledge. In the Effie Afton case, Lincoln went to the crash scene to better orient himself. Getting firsthand knowledge of a crime or accident scene is invaluable because it gives you a personal feel for the case being tried, which in turn provides for a more convincing argument. Moreover, when dealing with critical information, it is wise to never take anyone's word for what can be personally witnessed. Lincoln developed his information about the accident by taking measurements and surveying the river's currents. This allowed him to personally tailor his case to his observations.[7]

Another trial tactic that can be emulated was Lincoln's willingness to admit the obvious early in a case. Specifically, by admitting that the bridge was indeed a hazard, he took much of the sting out of the issue. Lincoln knew if he argued arcane points in front of the jury he would have lost credibility. Lincoln's point was that of course having something in the river was, on some level, a hazard to river navigation—but it was not an overly burdensome hazard, and it could have and should have been avoided. It is much more effective to admit your weak points in a case, be honest, and move on while holding on tight to your core points. Do not vainly attempt to argue a weak position if you have other, stronger points at hand, even if those points superficially appear to work against you. In other words, pick your battles.

Notwithstanding the lesson of cutting your losses on weak points, a trial attorney must be able to point a finger at someone or something else and lay the overall blame elsewhere. Lincoln admitted that the bridge was a hazard just as riding a horse is a hazard. Yet, the key in his argument was that the Effie Afton itself was the cause of the accident. If one rides a horse and falls off, it's illogical to say that since riding horses is a hazardous activity, the horse is at fault.

An additional reason for laying blame on your opponent is that it psychologically lets your client know that you are working for them. In a trial, a lawyer not only has to convince the jury that she is right, but she must also convince the client that she is effectively working for them. Lay clients do not always know why a lawyer uses certain tactics in a case. However, they will always understand when the lawyer blames the opponent.[8]

Another tool used by Lincoln in the Effie Afton case was his insinuation that the "accident" was not really an accident. He did this by pointing out that after the incident, all the river craft in the area gathered around the sunken boat and sounded their whistles in celebration. Because Lincoln could not "prove" the accident was intentional, he did the next best thing—he slipped in some supporting facts with the intention of letting the jury figure it out for themselves. Juries are not stupid, and they understand that if it looks and quacks like a duck, it is most likely a duck. The lesson here is that sometimes you cannot prove things, but it is important to get the information into the minds of the decision makers anyway; they will usually come up with the most obvious answer. However, it must be noted that if a subject matter is deemed inadmissible, it is unethical to "slip" it in. Therefore, a persuader must walk a fine line between manipulating the rules by making an argument that undermines the judicial system and mentioning details that are simply persuasive.

The closing in Effie Afton was typical of Lincoln's career. Lincoln often would appeal to a core American value in making his summations, as he did here with the "American Doctrine of Bridges." Lincoln appealed to the entrepreneur and frontiersman that is inside every American. Americans are proud and love to hear stories of their country growing and thriving. By arguing that the railroads were essential to America's prosperity, he keyed into that core trait. The adventurous spirit is still alive in America, making this type of argument relevant even today.

Also in Lincoln's closing, he touched the part of every American who believes that in a free country, everyone is entitled to free movement and the opportunity to succeed. By arguing that a man has as much right to travel over a river as he does to travel up it, he addressed the concepts of freedom and capitalism that are enshrined within the Constitution and the Declaration of Independence. This also had the effect of making it personal to each member of the jury—*you* are allowed to travel any way you see fit.

ぎ ぎ ぎ

The Chicken Bone Case

Shortly after midnight on October 17, 1855, the town of Bloomington, Illinois, was awakened by fire bells. The fire brigade fought to contain a fire that had started in the livery stable and was spreading to adjacent houses and buildings. By the time the firefighters won the battle, an entire block was destroyed, with only a bank and hardware store remaining. The fire claimed one life, that of William Green, and injured several others. One of the injured was Samuel Fleming, whose femoral bones were both broken when a chimney collapsed on his thighs.

Three doctors, Thomas Rogers, Jacob Freese, and Eli Crothers, treated Mr. Fleming. Dr. Freese worked on his left leg, while Dr. Crothers and Dr. Rogers worked on Fleming's right leg. All three doctors made house calls to Fleming for two weeks and opined that his recovery was going well. In a deposition taken in August of 1857, Dr. Freese stated that Fleming, "was getting along first rate, and that, were it not for the confinement, he would scarcely know that his thighs were broken—so little pain did he suffer."

However, the prognosis changed after the two-week mark, when Fleming started to have extreme pain at the fracture point in his right leg. Fleming's sister, who was caring for him, said she felt the fracture point and thought that the bones were not set properly. The doctors did not concur with the sister's assessment and agreed that the leg was healing normally. They increased his morphine for the additional pain. Dr. Crothers went on to tell Fleming that his pain was due to pleurisy and had nothing to do with his leg.

Nearly a month after the accident, Dr. Rogers called on Fleming to see how he was healing. To his surprise, after he took off the bandages, he discovered that Fleming's legs "were crooked as Ram's horns." After Dr. Rogers gathered the other two doctors, they measured Fleming's legs to discover that one was an inch shorter than the other. Before they redressed his legs, they changed the position of his splints hoping it would alleviate the problem. A week later the three doctors returned to Fleming's house and learned that while the left leg was healing properly, the right was still misshapen at the fracture point. Dr. Freese observed that the left leg was "doing well—but the right one had a considerable bend at the point of fracture. The fracture was originally oblique, and now we found the lower sharp point of the upper portion of the thigh bone bending outward from a proper line of the bone—when in sound condition."

The doctors recommended that Fleming have his leg rebroken and reset. Fleming, after prudent deliberation with his family and the doctors, relented and agreed to the procedure.

Fleming was put under anesthesia using chloroform. Once they believed that Fleming was unconscious, Rogers and Crothers started to manipulate the limb in order to refracture it. However, before they completed the procedure, Fleming began to scream in pain. Fleming ordered the doctors to stop, at which time the doctors insisted that if they did not finish the procedure his leg would be permanently misshapen. Nevertheless, Fleming ordered the doctors to cease; Fleming's family also told the doctors to stop, saying "let him alone, he had suffered enough." The doctors stopped the procedure and left but not before Dr. Crothers told Fleming "that he would not be responsible for the result."

As expected, when his leg had fully healed, it was deformed and Fleming walked with a severe limp. Because Dr. Crothers and Dr. Rogers had worked on his right leg, Fleming held them responsible for his deformity. On March 28, 1856, Fleming retained six lawyers to file a tort suit in the McLean Circuit Court. Fleming asked for ten thousand dollars in damages, a considerable amount for the day. He averred that the two doctors had negligently failed "to use due and proper care, skill and diligence" when caring for his leg. He also claimed but for this negligence, he would not have "suffered and underwent great and unnecessary pain and anguish," which resulted in his legs healing in "unsightly and unnatural a manner."

The doctors also hired an armada of lawyers. They hired four local attorneys: David Brier, Jessie Birch, L. L. Strain, and Andres Rogers. In addition, to counter Fleming's hiring of Leonard Swett—renowned for his specialty in medical malpractice cases—the doctors hired prominent Springfield attorneys John Stuart and Abraham Lincoln. Lincoln and Stuart were former partners, so they knew how to work together, which helped significantly considering they were hired last-minute and only had a week to prepare for the trial.

When the spring term opened in Bloomington on April 7, 1856, Lincoln made a motion to Judge Davis that a continuance be granted. The request for the continuance was based on the fact that Dr. Rogers was "so unwell as to be unable to attend the present term of court, and . . . his personal presence at the trial is necessary to enable them to conduct the defense of the case properly." Dr. Rogers was especially important for the defense because he had attended to Fleming more frequently than Dr. Crothers; it was argued that he had a "more intimate acquaintance with, and perfect knowledge of the whole case."

Judge Davis granted the continuance, scheduled the trial for the fall term, and ordered the defendants to pay the court costs for the delay.

When the fall term came about, Lincoln again asked for a continuance. This time the reason was because Dr. Freese had moved to Cincinnati and the defendants had not been able to depose him. Lincoln and the other defense attorneys argued that Dr. Freese's testimony was critical because he was present when the defendant doctors originally set the leg. In addition, Dr. Freese was present when the doctors decided to leave the leg alone and hope it would heal naturally. The defense also argued that Dr. Freese was necessary to explain the doctor's actions when they tried to re-break the leg in order to reset it. Again, Judge Davis allowed for the continuance and again made the defense pay for the court expenses and set the trial for the spring term of 1857.

In the interim, Lincoln thoroughly prepared his witnesses for trial. Notable in this preparation was his work with Dr. Crothers. Lincoln had the doctor run through the technical aspects of the injury itself, which is when he learned how a human bone changes with age. Dr. Crothers used a chicken bone to demonstrate this organic alteration, which Lincoln immediately recognized as a brilliant explanation—he understood the situation perfectly when a chicken bone was used to illustrate it. He realized that a jury would also find this demonstration crucial in understanding the medical evidence.

In the spring of 1857, a jury was sworn in to hear the case of *Fleming v. Rogers and Crothers*. The trial itself took a week to complete—a relatively long trial for the time. The plaintiff called an army of doctors to testify, fifteen in total, along with more than twenty other witnesses. Lincoln and the defense also called many doctors to contest the plaintiff's claim of events. However, it was Lincoln's wit and skills as an attorney that had the most effect on the outcome.

During the cross-examination of Fleming, Lincoln asked the plaintiff if he were able to walk. Fleming answered affirmatively, but also added: "one leg is short, so I have to limp." After Fleming finished his answer Lincoln turned to the jury and said: "Well, what I would advise you is to get down on your knees and thank your Heavenly Father, and also these two doctors that you have any legs to stand on at all!" The statement flustered Fleming and made a critical point to the jury—specifically that Fleming was indeed better off than he would likely have been with no treatment.

Lincoln saved the chicken bones for his closing argument. Referring to the medical evidence presented in the case, Lincoln held up one chicken bone from a middle-aged chicken and one bone from a pullet. He summarized the evidence that the jury heard during testimony and explained to the jury that each bone had its own consistency and pliability, with the bone from the young chicken being limber and flexible and the older chicken's bone being brittle. Lincoln then pointed out that Fleming was himself middle-aged. Lincoln then dramatically snapped the old chicken bone in two, showing the jury how brittle it was and how the fracture point was so severe that the doctors could not be held account- able for complications.[9]

The demonstration with the chicken bone had its intended effect on the jury. Before the trial started, it was rumored that a majority of the jury was predisposed in favor of Samuel Fleming. The defendants were wealthy and being tried in a humble town, and it can be assumed that the townsfolk would have liked to see the rich defendants punished (class prejudice ran in both directions.) Despite this inclination of the jury, because of Lincoln's closing argument, the jury hung and could not reach a decision after eighteen hours of deliberation.

The judge set the retrial of the case to the fall docket. However, when the fall court term came, the defense had lost yet another witness. Isaac Small, who administered the chloroform to Fleming when the doc- tors were attempting to reset his leg, had moved to Tennessee. Judge Davis allowed for another continuance. The defense then asked for a change of venue because they felt that Fleming had an "undue influence over the minds" of possible jurors in McLean County. The judge granted the motion for change of venue, and the case was transferred to Logan County.

The case was never tried in Logan County because a settlement was reached before the March 1858 court term began. The defense agreed to pay for fees that Fleming had incurred as a result of the dispute, which totaled about a thousand dollars.

It is noted that some scholars dispute that the *Fleming* case was a great victory for Lincoln—after all, he did not win. But the truth is that a hung jury is a near-win for the defense, and it is a loss (not a total loss—but a loss nonetheless) for the plaintiff. Obviously, a not guilty verdict is pre- ferred, but a do-over is the next best thing; it gives the defense a second chance with the knowledge of what the plaintiff's case will be. Also, as seen here, the hung jury allowed the defense to drag out the case and reach a settlement only one-tenth of the original demand.

The lesson here is about thorough witness preparation: Only after a lawyer personally prepares a witness will he fully understand how to ask questions that trigger the most effective responses. So, in addition to working with your witnesses on what you want them to say during examination, it is critical that an attorney learns from his clients and wit- nesses. It was from Dr. Crothers that Lincoln got the idea to use a chicken bone to demonstrate the aging effects on human bones, which played a substantial role in getting the hung jury. This account shows not only how Lincoln was meticulous in his witness preparation, but also that he learned from his witnesses and was not too proud to use a good idea, even when it came from someone else. The ability to absorb and adapt effective trial techniques is critical in becoming an effective oral advocate. Even the most gifted speaker can pick up tricks from others—that is often how they become speaking geniuses.[10]

Another lesson that can be learned from this case is Lincoln's ability to turn a damaging answer into a positive one with clever wording. In this case, when Fleming told Lincoln that he could walk but had a short leg with a limp, Lincoln, instead of backing down from the damaging response, turned the answer into a positive point for his clients by inferring that he would not be walking at all if not for his client's diligent work.[11]

No persuasive speaker will get the exact answer he wants all the time. The ability to recover from a damaging response is what separates average advocates from truly gifted advocates. Instead of letting Fleming gain sympathy in the jury for his leg, Lincoln attempted to make him seem ungrateful for a job well done. Of course, you must be careful with this technique; often attorneys attempt it and come across as heartless. It is possible that some on the jury might have thought Lincoln was making fun of Fleming, but the lesson remains the same—try to turn bad responses into supportive ones.

While the chicken bone demonstration was originally Dr. Crothers', Lincoln undoubtedly perfected the lesson for the jury. The ability to effectively communicate to the jury or an audience that you want to persuade is, in a nutshell, the key to effective oral advocacy. Whether using a chicken bone or quoting the Bible, the goal is the same: to connect with the decision makers without looking as if you are trying to manipulate their emotions. Here we see that Lincoln was talented at understanding his audiences. With simple country people, he used simple props they would all recognize. Most on the jury had probably butchered a chicken, creating a personal connection to Lincoln's analogy. Lincoln knew this, and knew that people will believe their past familiarity above almost anything else.

In addition to *how* Lincoln used the chicken bones, we can learn from *when* he used them. Lincoln well understood a jury's attention span. A jury will absorb some of the opening statements, some of the closing arguments, and bits and pieces of the actual testimony. Lincoln could have easily used the bone demonstration during his direct examination of Dr. Crothers—after all, it was his idea. However, Lincoln understood that saving his most effective demonstration for his closing would have the most dramatic effect and would be remembered the longest.

The last two lessons that can be learned from Lincoln in this case are his use of continuances and knowing when to settle. In total, the case was continued three times; although it is not suggested that the defense sought the continuances to undermine the proceedings, it is noted that by postponing a trial, the defense is more likely to gain a favorable settlement, especially from an anxious plaintiff. Also, legal wrangling motivates plaintiffs to settle—while legal hoops are probably what attorneys are hated most for by nonlawyers, Lincoln's use of the change of venue, without a doubt, combined with the continuances and hung jury, motivated Fleming to settle for roughly one thousand dollars, one-tenth of the original claim.

This brings up the last lesson, which is to settle when possible. Not every case can be won; it is the job of a good advocate to look into his crystal ball and advise his client when to cut their losses and settle. Settlement is almost always in the best interest for both sides—therefore, the possibility of settlement should always be on an advocate's mind.

❧ ❧ ❧

Notes

1. Allen D. Spiegel, A. Lincoln, Esquire: A Shrewd, Sophisticated Lawyer in his Time 159 (Mercer Univ. Press 2002).

2. Newton Bateman, Paul Selby, Charles Aesop Martin, Historical Encyclopedia of Illinois, vol. 2, 689 (Chicago Munsell Publishing 1915).

3. I was involved in a case as a Federal Prosecutor where the only elements that the government had to prove were that the defendant was deported at some point in time, he was not a U.S. citizen, and he had illegally returned to the United States. (8 U.S.C. § 1326). These are typically fairly easy cases for U.S. Attorney Offices. However, in this case, the defense attorney aptly came up with another theory, a totally off-the-wall theory, but a big enough backdoor for a juror to scramble through. The defense's theory was that because we did not have an expert from the government agency (USCIS) that keeps track of deportations in the United States, we did not prove beyond a reasonable doubt that the defendant in fact had been previously deported (despite having a witness who testified that he saw the defendant physically leave). The jury hung 11–1, with one juror buying into the alternate possibility.

4. I and another attorney (Assistant United States Attorney Anne Perry) retried the case that resulted in a hung jury. The same Federal Defender put on basically the same defense with the same backdoor. We not only were able to compensate a little and make the door smaller (by affirmatively addressing the record-keeping issue), but the jury in the second trial also simply did not buy the alternative theory—they returned a guilty verdict in a little over an hour.

5. In another criminal trial that I conducted (with Assistant United States Attorney Robert Huie), the opposing counsel made a huge deal over the lack of a signature on a particular document. In his closing, the defense attorney indignantly asked how the government could expect the jury to believe that his client was at this meeting when this very important document was not signed by him. As I listened, I remembered that there was another version of the document that was signed by the defendant. My rebuttal was short: I summarized that the defendant's case rested on a missing signature. I then presented a blowup of the alternate document, complete with the defendant's signature. The defense's weapon was turned around and was pointed right at them. The jury convicted in thirty minutes.

6. Lincoln spent a good portion of 1856 campaigning for the Republican Party, which took him away from his legal business. He often would fill his political coffers with fees from one big case.

7. For a relatively simple criminal case I tried, my co-counsel and I went out to the middle of the California wilderness to get a feel for the site where the defendant was apprehended. We took pictures of the site and the route where a foot chase had taken place. I offered the evidence of the foot chase through the agent's testimony and the pictures that were taken. I noted to myself how much

easier it was for me to walk the agent through the foot chase and apprehension of the accused because I had gone to the scene myself and walked the path with the agent. The testimony was more powerful because I, the questioner, had "witnessed" the chase myself, so I knew exactly what to ask and did not have to depend on the agent to tell me what he thought was important.

8. When I was first starting out in the courtroom, I could never understand why defense attorneys would irritate a judge by blithering on about facts that did not matter at that stage of the case—usually concerning how innocent their client was when the only issue was if the defendant understood the charges. A more senior attorney counseled me after I complained about a particularly longwinded attorney, and told me that the jabbering was really directed to the client and nobody else. He wanted the client to feel confident in him and their case.

9. Some accounts of the trial do not have Lincoln snapping the bone at the end of his summation.

10. I learned much of my courtroom skills from the opposing counsels I have faced. Not only did I learn what worked, because their effective presentations gave me a blow, but I also learned what did not work—what was unpersuasive. It is easier to watch the faces of a jury or a judge and gauge their response when you are not speaking. My first job out of law school was as a federal judicial law clerk in the Middle District of Pennsylvania. I learned more about good and bad legal persuasion (both oral and written) there than anywhere else—just by watching and reading the attorneys at work.

11. In asking these questions, Lincoln could have been setting up Fleming to respond in that way so Lincoln could checkmate him with his response. In that case, it just demonstrates Lincoln's ability to lead a witness the way a master walks his dog.

LAW AND POLITICS: A DUAL CAREER

For all the jokes our society has about lawyers, historically lawyers are some of our nation's greatest heroes. From the Founding Fathers to Lincoln himself, lawyers have a place in our history as leaders. It was a lawyer who wrote the Declaration of Independence, a lawyer who drafted the majority of the Constitution, and a lawyer who delivered the Gettysburg Address.

The practice of law prepares individuals to bring tranquility from chaos and resolution from battle. For this very reason, Lincoln's years as a practicing attorney made him a better president. There are few other professions that would have given him a more solid understanding of the human endeavor. His practice taught him more than the mere letter of the law or trial advocacy techniques—it provided him a Petri dish in which to view mankind and all of its foibles.

In his book, *America's Lawyer-Presidents,* Norman Gross summarizes: "Though many people might initially associate the law with legal technicalities, procedure, and documents . . . [it is really] an instructive mirror of the issues, institutions, events, and people that have shaped American history and continue to affect us on a daily basis."[1] Thomas Jefferson expressed the same sentiments when he said that, "the study of law qualifies a man to be useful to himself, to his neighbors, and to the public."

In writing the foreword to Gross's book, former Associate Justice Sandra Day O'Connor reinforces this theory by observing:

Lawyers have played a pivotal role in the shaping of the political and civic life of this country. Their role remains a vital one today. Legal education continues to provide the training ground for significant numbers of our nation's leaders. Individuals with law degrees currently occupy roughly half the state governorships, more than half the seats in the United States Senate, and more than a third of the seats in the House of Representatives.[2]

Because of "this powerful nexus between law and politics, it should be no surprise that twenty-six of our nation's forty-four presidents have been lawyers. Through a common profession, each followed a distinctive legal career and path to the high office."[3]

The warrior ethos that Lincoln displayed during the Civil War is the same that an attorney uses while battling in court for his client. Yet, in addition to being a warrior, a good attorney is also a diplomat, solving problems for his client. It is a truism taught in business school that many attorneys feel their prime purpose is to bring up obstacles; by eternally finding potential flaws (sometimes to the most trivial levels), they are (1) protecting their client and (2) proving how invaluable their services are. Many business books have cautionary tales about how important it is to rein in your legal team and to impress on them that the goal is to get the deal done—not to sink the deal by pecking it to death. These skills Lincoln learned while he mediated for his clients, and they later facilitated his ability to start the mending process for the country, a process cut short by an assassin's bullet.

In the end, being a politician made Abraham Lincoln a better attorney. And being an attorney made Lincoln a better president. Lincoln's skills as an attorney aided his political skills in at least four areas: first, his ability to campaign; second, his method of forming his cabinet; third, his handling of constitutional issues during his presidency; and fourth, his skill in handling the slavery issue.

ᡒ᠍ᡒᡒ

The Campaigning Lawyer

Lincoln had passion for the law, but became an attorney to get closer to his true love—politics. True, Lincoln was neck-deep in Illinois politics before he became a lawyer. However, it was not until after he became a member of the bar that his political career took off.

Lincoln was interested in a particular type of politics: legislative. He never sought a judgeship, apart from occasionally sitting in for Judge Davis on the Eighth Circuit. Furthermore, until he ran for the highest executive political office in the country, Lincoln generally stayed away from executive politics as well. Besides helping his friends David Campbell and Ward Hill Lamon by writing indictments and serving *pro tem* as the state's attorney, he was never appointed to an executive position, nor did he run for these offices.

When Lincoln joined the Stuart law firm, they practiced law just as much as they practiced Whig politics. However, it was not until his partnership with Herndon that Lincoln's political ambition grew to a national level. He had a strong desire to sit in Congress; he even wrote a letter to a friend that read, "if you should hear anyone say that Lincoln [does not] want to go to Congress, I wish you as a personal friend of mine, would tell him you have reason to believe he is mistaken. The truth is, I would like to go very much."

And go he did. In the 1840s, the Whigs were a minority in Illinois. However, the United States Representative seat for the Seventh Congressional District had a Whig majority. This one Whig seat in the midst of a Democratic state caused enormous competition between the Whig candidates. Lincoln sought the nomination in 1842 and again in 1844 with no success. He finally was nominated by the party in 1846 and won the congressional seat.

The freshman representative marched to Washington full of confidence, thinking he was an experienced politician because of his years in the Illinois General Assembly. However, it did not take long for the reality of the situation to sink in. Being a new member in the thirtieth Congress, Lincoln was closed out to the committees where the real governing took place.

However, despite feeling disenfranchised, Lincoln did make friends in Washington; one such friend was Alexander H. Stephens, who later became the vice president of the Confederate States of America. In addition to being disillusioned over Washington politics, Lincoln and his family were excluded to a great extent from the Washington social life, which was a great regret to Mary Lincoln.

During Lincoln's time in Washington, James K. Polk, a Democrat, was president. In May of 1846, President Polk asked Congress to declare war against Mexico due to a shooting incident against U.S. forces on what the president claimed was United States soil, and Congress did so.

Lincoln joined many Whigs in opposition to the war. He became one of the most vocal antiwar Congressmen and introduced several resolutions challenging the president's reasons for going to war.[4] He took on the president like an attorney in trial. One resolution, in particular, challenged the president's contention that the shooting happened on U.S. territory. Like a lawyer pleading for a more definite statement from their opponent, Lincoln asked the president to be more precise in the location where the hostilities started. In another resolution, Lincoln claimed that the American soldiers were in the disputed area against the commanding general's orders.[5]

While these resolutions went practically unnoticed on a national stage, they were bombshells for Lincoln back home. Illinois on the whole was in favor of the war; Lincoln's adversaries back home latched on to his unpopular position, calling him a traitor and nicknaming him "spotty Lincoln" after the resolutions he proposed disputing the "spot" on the ground that the shooting took place. Despite public disapproval of his stance on the war, Lincoln stuck to his guns, saying "that I shall be fully convinced of what I more than suspect already—that [our leader] is deeply conscious of being in the wrong; that he feels the blood of this war, like the blood of Abel, crying to Heaven against him."

Another national crisis that arose while Lincoln was in Congress was the extension of slavery into new American territories. Lincoln supported the Wilmost Proviso, which declared that any new land obtained from Mexico would be a free territory. Lincoln also helped present a plan that would abolish slavery in the National Capital; both the Proviso and the "free Washington" plan were unpopular and were not successful.

Although Lincoln may have come out on the unpopular side of these national events, particularly his stance on the war, his political career was not over. This was due in part to his shrewdness during the 1848 presidential election. Here, Lincoln supported the war hero Zachary Taylor instead of his political idol Henry Clay. When asked about the decision, he simply said "Mr. Clay's chance for an election is just no chance at all."

Lincoln supported Taylor because, despite wanting to run for a second term in Congress, he could not—because of the competition over the one Illinois Whig seat in Congress, there was a tradition that a Whig member would only serve one term then give his seat to the next in waiting. However, a bigger factor was that his antiwar position made him unpopular in Illinois. Thus, Lincoln reasoned that with no future in Congress, his best avenue for continuing his political career was to ride the coat tails of a war hero—Zachary Taylor. Unfortunately, despite his campaigning for President Taylor, the new administration could only offer him a governorship of the frontier territory of Oregon. He turned down the governorship after conferring with Mary Todd because he believed it could not save his political career. The only other professional goals he had left rested in his law practice. Returning from what he saw as a failed term in Congress with no political future, Lincoln returned to Springfield and began his practice again with a new fervor.

For all intents and purposes, Lincoln gave up politics until 1854, when Congress passed the Kansas-Nebraska Act—which energized Lincoln anew. The new law essentially created two new territories: Kansas and Nebraska. Further, the Act declared that at the date of their admission in to the Union, the new territories could be admitted as free or slave states as their constitution would prescribe. The Act's author was an important Democrat in Illinois, Senator Stephen A. Douglas. The Kansas-Nebraska Act rescinded the Missouri Compromise that was passed in 1820, which divided the country in two, with the North being free states and the South slave states.

"Immediately upon the passage of the Kansas-Nebraska Act, frayed party ties began to snap. Thousands of Northern Democrats withdrew in indignation from their party. The Whig Party, already split along sectional lines, ceased to function as an effective national organization . . . ."[6]

Senator Douglas introduced the bill as the Chairman for the Committee on Territories. Douglas was eager to develop the western territories because he saw it as the future of U.S. expansion (which he felt would help his presidential ambitions), but also, and maybe more important, he had a significant financial interest due to his huge speculator investments in the western region.

The Missouri Compromise set out that, except for Missouri itself, the land acquired under the Louisiana Purchase would be free territories. Douglas's bill lured in Southern Congressmen with the promise of expanding slavery to the territories, through the doctrine of popular sovereignty (the territorial legislatures would vote on the issue of slavery). It was common knowledge that the territories to the South would indeed vote to make their regions "slave territories."

This enraged Northerners and other anti-slave Americans. Those who were against slavery saw it as a direct attack on their values. Those who were indifferent to the issue saw the Act as a direct attack on the status quo (the Missouri Compromise), which had for decades kept the slavery issue under wraps.

Not only did the Act rip open a political war, but it was also the precursor to the Civil War, inciting open violence in Kansas. The Whig Party, which was already having internal issues, opposed the Kansas-Nebraska Act and died as a functioning party in the South. The Democrats lost the majority of their influence in the Northern states.

Because of the political upheaval, room was made for a new political party. As early as February 1854, cast-offs from the Democrat party, disgruntled Whigs, and Free-Soilers met to organize a new party with the purpose of resisting the extension of slavery into the territories.[7] Four months later in Jackson, Michigan, a similar group "adopted the name Republican in emulation of the Democratic-Republican Party of Thomas Jefferson."[8] Lincoln did not join the new party at first, deciding instead to try to stabilize the crumbling Whig party. After it became clear that there was no saving the Whig party, Lincoln jumped to the Republicans who welcomed him with open arms.

The Kansas-Nebraska debate brought Lincoln back to politics with a vengeance, though initially he did not envision himself holding office again. Rather, his sole purpose was to help Richard Yates get reelected to the Seventh Congressional District because Yates was an outspoken opponent of the Kansas-Nebraska bill. However, it did not take long for Lincoln's political ambition to get the better of him. Lincoln was always hungry for political office; when talking about Lincoln's ambition, Herndon wrote that the "man who thinks Lincoln calmly sat down and gathered his robes about him, waiting for the people to call him has a very erroneous knowledge of Lincoln." Herndon went on to describe Lincoln as, "always calculating, and always planning ahead. His ambition was a little engine that knew no rest . . . . During the anxious moments that intervened between the general election and the assembling of the Legislature he slept, like Napoleon, with one eye open." However, unlike others with vast ambition who become tyrants, Lincoln channeled his ambition and love for the law and became a statesman. Indeed, "[w]e can be certain that Lincoln, who had a natural humility, was not attracted to political leadership by megalomania or a cheap desire to lord it over other [people]."[9]

In the fall of 1854, Douglas was touring Illinois defending the Kansas-Nebraska Act and made a stop in Springfield. After one of many speeches Douglas made in Springfield, Lincoln was given the opportunity to respond. Lincoln was ready; in typical fashion, he had fully researched the speeches Douglas had been giving over the previous month. Each speech was essentially the same, and Lincoln felt confident that Douglas's address would be the same in Springfield. Armed with Douglas's talking points, Lincoln took off the gloves and proceeded to destroy each of Douglas's arguments in turn.[10]

Lincoln argued that the Kansas-Nebraska Act not only permitted slavery to expand, but it also was actually "legislating for slavery, recognizing it, [in addition to] extending it." Douglas's comments addressed slavery on a legal and political level. Lincoln assailed the legal and political arguments Douglas proffered. However, he also raised the tone of the debate to an issue of morality and good versus evil. Lincoln stated that "the slaveholder has the same political right to take his Negroes to Kansas that a freeman has to take his hogs or his horses. This would be true if Negroes were property in the same sense that hogs and horses are. But is this the case? It is notoriously not so."

Lincoln went on to argue that slavery and democracy are irreconcilable doctrines of the human existence. He stated that when a man rules himself it is called democracy, but when a man "governs himself, and also governs another man—that is called despotism. If the Negro is a man, why then my ancient faith teaches me that 'all men are created equal,' and that there can be no moral right in connection with one man's making a slave of another."

While Lincoln's speech was bold, he knew when the rhetoric helped and when it made matters worse. Because of this, he stayed away from arguments supporting universal emancipation. He stated that "I would not hold one in slavery, at any rate . . . [however] I will not undertake to judge our brethren of the South."

Lincoln spoke throughout Illinois after debating Douglas. People appreciated his arguments because of his moderation; this attraction made him a palpable candidate for higher office. Specifically, this attention brought Lincoln directly to a senatorial race, which he lost in 1855. The failure again brought Lincoln back to the law. For five more years Lincoln expanded his practice; however, instead of stepping away from politics as he had done after his two years in Washington, he used these years to bolster his new party and worked tirelessly for the Republicans. In 1858 he was nominated to run as the Republican candidate for the United States Senate. Not only was a seat in the Senate a dream of Lincoln's, it was Douglas's seat—this added to the political excitement.

When Douglas heard that Lincoln was his opponent, he foretold, "I shall have my hands full. He is the strong man of his party—full of wit, facts, dates—and the best stump speaker, with his droll ways and dry jokes . . . ." The stage was set for political history to be made.

*THIS PICTURE WAS TAKEN TWO WEEKS BEFORE
THE FINAL LINCOLN-DOUGLAS DEBATES.*

When the campaign began, Lincoln challenged Douglas to a series of debates, and although Douglas was reluctant, he agreed to debate Lincoln in each of the congressional districts left on his tour—a total of seven. Addressing the importance of the debates to the community and the candidates, Benjamin Thomas writes in his book:

> These joint debates marked the highlights of the spectacular campaign, but they represented only a small part of the effort put forth by the rival candidates. Between the debates each man spoke almost every day for four months to large crowds in the open air, and traveled incessantly between engagements, by railroad, steamboat, or horse and buggy, putting up with the scanty comforts and poor food of country inns, and never, so far as the record shows, missing a single engagement. At the end Douglas's voice was a hoarse croak, but Lincoln's seemed as strong as ever. [Likely because the years Lincoln spent on the circuit prepared him for such debates.][11]

Even though it was a Senate race, many voters outside of Illinois followed the Lincoln-Douglas debates. Lincoln was seen as one of the few who could hold his own against Douglas, the "Little Giant," who was renowned for his debating abilities. Moreover, Lincoln demonstrated to a national audience his incredible ability to defend a moderate position while not upsetting the abolitionists in his party.[12]

In one such debate, Lincoln cornered Douglas between his own catch phrases "popular sovereignty" (a notion that allowed states to decide whether they will be a free or slave state) and the *Dred Scott* decision (a decision preventing the government from interfering with owners' rights over slaves), which Douglas also supported. By doing this, Lincoln put Douglas in a position where he had to either abandon his position of popular sovereignty, admit the *Dred Scott* case helped the spread of slavery even to states that did not want it (a concept that directly contradicts popular sovereignty), or confess that the *Dred Scott* decision was bad law. All three options were impossible choices for Douglas, and Lincoln knew it.

Throughout the debates, Lincoln tried to force Douglas to take a stand and declare his interpretation of *Dred Scott*—a dilemma that Douglas could not escape. If he renounced the decision, he would lose the support of the South and tear the Democratic Party asunder. On the other hand, if he tried to appease the slave power and support the decision, his Illinois constituents would turn on him. Douglas did the only thing he could—he pacified his voters, endorsing his political theory of popular sovereignty and saving his Senate seat.[13] However, in doing so, Douglas started a chain of events that would eventually lead to the divide of the Southern and Northern Democrats and his losing the presidential race to Lincoln in 1860.

Despite his popularity and the fact that the Republicans outpolled the Democrats by four thousand votes, Lincoln lost the 1858 senatorial election to Douglas due to outdated and biased apportionment laws (the process of allocating political power among a set of defined constituencies or geographic area), which heavily favored the Democrats who had controlled the state for years.[14] Almost immediately after Lincoln lost to Douglas, newspapers started to mention him as a possible candidate for president. Lincoln disregarded the rumors, stating that there were more qualified candidates in the party. Lincoln knew that if he let it be known too early that he was running, his opponents would come out of the woodwork to attack him. In addition, while he was interested in the presidency, he thought his prospects were too tenuous. What he really wanted and thought was within his grasp was a Senate seat in the next election.[15]

As the national Republican Convention grew closer, some believed that Lincoln could be a viable vice presidential candidate. However, after it was announced that the convention would be held in his home state, although still a long shot, Lincoln's chances of receiving the nomination for the presidency increased slightly. It is interesting that Lincoln's objective for throwing his hat in the ring for the top nomination was not because he thought he stood a shot of getting the top seat, but rather because he thought it would bring him name recognition for his senatorial prospects.[16]

Yet, beating all odds, and due to the keen political ability of Lincoln and his friends, Abraham Lincoln became the first presidential candidate for the Republican Party. This astonishing win was made possible by Lincoln's friends descending upon Chicago to campaign for their colleague and friend. His former partner Logan made the trip, along with gubernatorial nominee Richard Yates, Leonard Swett, and a score of others. The campaign group was led by Judge Davis, who put his heart and soul into getting Lincoln the nomination. Day and night, Davis was "dickering with all the finesse he could command" on behalf of his mentee.[17] When Lincoln sent a telegram to Davis at the Republican Convention warning him that he would "authorize no bargains and will be bound by none," Davis responded with, "Lincoln ain't here," and continued to line up delegate support, promising the delegation from Indiana a Secretaryship of the Interior, and the Commissionership of Indian Affairs to the Pennsylvania delegation (which sealed the deal for Lincoln).[18]

Making the race more historic and dramatic, Lincoln's nemesis, Senator Douglas, got the nod as the Democratic nominee.

ðﾶ ðﾶ ðﾶ

The Campaign for President

One of the greatest skills that Lincoln developed as a lawyer was his ability to debate and impress his opinion upon an audience. Two noteworthy examples of this ability can be seen in the Douglas Ottawa debate and Lincoln's political speech at the Cooper Institute in New York.

The Ottawa debate was held on August 21, 1858, in Ottawa, Illinois. The significance of the debate is that it is a poignant example of Lincoln's ability to use his courtroom wit against an accomplished debater. Douglas gave his opening speech, which harshly ridiculed Lincoln's lack of experience and his stance on the Mexican War (inferring that he was not a patriot), and insinuated that Lincoln was jumping on the Republican bandwagon as a means to an end, not because of a true conviction. When it was Lincoln's turn, he refuted Douglas's charges in both an elegant and powerful way, just as he had done a thousand times before juries.

Lincoln started his retort by meticulously picking apart Douglas's historical data. Because he knew that a happy audience was an attentive

ABRAHAM LINCOLN, REPUBLICAN
CANDIDATE FOR THE PRESIDENCY, 1860.

audience, Lincoln added his dry humor as he carefully tore Douglas's argument apart. For instance, when an audience member yelled out for him to "put on your specs" (eyeglasses), Lincoln, without skipping a beat, responded by saying, "Yes Sir, I am obliged to do so. I am no longer a young man." (Apparently making fun of your own age was considered very funny in 1860—as many accounts of this debate specifically comment on this funny moment.) With a lighter style he created a lighter mood. Lincoln's main attack was centered on unraveling the "Judge's" (as Lincoln referred to Douglas) own statements and positions by tying Douglas's own words around him. One example:

> [The Judge] has read from my speech at Springfield, in which I say that "a house divided against itself cannot stand," [(Douglas had criticized this phrase during his opening remarks)]. Does the Judge say it can stand? I don't know whether he does or not. The Judge does not seem to be attending to me just now, but I would like to know if it his opinion that a house divided against itself can stand? If he does, then there is a question of veracity, not between him and me, but between the Judge and an authority of a somewhat higher character.

Just as Lincoln would corner a witness during cross-examination, Lincoln cornered Douglas with this loaded question. Douglas either had to admit he misspoke or admit Lincoln's slogan was correct. To twist the knife further, Lincoln set him up where he looked as if he was disparaging the Almighty's words (a "house divided" is a quote from Jesus) and insulting God himself—lawyering at its best.

The Cooper Institute speech, which will be discussed in detail in Chapter 5, is a prime example of Lincoln's ability to move an audience. In the last paragraph of the speech, when addressing slavery and the South's pressure to spread it to the free territories, Lincoln stated:

> Neither let us be slandered from our duty by false accusations against us, nor frightened from it by menaces of destruction to the Government nor of dungeons to ourselves. Let us have faith that right makes might, and in that faith, let us, to the end, dare to do our duty as we understand it.

Lincoln's message was delivered in a way that both stirred emotion and immediately got the audience's minds agreeing with his message. This passage also demonstrates the usefulness of rhetoric to inspire your audience. Lincoln often used such language in the end of his addresses and closing arguments with the goal of rousing the audience or jury into action for his cause, with his cause being a vote for him for office or a vote for his client from a jury.

There are numerous lessons that a persuasive speaker can learn from Lincoln's road to the presidency. In his speeches and debates with Douglas, Lincoln used several of his favorite devices to great effect: combining humor with a constant barrage of loaded questions and salient facts. Speakers who have the ability to show that they do not take themselves too seriously and have the ability to poke fun at themselves will typically resonate with their audience. By making your audience like you, they are more willing to listen to you. Nobody really likes a speaker who is drowning in self-importance or who has delusions of grandeur.

A highlight was his handling of the Mexican War issue while he was a junior congressman. Specifically, Lincoln's credibility was enhanced when he stuck to his convictions concerning the war, even when his position was unpopular at home. **By not wavering under pressure, you will deliver a more believable argument every time the issue arises**—people are more likely to believe what you say and respect your position if that position never changes. This is a useful lesson in all walks of life, especially in the public service world, in which ethical people have to make unpopular decisions on a daily basis. However, it must be noted that there is a fine line between loyalty to your convictions and plain stubbornness—the former is noble while the later is dangerous. It takes wisdom and maturity to determine where the line is.

When looking at Lincoln's decision to support war hero General Zachary Taylor for president over his political idol Henry Clay, it might appear at first glance to be a transgression against the lesson of sticking to your convictions. However, on closer inspection, there is a clear distinction. Lincoln had no moral or professional obligation to support Clay, and after a careful review, he determined that Clay was not electable. Thus, the lesson is two-fold: **never jump into a boat with an issue you know to be a loser unless there are principled reasons for doing so**. Second, **a good persuasive speaker must look several moves ahead**—meaning that if Lincoln had supported Clay knowing that Taylor would win, he would have severely limited his political career (the fact that supporting Taylor in the end did not help his career is of no consequence to the lesson). There is nothing wrong with riding the coattails of a winner, so long as you do not subjugate your values to do so. And since Lincoln ultimately supported Taylor's political positions (for the most part), his choice was both wise and politically expedient.

A critical lesson can be learned from Lincoln's first debate with Douglas over the Kansas-Nebraska Act. Lincoln, being a shrewd attorney, carefully studied the speeches Douglas had made prior to coming to Springfield. He knew that Douglas would likely give essentially the same speech he had been giving, so Lincoln formatted his responses to systematically refute each of Douglas's points. People (lawyers especially) tend to repeat the same arguments when faced with similar facts. Therefore, if an opponent in a case has argued cases involving a particular set of facts that are analogous to the facts in your current case, carefully examine the case and exhume what your opponent is likely to say again.

In this debate, it's also notable that Lincoln gave an argument that appealed to both the left and right side of the brain. Although the "brain side" concept was unknown in 1860, Lincoln was a masterful trial attorney and certainly understood that there are two distinct types of thinkers: the affective (right side of the brain) and cognitive (left side of the brain). Affective thinkers use emotion, their personal morality, and learned premises on how life works to make decisions. Cognitive thinkers, by contrast, reach logical decisions by accruing data and looking at the technical rules.

Knowing that people process information differently, and in order to communicate persuasively with the entire audience, Lincoln formulated his arguments to cover both types of individuals. Specifically looking at this debate, Lincoln said the Kansas-Nebraska Act was wrong in its "direct effect" and wrong "in its prospective principle." Lincoln first argued it was wrong in its direct effect by averring that the Founding Fathers' intent was to eventually end slavery, not for it to spread, as the Kansas-Nebraska Act provided for. He acknowledged the legality of slavery where it was already established, but decreed that its spread undercut the social fabric of the nation and was illegal under the provisions of the Constitution, thus undermining law and order and ultimately the stability of the nation. By arguing its negative direct effects, he appealed to the people whom today we call left-side thinkers.

For the individuals who were right-side dominant, Lincoln argued using passion and morality. He cited the Act's prospective principle of slavery being repugnant, which indicated that the spread of slavery was morally wrong. Lincoln also appealed to the same people by claiming the institution of slavery mocked the Declaration of Independence, which stated that "all men are created equal." Such a claim surely invoked strong emotion; the Declaration was considered nearly sacred to nineteenth-century Americans. **By proffering arguments that appeal to both individuals who "feel" their decisions and individuals who "reason" their decisions, you cover all your bases and will persuade a larger audience**.

This is similar to Aristotle's lesson that the goal of argumentative writing is to persuade your audience that your ideas are legitimate—or at least more legitimate than your opponent's arguments. Aristotle divided his means of persuasion into three categories: *ethos*, *pathos*, and *logos*.

Ethos is the appeal based on the credibility of the persuader—basically, people will believe those whom they trust and respect. *Pathos* is the appeal based on the emotions of the audience, and *logos* is the appeal based on pure reason. Aristotle taught his students that by using all three categories, they would reach the most people with their argument and therefore be more "legitimate" than their opponent.

Also, in argument, there is a time and place for everything. Lincoln had the ability to deliver enough fire without burning down the house—too much rhetoric about emancipation only would have incited his opponents, allowing them to marginalize his arguments by labeling him a radical. Lincoln downplayed the most radical parts of his antislavery positions and successfully kept his feelings for universal abolishment of slavery from becoming a weapon his opponents could wield. On the other hand, Lincoln knew that not enough speechifying would bore his audience and prevent them from absorbing his points. Lincoln knew that **there is a balance point in the middle of spouting fiery rhetoric and refusing to take a position where great persuaders deliver their messages.**

Finally, there are times when you just have to go for the jugular. Lincoln knew that Douglas's catch phrase of "popular sovereignty" was his pet theory, which he used to support the Kansas-Nebraska Act. By attacking the very foundation of Douglas's support for the Kansas-Nebraska bill, Lincoln put Douglas on the defensive, and very nearly brought Douglas's entire argument to its knees. It was also a weapon Lincoln used to maneuver Douglas into a trap. Indeed, a critical lesson to be obtained from Lincoln's squaring off with Douglas was his ability to box Douglas into an impossible situation, just as he would corner a witness he was cross-examining.

A power scheme to use against an opponent is to maneuver him into a situation where he has to answer a loaded question by picking one of two options. By design, the delivered options are damaging, so it's a win-win situation for the examiner. Furthermore, if the trap is designed properly, it leaves room for the opponent to pick his own ridiculous third option. This is sometimes the most favorable outcome—it usually both serves as an admittance that your point was right and spoils the opponent's credibility because he is trying to sell a ridiculous answer. A classic example of this (which is improper in a courtroom because it is considered argumentative or badgering) is to ask a man charged with hitting his wife: "Did you answer the phone before or after you stopped hitting your wife?" As seen, the question is clearly loaded with two options; the man either answered the phone before he hit his wife or after, but in both options he hit his wife. Douglas would have had to either abandon his theory of popular sovereignty, which would have made him look weak and beaten, or he would have had to disavow the *Dred Scott* decision, which was heavily supported by Southern Democrats. Douglas went with option "A," saving his favorite political theory and angering the Southern Democrats.

The Democratic Party was split in the 1860 election due in part to Lincoln cornering Douglas on his positions concerning popular sovereignty and the *Dred Scott* decision and pitting different factions of Democrats against each other. As a result, Abraham Lincoln—a farmer's son, born in poverty in a log cabin—became the sixteenth president of the United States of America.

&&& &&& &&&

Lincoln's Cabinet

A critical skill that transferred with Lincoln from lawyering to politicking was his determination to get a good result for his client, despite personal feelings or his own ego. During the Republican Convention, where Lincoln pulled off his dramatic upset, his political rivals were William Seward, Simon Cameron, Salmon Chase, and Edward Bates. However, in addition to being his same-party opponents, Lincoln also viewed them as strong, intelligent leaders. Putting aside any lingering bitterness, Lincoln offered them his first and most prominent political posts.

Seward was offered the State Department, Chase the Treasury, Bates the Attorney General position, and Cameron became the Secretary of War. Concerning these nominations, historian Benjamin Thomas commented that, "[f]or a President to select a political rival for a cabinet post was not unprecedented; but deliberately to surround himself with all of his disappointed antagonists seemed to be courting disaster."[19] Thomas went on to say that the nominations were a "mark of [Lincoln's] sincere intentions that [he] wanted the advice of men as strong as himself or stronger. That he entertained no fear of being crushed or overridden by such men revealed . . . surpassing naiveté or a tranquil confidence in his powers of leadership."[20]

Doris Kearns Goodwin dedicated her entire book, *Team of Rivals: The Political Genius of Abraham Lincoln*, to this very subject and observed that "the cabinet was evidence of a profound self-confidence and a first indication of what would prove to others a most unexpected greatness."[21] Despite Lincoln's choosing a "team of rivals" to make up his cabinet, he quickly distinguished himself as the undisputed leader of the pack. His former competitors, who had initially thought of Lincoln as a country bumpkin, were won over by his extraordinary talents and brilliant mind.

Some of the individuals chosen had personally affronted Lincoln during his law practice days. For instance, in 1855, Lincoln went to Cincinnati, Ohio, to appear for the defense in a federal patent infringement suit (*McCormick v. Manny*). However, Lincoln, despite being a well-respected attorney, was almost completely shut out from the case by the other defense attorneys, including Edwin Stanton—his second Secretary of War—and George Harding, his future Commissioner of Patents. Some commentary on the incident reported that Stanton was overtly rude to the future president. The attorneys had no faith in Lincoln's abilities and removed him from the closing argument spot, opining that his gangly look and lack of education would not play well for the jury. Lincoln was disappointed and his pride was offended, but he was ever the consummate professional, accepted the group's decision, and gracefully separated himself from the case—for the good of the case.[22]

Lincoln's appointments to his cabinet show his selfless dedication to the good of the country. The lawyer in Lincoln thought of his client first and his own ego second; and as president, his client was the nation. This aptitude for containing his own ego for the good of the cause may be the most difficult skill for anyone to master (especially lawyers). When he was first elected, Lincoln knew that the country was on the brink of a great upheaval. With the possibility of war on the horizon, he needed the most competent individuals in his cabinet, rather than his personal cronies. Looking at Lincoln's choices in the making of his cabinet the lesson is obvious: **never let personal feelings interfere with the good of your client**. This demonstrates Lincoln's commitment to the business proverb that first-rate people hire first-rate people and second-rate people hire third-rate people.

Ralph Emerson summed up this trait of Lincoln's by saying that "his heart was as great as the world, but there was no room in it to hold the memory of a wrong," especially when it came to saving the Union.

श्री श्री श्री

Presidential Power during the Civil War

Legal scholars have scrutinized whether Lincoln abused his power as president during the Civil War—this debate continues today. Another wartime president, Woodrow Wilson, said, "Mr. Lincoln did all things with a wakeful conscience, and certainly without love of personal power for its own sake; seeing substantial justice done, too, wherever he could. But the Constitution was sadly strained nevertheless." What is often missed by critics is that Lincoln did not take his extreme actions as president on a whim; he pondered them, sought counsel on them, and ultimately believed he was legally entitled to take such actions. There are as many valid arguments that his actions were perfectly lawful as there are arguments that what he did was illegal.

Was Lincoln a dictator? In some sense he probably was—but the significance of Lincoln's questionable acts, which will be discussed in detail in the following section, is that they were motivated by the desire to save the union with benevolent statecraft and not warfare. Lincoln, much like the ancient figure Cincinnatus, who gave up absolute power after saving Rome to go back to being a farmer, was willing to relinquish his dictatorial powers as soon as the peril had passed.

Thomas Jefferson understood this delicate balance, stating that "[a] strict observance of the written laws is doubtless one of the high duties of a good citizen, but it is not the highest. The laws of necessity, of self-preservation, of saving our country when in danger, are of higher obligation."[23] Jefferson went on to say that to "lose [the] country by a scrupulous adherence to written law, would be to lose the law itself, with life, liberty, property and all those who are enjoying them with us; thus absurdly sacrificing the end to the means."[24]

When Lincoln was sworn into office, he immediately faced the nation's greatest constitutional crisis. During this time of great constitutional upheaval, the country greatly benefited from the expertise of a lawyer in the decision-making chair. Who better to lead the country during a constitutional crisis than a lawyer? Yet more than a lawyer, the country needed a master of the Constitution. "Fortunately, Lincoln knew the Constitution well. Almost a worshipper of that instrument, he endeavored ever to solve the general governmental problems in a legal way compatible with the Constitution."[25]

"At every turn new legal and constitutional questions presented themselves for urgent consideration," noted Albert Woldman in his 1936 book *Lawyer Lincoln*. Woldman went on to say that "[t]o the solution of these grave and unparalleled problems, the Lawyer-President applied the broad principles of law and justice with which he had stored his fertile brain during the twenty-three years of practice in the courts of Illinois."[26]

While in office, Lincoln faced four significant constitutional issues. First was the president's legal right to wage war without the express permission of Congress. Second was the president's ability to arrest individuals without a warrant and suspend habeas corpus (to produce the body); specifically, habeas allows those arrested to challenge their detention by seeing a federal judge. Third, Lincoln was faced with the right of the president to increase the army and navy beyond the congressional authorized amount and to spend money from the national treasury to support the amplified Armed Forces. The last, and most significant issue Lincoln had to confront, one that all others stemmed from, was the legal right of the president to preserve the union by declaring the secession a rebellion and illegal.

Congress has the undisputed power to declare war, but when hostilities broke out at Fort Sumter on April 12, 1861, Congress was out of session, and not scheduled to reassemble until July. The president was therefore faced with waging war without Congress's express consent or allowing the rebels an unfettered string of victories.

Declaring war. The power of declaring war is explicitly reserved by the Constitution to the Congress. Yet, by ordering the blockade of Southern ports and mobilizing troops, Lincoln essentially declared war on the Confederacy. He defended his actions by arguing that they were "ventured upon under what appeared to be popular demand and a public necessity." He further explained that he trusted Congress to ratify his actions when they met—however, if they invalidated his action, he would immediately comply.[27] The Supreme Court later "upheld the legality of Lincoln's policies by declaring, in effect, that the President had not initiated a war, but had only taken necessary measures of resisting a war forced upon the Government."[28]

Habeas corpus. The Constitution dictates that the writ may be suspended when the country faces a rebellion or invasion and the need for public safety requires such extreme action—Lincoln declared the rebellion to be one of those times. The debate stems from the question: "who had the power to suspend the writ"? Lincoln answered by saying:

> Now, it is insisted that Congress, and not the Executive, is vested with the power. But the Constitution itself is silent as to which is to exercise that power, and as the provision was plainly made for a dangerous emergency, I cannot bring myself to believe that the framers of that instrument intended that, in every case, the danger should run its course until

Congress could be called together, the very assembling of which might be prevented, as was intended in the case, by the rebellion.

The draft. Later in his presidency, when the constitutionality of the conscription law was challenged, Lincoln's legal opinion, in the absence of an on-point Supreme Court decision, became the established legal opinion of the land.[29] Lincoln's argument was simply that when the Constitution states that Congress has the authority to raise and support armies—it inherently must have the right to draft such an army.

Secession. As for the greatest constitutional question—the secession— Lincoln gathered his resources using skills from both politics and the law. Lincoln's political assault started by first portraying the Confederacy as a lawless people who had committed a crime against the Constitution itself. The Constitution was revered by most Americans along with its drafters; portraying secession as blasphemy against the Founding Fathers and their prized work was a powerful strategy. His political attacks against the South continued throughout the war; he repeatedly espoused his belief that, since the act of secession was illegal, everything that followed from the act was without legal standing as well. Therefore, he would not recognize the South's new government as anything more than the head of a rebellion. "He confined the legal character of the conflict to a mere domestic uprising by insurgents who owed allegiance to the Government they were seeking to overthrow and who were obstructing the execution of the laws by combinations too powerful to be suppressed by the ordinary course of judicial proceedings."[30]

Lincoln's political attack on the rebellion became international in nature when he lobbied foreign governments to accept the position that secession was illegal and an attack on the United States itself. Lincoln made it clear to foreign governments that to recognize the South's government was to give cause to the United States to declare war.[31] "[T]he magnitude of the struggle soon compelled all to treat the Southern Republic as a belligerent under the principles of international law."[32]

The legal attack Lincoln waged against secession began with the posing of a legal question: was the Union of the American States a "perpetual, indissoluble, and indestructible unity, or was it merely a venerable treaty of alliance leaving each constituent State a sovereign body, with an indefeasible right to withdraw whenever it wished to do so?"[33] This was a typical Lincoln double-edged question, in that it was not so much a question as it was a clever way to paint the South as almost mocking the sovereignty of the United States. He continued to enforce this position by delivering legal arguments supporting his belief that the Confederacy was in fact an illegal rebellion.

The South tried to refute Lincoln's claim that the secession was unconstitutional; their basic argument was that because the States had joined the Union voluntarily, they never surrendered their sovereignty, so they should be able to voluntarily leave the Union. Lincoln assailed this argument, demanding that the South show where the Constitution expressly said that disunion was an available option. Using a classic legal rule of construction, Lincoln averred that nothing could be implied as law which leads to unjust or absurd consequences.[34]

Lincoln expounded on this argument by explaining that the Union was not established by a simple contract that could be breached at the will of one party; rather, it was established by supreme law, ordained and established by the *people* of the entire United States. The United States, in Lincoln's opinion, was cemented into an indivisible mass.[35] Consequently, because the Union was indissoluble, the states became organic to the nation itself—the South's assertion that the Constitution contained an ouster clause could not be implied.

When addressing the South's claim to state sovereignty, Lincoln maintained that the "States have neither more nor less power than that reserved to them in the Union by the Constitution . . . ."[36] He added that the states already held a strong standing in the Union, but it was that of a state and nothing more. Therefore, if they usurped more rank in the Union or *outside* the Union—for instance, recognition of being their own country—it could only be done contrary to law and by rebellion.

Lincoln forcefully called to attention the fact that it was the Union that procured independence from the British, the Union that bought land where other countries had been established, and the Union that was older, more solid, and more legal. Consequently, it was the Union's Constitution that was sovereign, and only through its proscribed methods—namely a Constitutional Amendment—could the states be allowed to gain complete sovereignty.

Lincoln also argued that even if the South were correct in its argument that the Constitution was merely a contract between states, then it followed that the only way the contract could be unmade was peacefully by *all* parties which made it; not by a select few. This is the well-established principle of law called mutual consent, where both parties of a contract mutually rescind the binding instrument. "It follows from these views," Lincoln argued, "that no State upon its own mere motion can lawfully get out of the Union; that resolves and ordinances to that effect are legally void and that acts of violence, within any State . . . against the authority of the United States are insurrectionary or revolutionary, according to circumstances."

Lincoln pointed out that in the history of mankind, no government had ever had a provision that allowed for its own termination.[37] In his July 4, 1861, message to Congress, Lincoln continued this argument by declaring that the crisis "embraces more than the fate of the United States. It presents to the whole family of man the question whether a constitutional government of the people by the people can or cannot maintain its integrity against domestic foes. . . . Must a government of necessity be too strong for the liberties of its people or too weak to maintain its own existence?" Lincoln was not only fighting for the good of the Union, but also for democracy as a form of government.

Lincoln's last legal argument against secession was based on the constitutional provision that guaranteed every state to enact a republican form of government. Lincoln argued, "[w]hat was to prevent any seceding State from adopting other than a republican form of government? Therefore . . . to ensure the maintenance of the guaranteed form of government, the Federal Government, of necessity, must have the right to prevent the secession of the States."

It was because Lincoln so adequately made clear that secession was illegal that he was able to act with military force. Without sufficiently making this argument to supporters, the North would have been unable, due to internal and international pressures, to wage such an expansive and devastating war. Despite Lincoln's extreme desire for peace, Lincoln the lawyer became Lincoln the warrior. Furthermore, because Lincoln saw the country as an indivisible whole, he was not only fighting to keep the South in the Union, but to prevent the Union as he knew it from crumbling.

Lincoln's determination to preserve the Union at any cost stemmed from his absolute devotion to the Constitution. An example of this is his handling of the Confiscation Bill enacted by Senator Lyman Trumbull. The bill essentially made rebellion a crime and allowed the president to seize all property of individuals involved with the rebellion. After confiscation, the property was to be sold and used to support the Union's military.

Despite the advantages the bill gave Lincoln in fighting the war, he intended to veto it. Lincoln thought that convicting the rebels of treason and then seizing and selling their property without a trial was a violation of the bill of attainder clause, the due process clause, and the taking without just compensation clause. Proponents of the bill argued that the Constitution was inapplicable in a time of such national crisis. Senator Sumner, a staunch supporter of the bill, said in an address before Congress that the "Constitution is made for friends who acknowledge it, and not for enemies who disavow it, and is made for a state of peace and not for the fearful exigencies of war."

Lincoln put his full effort into quelling this kind of thinking and worked diligently to stop the bill's passage. Lincoln insisted on preserving the Constitution as he saw it; he believed that if he were to fight a bloody war (that took the lives of 619,000 Americans) and trample the Constitution in the process, it would all have been in vain. Indeed, Lincoln believed, in direct contradiction to Senator Sumner, that it is during times of war when the country's Constitutional protections are paramount.

Lincoln handled the constitutional issues throughout his presidency with astonishing success; few of his interpretations and actions were overturned by the courts. In fact, Lincoln's overarching argument in defense of the Union was eventually adopted by the courts—[38]the U.S. Supreme Court stated that the "[t]he Constitution . . . looks to an indestructible Union composed of indestructible States."[39] It was "fitting and natural that the Supreme Court of the United States should give constitutional interpretation and definite written form to President Lincoln's great achievement . . . ."[40]

Maybe the greatest of Lincoln's accomplishments was the settling of the constitutional status of the states. Indeed, because Lincoln was able to put to rest the doctrine of state sovereignty and the widespread belief that the states could secede from the Union, he ensured the very survival of the Constitution. In addition he showed to the world that a constitutional democracy was possible, a government that could ensure the maximum liberty for its citizens and still maintain sovereign integrity.

ই▲ ই▲ ই▲

Combating a Constitutional Crisis

When addressing the case Lincoln made against the rebels, Lincoln used the tactic of vilifying his opponents to discredit their arguments. He did this by portraying the Confederacy's act as sacrilege against the Constitution. This had several effects. First, it made it easier to wage an unrelenting war against them—**it is always easier to kill a villain**. A similar tactic occurs in every war where the government supports derogatory names for the enemy in an attempt to lessen their humanity.

Second, by labeling your opponent a criminal you remove almost all credibility they hold with the fact finder. Here the fact finder was the American people, but this scheme also works with juries. In addition, this tactic allows you to completely control the argument because **once you have discredited your opponent, it is less important to address their arguments**.

A skill to be learned from Lincoln's attack on the legal right to secede was his gathering of international support for his campaign. When in a fight, it's critical to have friends on your side to attack with you. In addition, it is important to remove potential allies from your opponent by making it advantageous for them to stay loyal to you and painful for them to move to allegiance with your opponent. This tactic is not only used in armed warfare, but also seen regularly in court; both when you persuade your allies to prepare for testimony, and when you watch hostile witnesses closely to ensure they feel the pain of perjury if they should lie under oath in an attempt to be loyal to your opponent.

Lincoln used his deep understanding of the Constitution to counter the South's notion of a constitutionally valid secession by asking them to point out where in the Constitution it specifically said that a state could voluntarily leave the Union. Further, he supported his position by pointing out that the Constitution mandates that the federal government ensures that each state has a republican form of government. Therefore, Lincoln averred that in order for the federal government to carry out this mandate, it is logically impossible that the states can leave the union and prevent oversight altogether from the federal government.

There are two main lessons to be drawn here, and the first is obvious: **when the actual words in the law are to your advantage, emphasize it**. Lincoln played on the emotions of his audience when he did not have textual authority backing his position, but when the text of the law supported him, he would stand on the law and use it as his high ground. Second, it is easy to simply state what the law is and how it supports your position. However, **it is more effective to "show" what the law says**, which is exactly what Lincoln did here by showing how secession was incompatible with not only the text but also the spirit of the Constitution. Furthermore, Lincoln magnified the impact of this argument by pointing out that there was a legal method to secede spelled out in the Constitution—a constitutional amendment. This is an effective way to highlight your opponent's incorrect or illegal actions by contrasting to your fact finders how your opponents could have done it correctly.

Another lawyerly method Lincoln used during this time was to set up a hypothetical fact pattern using his opponents' facts to show how nonsensical their arguments were. Lincoln did this by showing that even if you assumed that the South was right in its assessment that the Union was a mere contract, it still follows, when applying contract law, that all parties must agree to its dissolution. This was a concept that the real estate tycoon in New York understood just as well as did the farmer who agreed to buy a pig from his neighbor. Lincoln was an expert at using simple logic that everybody could understand to drive home his arguments.

Another technique Lincoln used to discredit his opponents' arguments was to compare their arguments to history. Lincoln argued that no government in the past or present had formed a legal device for a select few to terminate their participation in the government. Lincoln explained that for a state to have such an organic law would destroy the government before it was even formed, due to the impossibility of a government pleasing all of its citizens all of the time.

Lincoln also demonstrated that there is power in consistency. **Being consistent in your arguments on every front denies your opponents the opportunity to use your own words against you**. This concept is demonstrated in the way Lincoln thwarted Congress's efforts to pass the Confiscation Bill, which Lincoln saw as a constitutional violation. Lincoln held that if you violate the Constitution in order to save it, you were not only being hypocritical but also counterproductive. Lincoln reasoned that if he signed the bill, he would be giving his opponents ammunition to attack his campaign to wage war to save the Union. We learn from Lincoln that the ends should justify the means, particularly when you are trying to defend a principle. Moreover, nothing will lose credibility faster than getting caught talking out of both sides of your mouth.

≈ ≈ ≈

Fighting Slavery

When you think of Lincoln, it's hard not to also think of slavery. As a lawyer, Lincoln's slavery cases represented three-tenths of one percent of his total caseload.[41] Despite this dearth of slavery cases compared to his mammoth lifetime caseload, they provide a glimpse into his attitudes toward the institution and how those attitudes influenced his practice and crossed over into his presidency.[42]

Lincoln believed slavery was an unbearable human torment and faced the issue head on in court, as he would go on to do in his presidency. For instance, in the case *Bailey v. Cromwell*, citing the Illinois Constitution, Lincoln was successful in appealing a circuit court's decision in the Illinois Supreme Court that allowed the selling of a slave girl within the state's borders.[43] The specifics of the case involved a young slave girl named Nance, who was sold to a man in Tazewell County, Illinois. Lincoln argued that according to the Northwest Ordinance of 1787, slavery was illegal in the Northwest Territories; therefore, the sale of a slave was also illegal. The case had far-reaching implications beyond releasing one

LINCOLN DRAFTING THE EMANCIPATION PROCLAMATION.

girl from the bonds of slavery—it established the principle that in Illinois every individual was free.

After Lincoln returned from Congress in 1849, the Lincoln-Herndon partnership no longer represented slave owners' interests in court. Moreover, not only did Lincoln refuse to represent slave masters, he also actively sought and accepted cases where he could defend fugitive slaves and free blacks.[44]

The first active step that Lincoln took against slavery was in 1837. The then young state representative joined a small minority to vote against a House resolution that declared the Right of Slavery as sacred to the slaveholding states. Lincoln not only voted "no" on the resolution, but also actively lobbied against the resolution, asserting that slavery was "founded on both injustices and bad policy."[45] Lincoln proffered his arguments against the resolution based on legal and constitutional principles; this reasoned approach was not enough to appease fervent abolitionists, but was a correct application of the law.[46] What gave Lincoln's position significance was his assertion that "'the promulgation of abolitionist doctrines tends to increase rather than abate [slavery's] evils'—for a young Illinois politician, this was a radical stance."[47] It was "radical" because it was so "moderate"; during the 1830s, there were the proslavery groups and the abolitionists, and everyone fell into one group or the other. Lincoln, on the other hand, shunned both groups—the proslavery crowd for their evil barbaric institution, and the abolitionists for their absolute disregard for the legality of slavery. That he advocated this third, moderate position was considered a "big idea" for the time; it was a position that both sides of the issue could tolerate.

As a lawyer, Lincoln understood that slavery was legally entrenched behind constitutional guarantees and historic promises. However, in the *Dred Scott* case, the Supreme Court ruled that the Missouri Compromise, which divided the country into slave states and free states, was unconstitutional. Dred Scott was a slave who had been taken into a free territory; on that basis, he sued his master, believing his presence in a free state should make him a free man. The case made it all the way to the Supreme Court.

On March 7, 1857, Chief Justice Roger Taney delivered his opinion for the Court's majority on the *Dred Scott* case to a live audience. The Court held that because of Mr. Scott's status as a slave, he could not become a citizen, held no constitutional rights, and could not be recognized to sue in court. Furthermore, because of his status as a slave, he was nothing more than property; and therefore Congress had no right to interfere with the slave owner and his property right in Mr. Scott. With this decision, the "most radical views of the Southern slave-powers [were] given judicial ratification by the highest tribunal in the land."[48] Lincoln viewed the *Dred Scott* decision as a disgrace to legal precedence and justice. It was Douglas's support of the decision and Lincoln's dissent that fueled much of their historic debates. Indeed, it was the debates between Lincoln and Douglas in the 1858 Senate campaign that became the center of gravity for the slavery issue.[49]

Unlike a good portion of the Republican Party, Lincoln was not an "extremist" when it came to slavery. He understood that slavery, as hateful as it was, had legal backing and was the law of the land. Lincoln believed that slavery would die naturally as the country matured. At the same time, he understood that it was critical to contain slavery and prevent its growth to new states.

While Lincoln served as a Representative in Congress, he had personally tried to diminish slavery by sponsoring a program to abolish slavery in the nation's capital. The program proposed a system of emancipation for children born into slavery after January 1, 1850. These free children would be entered into apprenticeship programs and learn a specific trade. For other slaves, the government would buy their freedom from their owners. Lincoln proposed the law in Washington, D.C., because, while he felt that Congress did not have the power to abolish slavery in the Southern states, it certainly had the power to regulate slavery in the District of Columbia. The legislation never actually came before Congress for a vote, but does demonstrate Lincoln's early propensity to erode the institution of slavery through legal and moderate means.

More than any president before or since, Lincoln dealt with issues of justice. This is true because as a lawyer, Lincoln regularly dealt with the rights of men and women under the law—and slavery can certainly be seen as the ultimate condition of law versus man and right versus wrong. Personally, "Lincoln hated slavery with every fiber in his being; he fervently wished that all men everywhere might be free."[50] However, as president of the United States, his personal feelings had to come second to his duty to the country. Slavery presented not only an issue of wickedness to Lincoln, but also an issue of law. Lincoln, therefore, devised a legal way to undermine the institution without violating the very instrument he was trying to protect by waging war—the Constitution.

It was clear to Lincoln and most legal thinkers at that time that neither the president nor Congress had any power to liberate a single slave. "It was his duty to uphold the Union and the laws. The barbaric institution was a part of the law of the land countenanced by the Constitution and sanctioned by the courts. It had existed even before the Constitution itself and had been accepted by [its] creators . . . ."[51]

During the campaign and after he was elected president, Lincoln took his case to the American people.[52] He argued that slavery was not being threatened in the states that already had it. He made it a point that while he opposed slavery personally and would fight to keep it out of the new territories, he would not advocate for the emancipation of a single slave. Lincoln went a step further to try and calm the Southern states by vowing to honor the current fugitive slave laws and return runaway slaves found in the North. Abolitionists were appalled by what they viewed as Lincoln's apathetic attitude toward the blight of slavery. One prominent abolitionist, Wendell Phillips, called Lincoln the "Slave Hound of Illinois." Yet what Mr. Phillips did not understand was that Lincoln's keen legal mind was planning a coup of the slavery establishment based on law, not emotion.

Lincoln consistently believed that if slavery were to be eradicated, it must be done in a way that was compatible with the Constitution. In addition, Lincoln understood that because the institution of slavery was so ingrained with the South's pecuniary structure, the immediate abolition of slavery would devastate their economy.[53] Because of this knowledge, Lincoln regarded the abolitionists' frenzied calls for emancipation profligacy and harmful, with complete disregard of the political, economic, and constitutional impacts to the country.

Woldman summed up Lincoln's attitude toward slavery versus the Constitution when he said:

> With all his sympathy for the downtrodden slave, with all his opposition to the extension of slavery, he took the anomalous position of supporting, defending, and preserving the Constitution, which forbade interference with this institution. So when the spirit of disunion ran wild, when sectionalism, bitterness, and partisan strife were at fever heat, when impatient extreme Abolitionists and rabid Secessionists were aiming a blow at the heart of the Nation, he never lost sight of the cardinal importance of preserving our constitutional form of government.[54]

However, soon after the War started, Lincoln reasoned that war brought forth different rules—now the Southern slave owners were rebels against the federal government, not just citizens engaging in repugnant but legal activities. By labeling slavery a tool that was helping the South's war effort, he was able to mount an attack on slavery as a legitimate course of action for winning the War. But Lincoln did not go on the offensive against slavery immediately upon assuming the presidency, because he was afraid the courts would overturn his actions and entrench the institution even further into the law. Lincoln was patient, and he waited for his opportunity to strike the first blow against slavery.

The legal device Lincoln used to challenge slavery was the Emancipation Proclamation. On September 22, 1862, Lincoln issued his preliminary edict of freedom for the slaves residing in the rebel states. He waited

THE EMANCIPATION PROCLAMATION.

to issue the proclamation until there was good news about the War he could bootstrap it to; that good news came in the form of the Union victory at the battle of Antietam, where General Lee's Army was driven out of Pennsylvania. The preliminary proclamation warned all Southern rebel states that if they did not lay down their arms and pledge allegiance to the Union before January 1, 1863, all slaves within their borders would be deemed free men and women. Because none of the rebel states returned to the Union by the first of January, the Emancipation Proclamation was issued.

The vested power that Lincoln cites in the proclamation was his power as commander in chief of a nation at war. A common misconception about the proclamation is that it abolished slavery nationwide. Rather, it freed those slaves who lived in the states that were in open rebellion against the Union. In other words, it only set free the slaves who were within the legal reach of the federal government because of the war. Not only did the proclamation surreptitiously weaken the Confederacy by prompting slaves to escape and hamper the South's ability to fight the war, it also overtly allowed for ex-slaves to join the Union Army and directly combat the Confederacy on the battlefield. By April 1865, approximately 186,000 black enlistees had joined the Union Army.

One concern with the Emancipation Proclamation was the international rule of postliminy, which states that property taken or altered will be restored to its pre-war status after hostilities have ceased. Thus, slaves who were liberated under the proclamation would return to their status as slaves after the War. Furthermore, it was "pointed out that the edict would have no effect upon the children of slaves born in the future."[55] Lincoln answered these criticisms by explaining that he never intended or claimed that the proclamation was anything other than a Union war tool and was frank when addressing the proclamation's legal shortcomings, while at the same time maintaining its good objective.

It is arguable that the final draft of the proclamation was Lincoln's finest moment as an attorney.[56] Lincoln wrote the proclamation with the full knowledge that his actions would be challenged in a federal court. Indeed, Lincoln anticipated the dispute reaching the Supreme Court and calculated that the proslavery Justice Taney, who was old and in poor health, would be retired or deceased by the time it got there. Lincoln wagered that he would have had the opportunity to fill Taney's seat with a Justice of his choosing before the case reached the Court.[57]

Because of this impeding legal battle, Lincoln was careful to base the proclamation on sound legal principles and not on passion or his personal hatred of slavery. As a written document, the Emancipation Proclamation is a simple, articulate, and concise document, written by a thoughtful lawyer.[58]

In Gross's book, *America's Lawyer-Presidents*, he notes that Karl Marx was working as a reporter for a London newspaper during the Civil War, and clearly recognized what Lincoln was attempting to do with the proclamation. Marx observed that the "most formidable decrees which he hurls at the enemy and which will never lose their historic significance, resemble—as the author intends them to—ordinary summons, sent by one lawyer to another."[59]

There is no doubt that Lincoln recognized the Emancipation Proc-lamation as a tenuous legal act—it was not the proclamation that Lincoln regarded as the most important tool to destroy slavery, but a constitutional amendment. An amendment would seal the fate of slavery and put to rest any lingering doubts about the institution's fate and the proclamation's legality.[60] "Lincoln's murder sanctified the Emancipation Proclamation 'and seemed to place it beyond controversy . . . .'"[61]

It is interesting that Lincoln originally viewed the Constitution as a perfect instrument of law; however, after battling the South and dealing with slavery, he viewed the Constitution as an instrument to promote the progress of mankind.[62] As mankind learned more, they needed to amend the Constitution with their new knowledge.

Lincoln's friend, senator from Illinois Lyman Trumbull, headed up the constitutional amendment in 1864; the Senate passed, but not the House. After Lincoln was reelected to a second term, the measure was reintroduced in the House and passed, partly because Lincoln personally got behind it. The amendment then went to the states for ratification. Unfortunately, the necessary twenty-seven of the thirty-six states did not ratify the amendment until December 18, 1865, eight months after John Wilkes Booth's bullet killed Lincoln. The Thirteenth Amendment is in some ways Lincoln's greatest gift to the Constitution, a single writing that delineates his philosophy for our country—equality and the absolute rule of law.

🐍 🐍 🐍

Legal Lessons of the Fight Against Slavery

The slavery issue confronted Lincoln with questions of morality versus questions of law. Lincoln loathed slavery, but at the same time he knew it was constitutional—this internal conflict is similar to a defense attorney representing a client who he knows is guilty of murder. The attorney may hate his client, know it would be an atrocity to let him on the streets, and strongly believe that he would kill again if let free. However, when faced with such a dilemma, the right answer for the defense attorney is to zealously defend the client, because he knows that he is really defending something bigger—the Constitution. This is not to say that anyone should ever surrender his or her morals or convictions—only that, when faced with terrible decisions, we must weigh the consequences, as Lincoln did.

Adding to the lesson above, we can also learn from Lincoln's change in strategy. Lincoln would not wage war against slavery directly because he knew as a lawyer it was a legally recognized institution. However, after the War began, Lincoln was able to use a different weapon from his arsenal as commander in chief. Lincoln drafted and implemented the Emancipation Proclamation as a wartime weapon. Here we can **learn to shift weight on issues and use backdoors to come at our opponents from different directions**. Lincoln could not dissolve slavery legally, but he could use freedom of the Southern slaves for military purposes. Therefore, when your opponent changes the rules (the South seceding), you can respond to this and even reframe the rules yourself (enacting the Emancipation Proclamation).

Numerous historians and scholars have criticized Lincoln's words in the proclamation as not going far enough, as having "all the moral grandeur of a bill of lading."[63] However, what these commentators fail to recognize is that Lincoln did not tone down the proclamation because he was a political propagandist, but rather because he was a brilliant attorney and pragmatist. The dullness of the Proclamation was, by design, not due to a lack of enthusiasm; it is clear that Lincoln was able to write and deliver a moving statement. But he understood for this issue that what the country needed was the skills of a prairie lawyer—not a dramatic orator.[64] This is precisely why the proclamation was lacking "isms" and pleas for worldwide justice for all. Lincoln knew he was on thin ice legally and politically when he wrote the proclamation. Therefore, it was designed as a tightly drawn document that was only to be the opening salvo of a campaign, the Thirteenth Amendment being the culmination. Lincoln knew that the War was about freedom, and so did many citizens. However, if he announced this purpose openly, he would have lost support, especially with the proslavery border states that were still loyal to the Union. So with the proclamation, Lincoln, a man who had no equal when he desired to inspire, made a conscious decision to be pedestrian.

A persuasive speaker should always care more about the *effects* of his words rather than the *style* in which they are wrapped. Sometimes a simple, boring written argument will go farther than a forceful one; it may not even be thoroughly read by your opponents, leaving them unprepared to address your points. There is a time and place for everything; sometimes the most effective communication is making a powerful and moving speech, and sometimes working under the radar will be your most persuasive strategy. Some historians report that this is precisely what happened with the Emancipation Proclamation: it was overlooked by many of Lincoln's naysayers.

The final lesson to be learned from Lincoln with regards to how he took on the slavery issue was his ability to change his opinion when necessary. Lincoln's original and deeply held belief was that the Constitution was a perfect instrument that did not need to be changed; after fighting a bloody war over a dispute in the Constitution, he amended this conviction, believing that the nation's document needed to be modified, specifically in the area of slavery and states' rights.

It is *critical* for a persuasive speaker to be able to admit when he's wrong and move on. Despite how important this skill is, it is the one most often ignored. This is essential for several reasons; first it allows you to develop a more effective argument. If your ego is so enveloped with your own opinions, you will never be able to see your own blunders, and you will never be able to dump your bad arguments and take successful ones from others. Moreover, you can lose credibility when you are seen as never admitting you are wrong. As discussed, you should always stay true to your principles and values; however, when new information surfaces and you are clearly wrong, sticking to your position will often be seen as stubbornness, not as being principled—giving the impression you would rather lie than admit a mistake.

Lastly, while the intent of this book is not to proffer a personal opinion concerning Lincoln's philosophy, I do feel it is important to address a particular issue I have with Lincoln's reasoning in this regard. When the law dictates *over* us instead of acting as a buffer *between* us, we are no longer a society of law but rather a "law society." Lincoln was conflicted over the issue of slavery—its moral repugnance but its legal protection. In general, it is true that in order for a civilization to prosper, its citizens must obey the law—regardless if they agree with it or not. That is the purpose of elections.

However, resistance against the transparently unjust is a human responsibility. As St. Augustine said and Dr. Martin L. King Jr. quoted, "an unjust law is no law at all." This is the legal conundrum that has plagued nations since laws were first written—unjust to whom? During Lincoln's time, people who hid runaway slaves thought they were helping subjugated people. To other people, they were outlaws. The point is: it is easy to criticize Lincoln over his misfeasance on the slavery issue one hundred years later, knowing all we know about the human endeavor. Was he wrong in his view that the laws of slavery should be abided by regardless of their inherent inequities? Yes. Was he a brilliant man trying to bring forth a better world while staying true to his belief in the sanctity of the constitution? Yes.

 è² è² è²

Notes

1. AMERICA'S LAWYER-PRESIDENTS: FROM LAW OFFICE TO OVAL OFFICE xiii (Norman Gross ed., Northwestern Univ. Press 2004) [hereinafter GROSS].

2. Gross, *supra* note 1, at ix.

3. *Id.*

4. Although Lincoln opposed the war, he voted for every appropriations bill to support the troops fighting it.

5. The general was Zachary Taylor, who became the twelfth president. Taylor's ascension to the White House was due in part to his efforts in the Mexican War; it never hurts to be a war hero in America.

6. BENJAMIN P. THOMAS, ABRAHAM LINCOLN: A BIOGRAPHY 144 (Barnes & Noble 1994) (1952) [hereinafter THOMAS].

7. *Id.*

8. *Id.*

9. RICHARD CARWARDINE, LINCOLN: A LIFE OF PURPOSE AND POWER 13 (Alfred A. Knopf 2006).

10. Twelve days later in Peoria, Illinois, Lincoln gave the same speech, thus is called the Peoria speech.

11. THOMAS, *supra* note 6, at 184.

12. *Id. at* 193.

13. ALBERT A. WOLDMAN, LAWYER LINCOLN 266 (Carroll & Graf 2001) (1936) [hereinafter WOLDMAN].

14. *Id. at* 192.

15. *Id.* at 195.

16. THOMAS, *supra* note 6, at 201.

17. *Id.* at 210.

18. *Id.* at 210–11.

19. THOMAS, *supra* note 6, at 235.

20. *Id.*

21. DORIS KEARNS GOODWIN, TEAM OF RIVALS: THE POLITICAL GENIUS OF ABRAHAM LINCOLN xvi (Simon & Schuster 2005).

22. *Id.* at 173–75.

23. Donald Kerwin & Margaret D. Stock, *The Role of Immigration in a Coordinated National Security Policy,* 21 GEO. IMMIGR. L.J. 383, 428 (2007) (citing Letters from Thomas Jefferson to John B. Colvin, Sept. 20, 1810).

24. *Id.*

25. WOLDMAN, *supra* note 13, at 298.

26. *Id.* at 287.

27. Further, the Founding Fathers specifically gave Congress the power to *declare* war, rather than to *make* war. The drafters wanted to enable a president to be able to act on his own accord in emergencies—for Lincoln, a third of the country was in rebellion. Moreover, Lincoln turned to Congress for approval when they came back into session.

28. WOLDMAN, *supra* note 13, at 292.

29. *Id.* at 297.

30. *Id.* at 290–91.

31. *Id.* at 299.

32. *Id.* at 299–300.

33. *Id.* at 286.

34. *Id.* at 289.

35. *Id.* at 289.

36. *Id.* at 331.

37. *Id.* at 289.

38. *Id. at* 287.

39. Texas v. White, 74 U.S. (7 Wall.) 700, 725 (1869).

40. WOLDMAN, *supra* note 13, at 341.

41. Gross, *supra* note 1, at 133.

42. *Id.* at 133.

43. *Id.* at 134.

44. *Id.* at 134–35.

45. *Id.* at 134.

46. *Id.* at 133–34.

47. *Id.* at 133.

48. WOLDMAN, *supra* note 13, at 256.

49. *Id.* at 257.

50. *Id.* at 333.

51. *Id.*

52. Gross, *supra* note 1, at 135.

53. WOLDMAN, *supra* note 13, at 333.

54. *Id.* at 333–34.

55. *Id.* at 337.

56. Gross, *supra* note 1, at 136.

57. *Id.* at 136.

58. WOLDMAN, *supra* note 13, at 336; "In all probability, had the legality of the Proclamation ever been tested in an actual court case, it would have been upheld as a proper exercise of the President's powers as Commander-in-Chief of the armed forces, and as freeing in law those slaves who obtained actual freedom in consequence of the edict." *Id.* at 337.

59. *Id.* at 136–37 (citing Karl Marx who was reporting for a London newspaper at the time.)

60. *Id.* at 133.

61. Henry Cohn, 53(8) FEDERAL LAWYER 53 (Sept. 2006) (book review citing HAROLD HOLZER, EDNA GREENE MEDFORD, & FRANK J. WILLIAMS, THE EMANCIPATION PROCLAMATION: THREE VIEWS (Louisiana State Univ. Press 2006)).

62. WOLDMAN, *supra* note 13, at 338.

63. A quote made famous by historian Richard Hofstadter. *See* ALLEN C. GUELZO, LINCOLN'S EMANCIPATION: THE END OF SLAVERY IN AMERICA 2 (Simon & Schuster Paperbacks 2004).

64. Gross, *supra* note 1, at 136–37.

EXAMPLES OF GREATNESS

It's true that Lincoln's reputation as a great lawyer is not universally agreed upon. He was a complicated man, and his practice in part reflected his peculiar personality. In addition, the legal matters he handled were more complex and nuanced than most. Indeed, the man who best knew him as a lawyer, William Herndon, said that "[n]othing in Lincoln's life has provoked more discussion than the question of his ability as a lawyer. I feel warranted in saying that he was at the same time a very great and very insignificant lawyer." An attorney who practiced with Lincoln from time to time said of Lincoln's greatness that "[h]e could not be called a great lawyer, measured by the extent of his acquirement of legal knowledge; he was not an encyclopedia of cases; but in the text-books of the profession and in the clear perception of legal principles, with natural capacity to apply them, he had great ability."[1]

Notwithstanding the near deification of Lincoln in this country, when his legal career is viewed through a microscope, blemishes can be found. Despite this, if you look at Lincoln's legal career—forgetting about his consecrated name and the folklore that surrounds him—his ability as a lawyer is nothing less than great. In this chapter we look at Lincoln's talents and aptitude for greatness, examining each to learn all we can from these facilities with the intent and ambition to imitate them.

God-Given "Talents"

It is indisputable that some of Lincoln's talents that made him great were innate—and the most obvious endowment possessed by Lincoln was his commanding height. In a time when the average height of a man was five feet seven inches, Lincoln towered over his opponents at six feet four inches. His height is significant because studies today show that people who are "tall" excel in life, not only in getting competitive jobs, but also in being trusted. Since the turn of the century, the taller man in an election has won the presidency seventeen times, while the shorter man only eight times. The reason for this is important; height gives others the impression of being in charge. Thus, while we cannot change our height (save expensive and painful medical procedures), we can be aware of the impact of height on a jury or someone we want to sway. Someone who is "vertically challenged" can compensate for this apparent disadvantage by paying extra attention to other ways to impart a commanding presence, such as their dress, voice inflection, choice of words, and body language.

Another natural talent Lincoln possessed was his strong voice. Contrary to the popular view—that he spoke like Darth Vader—Lincoln's voice was in fact high pitched, but it carried very well. The ability to be heard by a large audience was extremely important in a time without microphones. **Use the volume dictated by your environment. If people cannot hear you, they cannot be convinced by you**.

かい かい かい

Master of the English Language

Many modern day surveys rank public speaking as the number one reported fear, which is surprising considering this means that some people would rather be eaten by a shark than speak to a crowd. Despite Lincoln's incredible ability in front of a jury, he always suffered from a degree of stage fright. This proves that you can be nervous, yet effective—fear not only can keep you sharp, but also can help you prove to yourself that you can overcome a great trepidation.

Lincoln's skills in written and spoken language saved him from a life of poverty and his worst fear: a life of insignificance. Lincoln spent his life trying to articulate his own thoughts, his clients' positions, and eventually the sentiments of a nation. He was a passionate lover of poetry; his favorite was Robert Burns. He was also a deep admirer of Shakespeare and reread his works numerous times. Lincoln's love of the artistic manipulation of English was a root of his exceptional ability to communicate with precision.

Lincoln so much admired the ability to effectively communicate that he was continually studying others with this ability, trying to better his own skills in this area. When Lincoln was young, he attended a murder trial at which the accomplished attorney John A. Brackenridge[2] was pleading a case. Lincoln was so awed by the articulate and powerful speech that he said he listened as if his own life was balanced on the lawyer's persuasiveness.[3] Many years later, President Lincoln met Brackenridge and told him that he felt at the time that "if I could ever make as good a speech as that, my soul would be satisfied."

Lincoln desired to become a great writer, and as a result, he excelled at written communications. Douglas L. Wilson dedicated an entire book to Lincoln's power of persuasion with *Lincoln's Sword*.[4] According to Wilson, Lincoln has become "one of the most admired of all American writers. . . . If one were to judge the importance of a writer by the familiarity of his words and the depth of meaning and feeling they evoke, few if any American writers would compare with him."[5]

People often become what they admire; most professional athletes will state that while growing up, their role models were other accomplished athletes in their respective sports. Looking up to heroes is not enough to make greatness—it takes skill, determination, and practice—but having heroes is often what sparks the desire to follow a particular path.

Holding His Tongue

What a persuasive speaker does *not* say is often just as important as what he does say. Without lying, Lincoln was skilled at organizing his arguments in a way that did not highlight weaknesses in his arguments.

In 1847, before Lincoln swore off representing slave owners, he represented Robert Matson, a slave owner. The opposing party in the case was the Bryant family, whom Matson had brought from Kentucky to work on his Illinois farm. The Bryants fled after they learned that they were to be returned to Kentucky, but they were apprehended after Matson swore an affidavit in front of a justice of the peace claiming them as property. Lacking certificates of freedom, the Bryants were taken into a local jail where they (with the help of local abolitionists) filed a writ of habeas corpus asking the judge to let them go free. The legal question of the case was whether Matson was entitled to take his "property" back to a slave state after residing with the slaves in the free state of Illinois. Despite this being the crux of the case, Lincoln avoided the subject entirely. Instead, he focused his argument on a legal technicality; specifically, whether a habeas corpus petition was the proper proceeding to answer the legal question of ownership of property. This strategy skillfully slighted the very question (despicable as it was) of the case. Despite the legal tactic, Lincoln lost the case—the Bryants were declared free and resettled in Liberia.[6]

Almost every persuasive speaker will at some point have to try to sell a story or product they do not fully believe in; attempting to divert attention from the malevolent issue altogether can be an effective strategy. **If you need to take a position that is morally repugnant, try to rephrase the argument or do not present it at all.**

Another area on which to keep silent in the courtroom: **it is generally not wise to air your client's dirty laundry in the open.** This is especially true if the decision makers are already biased against your position. For example, if you are court-ordered to represent a contemptible client who is accused of sexually abusing a child, it would not be judicious to try to build up his credibility by discussing his impeccable work record at the local child care center.

Many lawyers believe that zinging one-liners makes their case more persuasive. Lawyers trade stories at happy hour on how they "got one in." But I have yet to read an opinion from a judge or read any trial technique literature that supports this contention. **Judges generally instruct lawyers to focus on persuasion, not "wit."**

It is critical to understand that a persuasive speaker must speak to his audience or jury as if every word matters. Complex arguments are also generally not a good strategy; it is often better to hold your tongue than to present an almost-incomprehensible argument.

Cross-Examiner

Lincoln's mastery over the spoken word also gave him an advantage when cross-examining witnesses. He had a natural gift for detecting contradictory logic. Part of his success at cross came from his ad hoc approach that often lowered his witness's defenses; however, his successful cross-examinations were mostly due to his daily practice in court. With each cross-examination he performed—as well as those made by his opposing lawyers—he learned more about the art. Lincoln knew the answers before the witness took the stand, which allowed him to lead the witness accordingly, without actually appearing as if he was leading them.

Isaac N. Arnold, a legal contemporary of Mr. Lincoln's, said that Lincoln possessed the skill to "perceive with almost intuitive quickness the decisive point in the case. In the examination and cross-examination of a witness he had no equal. He could compel a witness to tell the truth when he meant to lie, and if a witness lied, he rarely escaped exposure under Lincoln's cross-examination."[7] A newspaper reporter from the Danville *Illinois Citizen* echoed Arnold's assessment with maybe the most profound statement concerning Lincoln's persuasiveness:

> In his examination of witnesses, he displays a masterly ingenuity and a legal tact that baffles concealment and defies defeat. . . . And in addressing a jury, there is no false glitter, no sickly sentimentalism to be discovered . . . [s]eizing upon the minutest points, he weaves them into his argument with an ingenuity really astonishing. . . . Bold, forcible and energetic, he forces conviction upon the mind, and by his clearness and conciseness, stamps it there not to be erased. . . . Though he may have his equal, it would be no easy task to find his superior.[8]

Lincoln's great success as a cross-examiner came not only from his natural talent, but also from trial and error and studious observations of other attorneys. The famous law professor Irving Younger said that to be a "maestro" cross-examiner you must have three things: first, you must have some natural ability; second, you must master the rules of evidence; and third, you must gain significant experience in court. However, he notes that you can be a "really good" cross-examiner if you nail down number two and three.

Sound Bites

In today's society of fifteen-second news clips, we are all aware of the benefit of having snappy quips. While the public was more receptive to long speeches during Lincoln's time, Lincoln was well aware that short punch lines were easier to remember and imprint in the minds of all Americans.

Some of the most prevalent examples of sound bites in American history are Teddy Roosevelt's "walk softly and carry a big stick"; Franklin D. Roosevelt's "the only thing to fear is fear itself"; and John F. Kennedy's "ask not what your country can do for you, but what you can do for your country." Lincoln's career was filled with such sound bites from his time as a lawyer and into his presidency. Some of his most famous quotes used in the courtroom and while politicking are:

- "Force is all-conquering, but its victories are short-lived."
- "Better to remain silent and be thought a fool, than to speak out and remove all doubt."[9]
- "I will prepare and some day my chance will come."
- "Whatever you are, be a good one."
- "Whenever I hear anyone arguing for slavery, I feel a strong impulse to see it tried on him personally."
- "You cannot escape the responsibility of tomorrow by evading it today."
- "Truth is generally the best vindication against slander."

Try to develop a memorable phrase before your persuasive endeavor. For instance, if you are selling high-priced widgets, the phrase "quality not quantity" could be effective; when representing an auto accident victim who lost a leg, the sound bite "making my victim whole" is easily remembered.

By providing a theme to your audience, you reduce the likelihood of your audience making up their own theme—possibly a theme that does not emphasize the point you'd like it to. In addition, as mentioned, a short bit of information is easier to remember, giving a lasting effect to your message.

Bottom Line Up Front

The phrase "bottom line up front" (BLUF) originated in the United States military. This skill is taught to military leaders to help them become more effective writers and communicators. The basic premise of BLUF is to state your ultimate message up front.

The sparse Lincoln legal briefs and personal letters that have been preserved demonstrate this trait in his system of reasoning. Most of his writings are distinguished not only by their brevity but also their frankness. A colleague of Lincoln's, Isaac N. Arnold, said that "[h]e was so straight-forward, so direct, so candid, that every spectator was impressed with the idea that he was seeking only truth and justice."[10]

Audiences have a limited attention span, especially when the mode of persuading is written text. **It is critical to get your point across**

immediately. Studies have shown that when people read material, they only give their full attention to the first few lines. Whether you're making a sales pitch on paper or presenting your client's argument, state your intentions and your reasoning up front.

Dangerous with a Pen

Lincoln was a great writer in part due to his frankness and brevity. While there is little doubt that his most famous writing was the Emancipation Proclamation, it is but one of his manuscripts. Lincoln was a voracious writer, and as both lawyer and president, he sent a "constant stream of small notes and endorsements to various government offices"[11] and clients. He wrote frequently to his generals, offering advice or just keeping in touch.[12] Lincoln also wrote defensively during both his careers. Obviously as a lawyer he would defend his clients (and himself on several occasions), and as the president he found himself "operating in a perpetual cross fire from congressmen, governors, generals, . . . ordinary citizens—all dissatisfied, and many sincerely convinced that he was incompetent and leading the nation down a path of destruction. His writings were an important part of his effort to respond to this pressure."[13]

Lincoln's son, Robert Todd Lincoln, said this about his father's writings: "He was a very deliberate writer, anything but rapid. . . . He seemed to think nothing of the labor of writing personally [and i]n writing a careful letter, he first wrote it himself, then corrected it, and then rewrote the corrected version himself."[14] As with his oral skills, Lincoln was careful and precise in his written communications.

One of Lincoln's most brilliant writings was to a Kentucky newspaper editor, Albert G. Hodges (the piece is known as the Hodges Letter). Hodges had come to Washington as part of a delegation from Kentucky to present their views to the president, specifically their objections to the deployment of black soldiers in the Union Army.[15] President Lincoln made some remarks that impressed Hodges, and Hodges asked for a copy of the remarks to take back to Kentucky. Lincoln informed the editor that he did not have any notes about the meeting, but he would think about what he said and commit it to paper. What Hodges received is an incredible example of written advocacy (read the entire letter in Appendix 6).

> My dear Sir: . . .
>   I am naturally anti-slavery. If slavery is not wrong, nothing is wrong. I can not remember when I did not so think, and feel. And yet I have never understood that the Presidency conferred upon me an unrestricted right to act officially upon this judgment and feeling. It was in the oath I took that I would, to the best of my ability, preserve, protect,

and defend the Constitution of the United States. I could not take the
office without taking the oath. Nor was it my view that I might take an
oath to get power, and break the oath in using the power.

I understood, too, that in ordinary civil administration this oath even
forbade me to practically indulge my primary abstract judgment on the
moral question of slavery. I had publicly declared this many times, and
in many ways. And I aver that, to this day, I have done no official act
in mere deference to my abstract judgment and feeling on slavery. I
did understand however, that my oath to preserve the constitution to
the best of my ability, imposed upon me the duty of preserving, by
every indispensable means, that government—that nation—of which
that constitution was the organic law.

Was it possible to lose the nation, and yet preserve the constitution?
By general law life *and* limb must be protected; yet often a limb must be
amputated to save a life; but a life is never wisely given to save a limb. I
felt that measures, otherwise unconstitutional, might become lawful, by
becoming indispensable to the preservation of the constitution, through
the preservation of the nation. Right or wrong, I assumed this ground,
and now avow it. I could not feel that, to the best of my ability, I had
even tried to preserve the constitution, if, to save slavery, or any minor
matter, I should permit the wreck of government, country, and Constitution all together.

. . . .

. . . [I]n March, and May, and July 1862 I made earnest, and successive appeals to the border states to favor compensated emancipation, I
believed the indispensable necessity for military emancipation, and arming the blacks would come, unless averted by that measure.

They declined the proposition; and I was, in my best judgment,
driven to the alternative of either surrendering the Union, and with it,
the Constitution, or of laying strong hand upon the colored element. I
chose the latter. In choosing it, I hoped for greater gain than loss; but of
this, I was not entirely confident. More than a year of trial now shows
no loss by it in our foreign relations, none in our home popular sentiment, none in our white military force,—no loss by it any how or any
where. On the contrary, it shows a gain of quite a hundred and thirty
thousand soldiers, seamen, and laborers. These are palpable facts, about
which, as facts, there can be no caviling. We have the men; and we
could not have had them without the measure.

. . . .

. . . If God now wills the removal of a great wrong, and wills also
that we of the North as well as you of the South, shall pay fairly for our
complicity in that wrong, impartial history will find therein new cause
to attest and revere the justice and goodness of God.

Yours truly,

A. Lincoln

It is not clear why Hodges wanted Lincoln's oral remarks committed to paper. By all accounts, he persuaded Hodges and the other delegates during the face-to-face meeting.[16] Hodges could have requested the written version because he was in the news business and this was news, or he could have been so persuaded by Lincoln's point of view that he wanted to share "its force and appeal with his fellow Kentuckians."[17] However, if he hoped—and Wilson suggests this as a possibility—that Lincoln's remarks "would seem lame and ineffective if translated into writing—his request would have ordinarily have been a very promising gambit."[18] But not with Lincoln. He was just as dangerous with a pen as he was on a stump.[19]

ॐ ॐ ॐ

Great Speeches

Aside from the Gettysburg address, Lincoln's three most influential and successful speeches were his stump speech at Cooper Union, his first inaugural address, and his second inaugural address.

Cooper Union

The Cooper Union speech was delivered on February 27, 1860, to a fervent audience of more than fifteen hundred people in New York. While the political importance of the speech was enormous, Lincoln's enthusiasm prior to delivering it was wanting. Robert Lincoln later joked that the speech that was the catalyst to his father's career never would have happened if Robert had not done so poorly on the Harvard entrance examinations. In 1860, Lincoln had enrolled his son in Exeter, a school

This Photograph was Taken on February 27, 1960, in New York City, the Day Lincoln Delivered the Cooper Union Speech.

that specialized in getting young men ready for elite college examinations. Lincoln went to interview his son's teachers to account for his progress at the expensive school. It was only because he was in the area on February 27, 1860, that he agreed to speak at Plymouth Church, Brooklyn, which later changed the venue to Cooper Union, a college in Lower Manhattan.

The speech is remarkable for its ability to convince an audience through logic and reasoning (read the speech in Appendix 4). He achieved this success not with just good luck and a passion for the subject—he committed a substantial amount of time preparing for the speech. In addition to delivering a compelling argument for his party, Lincoln also answered the Southern criticism of the Northern states and the Republican Party, preempting counter-arguments before they could be fully developed by his opponents.

The tactic of preempting arguments is useful because it often discourages your opponent from raising them to begin with. However, it does have its drawback, in that it may present an argument to your opponent that he had not considered.

Another noteworthy aspect of the Cooper Union speech was its structure. Most law schools teach a basic form for persuasive communication, typically called IRAC or some variant there of. IRAC stands for Issue (note that the issue is up front, as the BLUF rule dictates), Rule, Analysis of facts, and Conclusion. By following this format, a lawyer is able to be the most effective in his arguments in the smallest amount of space.

Lincoln followed this structure to the letter in his Cooper Union speech. He started by stating the reason for his speech: to combat Senator Douglas's position on slavery. After he successfully established the premise of his speech, he talked about the rules that govern his issue; specifically, the Constitution of the United States.

The meat of Lincoln's speech and the IRAC argument structure is the analysis of the facts. Here, Lincoln laid out a detailed but concise examination of the facts leading up to Douglas's stance on expanding slavery to the territories. In doing this Lincoln put the argument at the feet of what he calls the "thirty-nine fathers," a reference to the signers of the Constitution.

Lincoln pointed out that while George Washington was president, he signed a bill that prohibited slavery from expanding into the Northwestern Territories; the bill was unanimously passed by the first Congress. To sum up his factual review of the "thirty-nine," Lincoln emphatically said:

> But enough! Let all who believe that our fathers, who framed the Government under which we live, understood this question just as well, and ever better, than we do now, speak as they spoke and act as they acted upon it. This is all Republicans ask—all Republicans desire—in relation

to slavery. As those fathers marked it, so let it be again marked, as an evil not to be extended, but to be tolerated and protected only because of and so far as its actual presence among us makes that toleration and protection a necessity. Let all the guaranties those fathers gave it, be, not grudgingly, but fully, maintained. For this Republicans contend, and with this, so far as I know or believe, they will be content.

After Lincoln thoroughly analyzed the issue, he stated the only conclusion that his facts could support—that the expansion of slavery to the territories was not a plausible or logical position based on the facts. He ended his speech by stating, "let us [not be] frightened . . . by menaces of destruction to the Government nor of dungeons to ourselves. Let us have faith that right makes might, and in that faith, let us, to the end, dare to do our duty as we understand it." By adding this line, Lincoln gave his speech the ring of power, letting his audience feel as if they had just witnessed history in the making.

Charles C. Nott was the leader of the Young Men's Republican Union. It was Nott who, with Lincoln's permission, annotated the speech and published it. In Nott's words, "[f]rom the first line to the last—from his premises to his conclusion, he travels with swift, unerring directness which no logician ever excelled—an argument complete and full, without the affection of learning, and without the stiffness which usually accompanies dates and details." Lincoln's speech at Cooper Union was not only a great political speech and legal argument against Douglas's party, it also provided a banner under which an entire movement—the Republican Party—could rally. This is much the same way the Declaration of Independence acted as a banner to the Minutemen and other American revolutionary fighters.

Nott was not the only one to realize the speech was groundbreaking. The *New York Tribune* called the speech "one of the happiest and most convincing political arguments ever made in this City." Similarly, The *New York Times* reported that:

> a lawyer with some local reputation in Illinois, was at his best. Without any attempt at flowery rhetoric of flighty oratory of play upon emotions, but with lawyer-like arguments and invincible logic, simply, calmly, and dispassionately he presented the case against slavery. Masterfully he arrayed his facts and historical and legal data concerning the controversy. His hearers were people of intelligence—"a great audience, including all the noted men—all the learned and cultured—of his party in New York: editors, clergymen, statesmen, lawyers, merchants, and critics."[20]

In general the address was acclaimed as "one of the most scholarly, effective, and convincing discourses of an argumentative nature heard in all that turbulent era of stirring political events. This masterful address contributed much toward making Lincoln a national figure and one of the leaders in the supreme crisis of our history."[21]

A student of persuasion can learn much from the structure of the Cooper Union speech. First, if you have the greatest argument combined with the greatest idea, but it's not organized in a concise, logical, easy-to-follow manner, it is worse than a poor argument that flows persuasively. Though it is not the only effective argument structure, the IRAC method works, especially for legal arguments. The structure of an argument should both lead the audience to understand the argument in the least amount of space and time, and convinces them that it's a winner.

Another lesson from the speech can be seen in Lincoln's factual analysis. While it is not always appropriate to "argue" while you are presenting the factual outline of your case, **you can present the facts in such a way that the only appropriate conclusion is yours**. By vicariously presenting the facts through the Founding Fathers (the "thirty-nine"), Lincoln effectively forced any opponent to have to argue not only against his elegant words, but also against the words of the Founders of the American government.

The First Inaugural

The second great speech in Lincoln's career was his first inaugural address, delivered in Washington, D.C., on March 4, 1861. To prepare for this important speech, Lincoln asked Herndon to bring him some books. "His law partner was amazed to observe that the list included only Henry Clay's great speech delivered in 1850, Andrew Jackson's proclamation against nullification, and a copy of the Constitution. Later Lincoln also asked for Webster's reply to Hayne, which Lincoln regarded as the finest specimen of American oratory."[22] With the sparse material, Lincoln locked himself in a room and wrote his famous speech (read the speech in Appendix XX).

Lincoln took a conciliatory tone during this address, appealing to the nation for peace and patience. While the speech was delivered to the entire country, he directed his soothing tone to a fearful South. He was direct with his intentions, stating, "I have no purpose, directly or indirectly, to interfere with the institution of slavery where it exists. I believe I have no lawful right to do so, and I have no inclination to do so."

While trying to present a pacifying atmosphere was Lincoln's primary goal, he also addressed his concern for obedience to the law. In stressing this, he made numerous references to the Constitution as the ultimate law. For example: "*All* members of Congress swear their support to the *whole* Constitution—to this provision as much as to any other" and "I hold, that in contemplation of universal law, and of the Constitution, the

Lincoln Delivering his First Inaugural Address. Photograph shows participants and crowd at the first inauguration of President Abraham Lincoln, at the U.S. Capitol, Washington, D.C. Lincoln is standing under the wood canopy, at the front, midway between the left and center posts. His face is in shadow but the white shirt front is visible.

Union of these States is *perpetual*. Perpetuity is implied, if not expressed, in the fundamental law of all national governments."

The speech remains a masterpiece in the art of persuasiveness. Here, Lincoln the lawyer, "who so often in the past endeavored to discourage litigation and to persuade litigious clients to compromise their differences with their adversaries, now as the Chief Magistrate of the Nation was pleading with his millions of new 'clients' to refrain from quarreling and to remain friends."[23]

While an aggressive stance can be an asset in persuasive speaking, **it is sometimes more effective to be appeasing and to speak with a benevolent tone**. Lincoln understood that a fist-pounding speech, threatening the South with military action if it did not stop its rebellious behavior, would surely cause a bloody rift in the Union. Instead, he tried to heal the hostilities with mollifying words. Of course, despite Lincoln's peace-making efforts, he was unsuccessful at preventing war, and on April 12, 1861, after Fort Sumter was attacked, the United States went to war.

LINCOLN DELIVERING HIS SECOND INAUGURAL ADDRESS. PHOTO SHOWS PRESIDENT LINCOLN STANDING IN THE CENTER OF THE PHOTO (BELOW THE FLAG AND TO THE LEFT).

Second Inaugural

Lincoln's Second inaugural address was succinct and profound (read the speech in Appendix 3). Unlike the first, the second inaugural had a sad but hopeful theme to it. Four years of war had waged, costing 618,000 American lives. Instead of being conciliatory, Lincoln acted as a judge, seeking mediation and settlement to a devastating case.

> Both parties deprecated war; but one of them would *make* war rather than let the nation survive; and the other would *accept* war rather than let it perish . . . . With malice toward none; with charity for all; with firmness in the right, as God gives us to see the right, let us strive on to finish the work we are in; to bind up the nation's wounds; . . . to do all which may achieve and cherish a just and lasting peace, among ourselves, and with all nations.

When the speech was delivered, the audience was taken aback at its brevity. Much like the Gettysburg Address, by keeping the speech concise and precise—a mere 703 words delivered in about ten minutes—he focused all of the speech's power and persuasiveness on one subject: ending the War. **A short but precise argument directed at the heart of a dispute will more often than not be more effective than an exhaustive but drawn out argument.**

Often a case will have several issues, with one issue being the foundation or "head" of the case in controversy—by destroying the head of the issue, there is no need to attack the "pinkie" of the case. This is a mistake made all too often by lawyers, who are trained to be meticulous in making arguments. However, what is often thought of as thoroughness is all too often received as tedious by the audience. On March 4, 1865, when Lincoln gave his second inaugural address, I am sure there were issues that were of concern to the national government concerning taxes, infrastructure improvements, and the increase in bankruptcies in the country; but what were those but petty compared to the bloody civil war that was waging.

è&. è&. è&.

Dedication to Clients

Lincoln had a profound sense of commitment to the representation of his clients. When his client became the people of the United States, he fought with the same industriousness that he did for his legal clients.

Use the Press When Appropriate

In the *General James Adams* case, we can see Lincoln's audacity in the representation of his clients. Lincoln was representing a woman who was being taking advantage of by the general because of her disenfranchised status as a widow. General Adams had forged a deed with the intent to swindle the widow out of her property. Lincoln knew that General Adams was an aspiring politician and would be hurt most by bad press over the dispute. Because of this, Lincoln launched a media war against the general by writing articles for the *Sangamon Journal*, making the clash the biggest news of the state. Use public attention when it helps your case. However, a more important and useful take-away is to **find your opponent's fear and exploit it.**

Work Ethic

Lincoln was not a great lawyer because of his immense breadth of legal knowledge; he lacked the proper education for that. Lincoln was a great lawyer because he was willing to work harder for his client than anybody else was.[24] This represents one of the greatest things about our country— that with hard work you can be great. Lincoln came from humble beginnings to become a great leader of a great country during an extraordinarily difficult time.

When some students asked Lincoln how to succeed, he replied, "Work, work, work, is the main thing."[25] The effort and endeavor of hard work are "not only good in themselves but the means to financial self-sufficiency."[26] Indeed, Lincoln had a deep loathing of sloth; he once said that "the leading rule [of men] is diligence. Leave nothing for tomorrow which can be done today."[27]

The lesson here is more reassuring than anything: if you are not at the head of your class, you can still win. **In a battle between work ethic and craftiness, work ethic will win almost every time.**

Leave Your Ego at the Door

A key trait in being a good trial attorney or salesperson, or excelling at any other person-to-person profession is the ability to swallow your pride and do the right thing for your client, employer, or consumer. While it appears that Lincoln was egotistical at times—for one thing, he was resistant to people altering his speeches for publication—he never let his ego interfere with the representation of his clients.

Most lawyers seem to care more for their record and reputation than for the needs of their clients. Not Lincoln. In the case of *Banet v. Alton and Sangamon Railroad*, Lincoln effectively argued on behalf of the railroad that a stock subscriber was required to make payment on his subscriptions, in spite of the fact that the railway changed the route of the rail. The state supreme court agreed that the public interest in the railway outweighed that of individual rights in property. This case was a substantial success for Lincoln in that it gave him some free advertising, and the precedent decision was beneficial to the rail industry, which represented a sizeable profit for Lincoln. Despite this, Lincoln argued twice against his legal position in the *Banet* case, seeking to overturn the decision—not because he felt the decision was bad policy—quite the contrary—but because it was detrimental to his current clients' position. **When you represent a client, you represent the client's interests—never your own.**

President Lincoln, on numerous occasions, shifted acclaim from himself to another individual or assumed fault that was not his own. He was always concerned with the needs of the Union first. When General Grant arrived in Washington in March of 1864 after his victories at Vicksburg and Chattanooga, he was received by the city as a hero. At the White House, Lincoln stood to the side, giving the place of honor normally occupied by the president of the United States to his general. Few other ambitious politicians would have given up the opportunity to stand with the new Union hero and receive acclaim along with him. But Lincoln realized that the nation needed a hero, and Grant served the role well; Lincoln knew the country needed to regain some confidence and pride in the Union's military leadership. The message must come before your own gain.[28]

ða ða ða

Preparedness Is Next to Godliness

It is true that at trial, Lincoln would often depend on his shrewdness and speech-making abilities over thorough research and preparation. However, when conducting appeals, he would reinforce himself with every available precedent and argument, working the case from all directions, making sure he was prepared to answer any question from the presiding judges. Criticism of Lincoln's preparation is not without some merit, but that is not the whole story.

Lincoln began by studying the case and mapping out his predictions on how the case would play out in court. He would give judicious attention to his opponents' case—trying to win their case in his mind's eye, with their evidence. Because of this, Lincoln was rarely surprised by the strength of his opponents' case or the way the facts were revealed at trial. Another example of Lincoln's preparation was his tremendous ability to preserve the record for appeal. He would predict legal problems in a case and be sure to object to them at trial to preserve his issue on the record—this allowed for an appeal on that issue.

This lesson does not only apply to lawyers. For instance, when selling a car, one of the most critical tasks is to preserve the record; the most successful car salesman is not the one who gets the most potential customers, or "ups," as they call them; rather, it is the one who preserves the relationship with his potential customers and past customers. When they are ready to buy, or when they are ready to buy again, they will come back to you. Several years ago, I read a story about a successful car salesman. His secret: sending personal holiday cards to all of his contacts, whether they bought a car or not—after several years of this practice, he was a millionaire.

ɛ⃝ ɛ⃝ ɛ⃝

Master of the Facts

Some people have a "steel-trap" mind—Lincoln did not. It took some time for him to memorize facts or occurrences. He once compared his mind to a piece of metal: hard to scratch, but once blemished, impossible to remove.

When Lincoln took a case, he would study the facts of that case but also the background of those facts to understand the entire subject. In this way, he completely understood the facts and how to best relate them to the jury. In a lawsuit over a patent involving mechanical reapers, for example, he had numerous reapers brought before the jury to show them the differences. He crawled around the floor of the courtroom, showing the jury every part, how each part worked—the jury was so enthralled with his simple explanation of a complicated machine they got out of the jury box and got on the floor with him, to get a better vantage of the part he was talking about. **This ability to easily digest facts and effectively use the information in a trial or a presentation comes with practice**.

ба ба ба

The Edges of the Law

In a world of television shows such as *Perry Mason* and *Law and Order*, people think a victory in a case has to be made with a dramatic ending—having a witness admit he was the murderer on the stand or introducing a document that conclusively proves the insurance company illegally refused coverage for an eight-year-old cancer patient. However, what Lincoln and other great trial attorneys or persuasive speakers know is that a victory is a victory. It is always preferable to win on the merits of your argument, but winning on a legal technicality is a win, too.

Lincoln had an almost uncanny ability to see the edges of the law—a marriage of the letter of the law and a thorough understanding of jurisprudence and all its implications. He was a formidable force on both the merits and technicalities of the case at hand. Although Lincoln had no love for winning on mere procedure, he considered it a greater travesty and dereliction of duty to his client to lose when a technical defense was available. He understood "that the pleas of limitation, infancy, usury, and other technical safeguards are absolutely necessary for a proper and equitable administration of justice. Having undertaken a case, a lawyer's duty compels him to array the facts and to present every phase of the law helpful to his client's cause."[29]

Despite his willingness to win on a possibly trivial point, available records show that, while he would raise a technical defense for his client's interests and would press such technicalities ferociously, he never did so at the expense of fair play. He never told half-truths or played deceitful tricks to gain an advantage. Lincoln's most famous technical win is the criminal defense of John Bantzhouse. Bantzhouse was a tavern owner in Sangamon County who was so incensed about noise outside his tavern that he fired a shotgun through the window, killing Walter Clark. James B. White was the state's attorney; he had held the office for less than a year and was fairly inexperienced, especially compared to the seasoned Lincoln.

Lincoln first moved to change venue and filed for a continuance in order to locate witnesses. Both motions went without protest from White. However, because of the continuance, White inadvertently violated a state statute that mandated that, after a suspect is charged with murder, he or she must be tried within two court terms or face a speedy trial violation. Because of the violation the court dismissed the case, and before White could bring another indictment at the earnest requests of Clark's brother,

Bantzhouse fled. Here, we see Lincoln very willing to take advantage of the naiveté of his opponent to benefit his client's interests.

In a civil case, *Dorman v. Lane*, Lincoln wrote to his associate in the case, attorney Samuel D. Marshall, laying out his plan to win on a statute of limitation:

> I learned today that Lane, to avoid paying the cost of taking the case between Dorman and him back from Supreme Court, has commenced a new proceeding in your Circuit Court. Write me, if this is so; and I, together with Judge Logan, will try to frame a plea either in bar or in abatement, out of the fact of the pendency of the old case, that shall blow them up on their new case.
>
> By the way, if they fail for more than a year (which they have nearly done already) to take the old case down from here, I think we can plead limitation on them, so that it will stick for good and all. Don't speak of this, lest they hear it and take alarm.[30]

Lincoln was more than willing to let another attorney win his case for him due to the other attorney's neglect. Again, Lincoln would not have tricked his opponents to think they had more time, but he had no problem letting them find out the hard way.

In another civil case, *Maus v. Worthing*, Lincoln argued a technicality; an appeal bond was not properly signed, so Lincoln successfully had his opponent's appeal dismissed. Here, Lincoln won on the simplest procedural mishap. A judge determines the law and the jury the facts; you can win on rhetoric and emotions in front of a jury, but a judge wants a legal reason, and even the smallest will do. "A lawyer usurps the province of the judge and jury when he determines in advance the justice of his client's cause. He is unfair to his client when he fails to protect his interests with every proper device of the law."[31]

Not using every tool in the bag is a discredit to your client and yourself. However, when dealing in technicalities, it is easy to go from practicing at the edge of the law to practicing in the abyss of the law. If you feel you are too close to the edge, you probably are, and in some instances you might have already fallen over. While "play hard, but not too hard" may seem like an impossible standard, it is important to note that 99 percent of these situations can be resolved with simple common sense. Most people know if they are being dishonest—if you cannot make that determination, maybe you should be looking for employment where you will not be put in situations where you have to make these calls. A simple rule is if you have to internally justify your actions, you are most likely playing too close to the edge.

ಶಿ ಶಿ ಶಿ

Selling Himself as the Folksy Storyteller

Lawyers have more in common with salespeople than they like to admit. They are both selling a product; with the salesperson, it's an insurance policy, a car, a microwave, and so forth; with the lawyer, it's his client's story. In addition, critical to any successful trial lawyer or salesperson is the ability to sell oneself. If you can't sell yourself as a trustworthy individual, it does not matter if you have the greatest widget at the greatest price, or the greatest and most compelling story—people will not buy your product. Lincoln understood this concept with intensity. He was diligent in selling his clients' stories and selling himself, humbly and with dignity, as a person of high character.

An interesting aspect of Lincoln's approachable nature is that it was partly artificial. Lincoln was alert to the political rewards of projecting himself as a folksy lawyer from humble beginnings.[32] But this is not to say that "there was anything contrived about his interest in the common folk. He empathized with those who were, as he had been, struggling self-improvers; he had . . . a deep faith 'in the honesty and good sense of the masses.'"[33]

Lincoln had hundreds of friendships, but he took very few people into his confidence. Those select few would describe Lincoln as easygoing, amenable, and trustworthy, but they would also describe a "barrier of dignity," which was never breached. Indeed, with Lincoln, he "did not appear the great man that he really was."[34]

Plain Spoken

Lincoln's quality skill as a communicator was not born from an Ivy League education. And despite being self-conscious about his meager schooling, it was because of this paltry education that he retained the ability to use homespun language that the jury could appreciate and relate to.

Lincoln knew that people would believe what they understand more easily than what needs to be explained to them. We all have had this experience: when a salesperson is trying to sell you a car and explains that the extra price comes from the engine containing VTEC intelligence technology that allows for a systematic piston rhythm, we feel like he is trying to take advantage of our naiveté. However, if the salesperson says that the car costs more because the engine is designed to give more power and consume less fuel, we feel that the extra money may be worth it.

Lincoln was a firm believer that simple talk gained credibility with the jury. When advising his junior partner, William Herndon, Lincoln said, "Billy, don't shoot too high. Aim lower and the common people will understand you." He went on to say, "they are the ones you want to reach—at least they are the ones you ought to reach. The educated and refined people will understand you anyway. If you aim too high your ideas will go over the heads of the masses and only hit those who need no hitting."

Lincoln would always talk *with* a jury or audience, never *at* them. Many people observed that when Lincoln was in front of a jury, it seemed more like a two-way conversation than a speech. John Hill, a contemporary of Lincoln's, said of his speaking ability: "Mr. Lincoln was the plainest man I ever heard. He was not a speaker but a talker."[35] The colleague went on to say that "[h]e talked to jurors and to political gatherings plain, sensible, candid talk, almost as in conversation, no effort whatever in oratory. But his talking had wonderful effect. Honesty, candor, fairness, everything that was convincing, was in his manner and expressions."

By using the local vernacular, Lincoln made his audience feel as if one of their neighbors was speaking. His audience felt Lincoln was one of them and knew immediately that he came from their ranks, rather than being a pompous, highbrow, slick-speaking lawyer.

Storyteller

Often Lincoln would win over his juries with quaint expressions or stories to put things in perspective. In the Wyant murder case, an insanity case that he tried when he was temporarily serving as the state's prosecutor, he was trying to deflate the defense's impressive medical testimony. During the trial, a doctor stated that one reason he believed the defendant was insane was because he picked at his head. Lincoln responded with: "you say, doctor, that this man picks his head, and by that you infer that he is insane. Now, I sometimes pick my head and those joking fellows at Springfield tell me that there may be a living, moving cause for it, and that the trouble isn't at all on the inside. It's only a case for fine-tooth combs." This self-deprecating story gave the jury an alternative reason for the defendant's picking at his head (basically dandruff) that everyone could understand and relate to.

When defending a man accused of assault and battery, Lincoln's theory of the case was that the "victim" was in fact the aggressor, and his client was merely defending himself. To explain this theory, Lincoln told the jury a made-up story of a fellow who was "going along the highway with a pitchfork on his shoulder, and was attacked by a fierce dog that ran out at him from a farmer's yard. In parrying off the dog with the pitchfork, its prongs stuck into the brute and killed him." At that point the dog's owner came upon the traveler and asked "what made you kill my dog?" Such a question elicited the response "what made him try to bite me?" from the traveler. The farmer then asked, "But why did you not go at him with the other end of the pitchfork?" Lincoln's make-believe traveler responded with: "Why did he not come after me with his other end?" The humorous story not only got a laugh out of the jury, but it also helped them understand that self-defense is an acceptable plea of justification when the victim is the aggressor, even when the defendant uses extraordinary force. Lincoln's client was freed.

In another case, while Lincoln was trying to convey the legal standard of proof, "preponderance of the evidence," he recognized in the jurors' faces that they were confused. He said: "if you were going to bet on this case, on which side would you be willing to risk a picayune [a Spanish coin of little value; it was actually slang in the 1800s for 'of little value']? That side on which you would be willing to bet a picayune, is the side on which rests the preponderance of evidence in your minds." He went on to explain, "[i]t is possible that you may not be right, but that is not the question. The question is as to where the preponderance of evidence lies, and you can judge exactly where it lies in your minds, by deciding as to which side you would be willing to bet on."[36] Through this simple story they were able to understand the legal concept and answer the question in favor of his client.

Being a good storyteller is extremely helpful, if not essential, to being a successful persuasive speaker—**when you are the storyteller, you are the narrator of events and have the ability to insert facts that make your case appear more favorable to the decision maker**.

ἐ▲ ἐ▲ ἐ▲

Loved by the Court and His Colleagues

It is well known that Lincoln was the star of the bar during his time. While his contemporaries did not unilaterally love him, most genuinely enjoyed his company, and more important, enjoyed working with him. The following traits can win you friends and respect.

Humility

His fellow lawyers loved Lincoln for the same reasons juries did—he was not pompous and could speak and relate to anyone, despite his great talent. On the circuit, while not in front of the bench, Lincoln was known for being a great storyteller who would attract sizable groups of attorneys. Entertainers always have a following, and Lincoln's stories were often funny at his own expense, usually involving his height, dress, or homely looks.

Despite his popularity and heightened status in the bar, he was humble and never showed self-importance at the expense of others. For instance, on the circuit, innkeepers would often reserve the head of the table for him. On one occasion, Lincoln sat in a seat other than the head position. When the innkeeper tried to move him to the seat of honor, Lincoln asked, "have you anything better to eat up there? If not, I'll stay here."

And remember—Lincoln's friends from the bar almost single-handedly won him the Republican nomination.

Kindness to the Staff

More than making friends with his colleagues, Lincoln was also well received by those who worked for him, as well as the employees of the court. These individuals saw Lincoln as an authentically nice, kind man. He had the ability to leave people feeling better about their surroundings and themselves than they did when he found them.

More often than not, a decision maker is highly influenced by his support staff. A judge's personal staff and law clerks have a wide range of discretion in the handling of cases outside their judge's conscious daily workload. A common mistake of salespeople is to focus on the breadwinner, not realizing that the supporting spouse is often critically influential or is the actual decision maker.

Willing to Mentor Young Attorneys

Lincoln was especially popular with young attorneys. This was primarily due to his willingness to help them; he was kind, patient, and courteous while advising them on their legal problems. He possessed the happy faculty of being able to set his young associates at ease, encourage them, and instill them with self-confidence.[37] One young attorney said on this subject: "No young lawyer ever practiced in the courts with Mr. Lincoln who did not in all his after life have a regard for him akin to personal affection."

Be helpful to the next generation; not only is it a kind and gracious thing to do, but as Lincoln discovered, it can also be lucrative. As a result of being the bar's father figure to young attorneys, Lincoln received a tremendous amount of work through referrals from new attorneys who felt over their heads. These individuals later became fervent political supporters of Lincoln's, helping him win elections and eventually the presidency.

ได ได ได

Professionalism: Never Make It Personal

Lincoln earnestly tried to avoid personal animosity with his opponents during cases. Lincoln's close friend and fellow attorney, Ward Hill Lemon, said that Lincoln "knew how to try a case without making a personal issue between counsel. He could utter effective replies without insulting his opponent, and during all his practice he never made an enemy in the ranks of the profession." Lemon went on to observe "that no one but a lawyer can appreciate what this means; but it requires generosity, patience, tact, courtesy, firmness, courage, self-control, and a big-mindedness which few men possess."

Along with the ability to avoid personal conflicts with other attorneys, Lincoln was also able to mend wounds and deal with strong egos. It is well known that attorneys have fairly large egos. Doris Goodwin, in her book *A Team of Rivals*, described this ability of Lincoln's as an

> extraordinary array of personal qualities that enabled him to form friendships with men who had previously opposed him; to repair injured feelings that, left untended, might have escalated into permanent hostility . . . . His success in dealing with the strong egos of the men in his cabinet suggests that in the hands of a truly great politician the qualities we generally associate with decency and morality—kindness, sensitivity, compassion, honesty, and empathy—can also be impressive political resources.[38]

Today's legal community is known for its gladiator, no-holds-barred style. As attorneys, we could learn a lot from Lincoln here; **you can represent your client zealously without stepping on your brothers and sisters of the bar.**

છ ઢ ઢ

Love Your Job

Lincoln truly loved the practice of law; one proof of this is that he became so good at it with no shortcuts. True, Lincoln had some natural abilities; however, he plugged away and became great the old-fashioned way—pure experience.

Lincoln gained his experience through several avenues. First, he did so by keeping a busy caseload. For twenty years he handled hundreds of cases and was well known as the hardest worker on the circuit. Lincoln also gained experience from other attorneys—by listening to their cases, picking the traits that worked with his style, and using those traits himself. When his office was above the U.S. Circuit and District courtrooms, he would open a trap door in his office's floor, and he and Herndon would listen in on the proceedings.

An aspiring persuasive speaker must understand that the vast majority of the greats in every profession became great through perseverance, not thorough supernatural talent. With a few exceptions, every lesson learned in this book was a lesson that Lincoln learned from hardcore practice. We have the benefit of skipping some steps by looking at his career and emulating his successes. However, reading about how Lincoln performed great cross-examinations is not enough—you must practice those techniques and execute them yourself.

As discussed earlier in the book, Lincoln was approached in 1860 by the president of the New York Central Railroad, Erastus Corning, who was so impressed by Lincoln's speech at Cooper Union that he wanted Lincoln's skills on the Railroad's staff. Mr. Corning invited Lincoln to become the New York Central Railroad General Counsel at an annual salary of ten thousand dollars (an enormous sum at the time). As the story goes, Lincoln flatly refused the offer, despite the extremely lucrative salary. He did so because he liked what he was doing; he loved his circuit practice.[39]

Attempt to shine at everything you do; you never know where it will take you. You never know who your client is, or for that matter who is listening. However, stay with what you like. Taking a job simply because it pays more can lead to unhappiness—know yourself well enough to know what will make you happy.

When Lincoln was the president-elect, he told his wife that they would "go back to Illinois and I will open a law office in Springfield." Lincoln also made this desire known to Herndon when he told him to let the old Lincoln & Herndon practice shingle "hang there undisturbed.

Give our clients to understand the election of a President makes no change in the firm of Lincoln and Herndon. If I live I'm coming back some time, and then we'll go right on practicing law as if nothing had happened." Woldman sums up this sentiment best when he stated "[a]s long as that sign hung there he would feel that he was still the lawyer and belonged in Springfield."[40] Lincoln loved the practice of law—after serving as president, he was planning to return to a messy office to work on inconsequential cases with minor clients for the love of justice. **If you love what you do, you will be better at it.**

ૐ ૐ ૐ

Love to Learn

Most professions that engage in persuasion are in a constant flux, especially the legal profession, which changes with every court decision. **You must have the ability to learn, and to use what you've learned.**[41]

Lincoln would learn anything to help his clients, including incorporating new technology into his cases after he'd first mastered it himself. A comparable example today would be a prosecutor mastering DNA science. During the Civil War, Lincoln read every available military science book in order to better understand how to win and how to instruct his army.

In addition to learning, Lincoln was a great teacher. Part of loving to learn is loving to teach—you have truly mastered a profession when you can teach it. When a junior attorney would come to Lincoln for help on a case, Lincoln never took over the case and split the fee. Rather, he would counsel the younger lawyer and insist that the lawyer fully participate in the trial. On one such case Lincoln induced the inexperienced attorney to give the opening statement and counseled him, "when you are doing it talk to the jury as though your client's fate depends on every word you utter. Forget that you have any one to fall back upon, and you will do justice to yourself and your client."[42]

ॐ ॐ ॐ

Cold, Clear, Calculating Logic

Lincoln once observed that he "pondered the meaning of life with such 'intensity of thought,' that he wore ideas 'thread bare' and turned them 'to the bitterness of death.'" His partner Herndon remarked that Lincoln thought more than any man in America and was "pitiless and persistent in the pursuit of truth." "Lincoln thought, slowly, methodically, deeply, as he tried to find the 'nub' of a question and strip it of irrelevancies."[43] Lincoln's close friend Henry C. Whitney said of Lincoln's critical thinking: "when it came to cases with no well defined precedent, Lincoln had a powerful advantage [over his adversaries] for he had no superior, certainly, and but very few equals at our bar in original reasoning."

Lincoln's reputation of being a logician was well deserved; he won numerous cases on nothing more than logic, or what he called common sense.

Common Sense

Lincoln sought to prevail in his cases through practical methods; he usually stayed away from flashy demonstrations. He could and often would win a case without making a single legal argument; instead, he would lay out the facts in a way that made it painfully obvious that his position was the only plausible one. "All his colleagues agree that for lucidity of statement, clear reasoning power, and analogy Lincoln had no superior at the bar of Illinois. His mental aptitude was to comprehend not only the technical rules of the law, but to discern the philosophy and the spirit which undergirds those rules."[44]

His excellent common sense was reinforced with a mind that was endlessly calculating. Lincoln believed in the governance of people through reason. He once said in a lecture that the nation should rely on "cold, calculating, unimpassioned reason." Lincoln believed that "the law" was essentially common sense, logic codified and printed in books. He therefore presented most of his legal arguments using the principles of natural justice (right versus wrong), believing the law would ultimately support his position.

This reverence for logic explains a great deal about Lincoln. Lincoln mastered the art of censoring his emotions; even his close friends regarded him as enigmatic when it came to his feelings. David Davis, a close friend of Lincoln's, once said that Lincoln was "the most reticent, secretive man I ever saw or expect to see." He could charm a single juror or a fifteen-thousand-person audience without exposing his intimate self. Lincoln never took anything on faith—to believe it, he had to prove it to himself. By never laying it all on the table, he allowed an inner sanctum to think, ponder, and reason.

President Wilson, when giving a speech, explained why this quality made Lincoln a better attorney:

> But one interesting thing about Mr. Lincoln is that no matter how shrewd or penetrating his comment, he never seemed to allow a matter to grip him. He seemed so directly in contact with it that he could define things other men could not define; and yet he was detached. He did not look upon it as if he were part of it. And he was constantly salting all the delightful things he said, with the salt of wit and humor. I would not trust a saturnine man, but I would trust a wit; because a wit is a man who can detach himself, and not get so buried in the matter he is dealing with as to lose that sure and free movement which a man can only have when he is detached.

You cannot be logical and calculating if you are losing control of your emotions. Lincoln possessed one of the most even-keeled dispositions in history. Indeed, during the most troubling days of the Civil War, Lincoln retained the ability to function and make wise decisions. He had the ability to diffuse his internal anxiety by practical methods. (Ironically, one way he dispelled stress was by going to the theater.)

During trial, Lincoln never expressed excitement—he remained calm and docile. He did, however, strategically use emotion for persuasion or to shock the court into acting justly. Lincoln's partner Herndon never fully appreciated how his senior partner achieved such spectacular results with so little noise; he wanted to see exhilarating rhetoric and tears in the jury box. But Lincoln was a courtroom tactician, and he resorted to theatrics only when absolutely necessary.

On the circuit, Lincoln often told the story of the Revolutionary War hero Ethan Allen and his trip to England on the heels of the war. Lincoln recounts that Allen was subjected to constant ridicule by the British making fun of the primitive Americans. When they were unable to rile Allen, they started mocking the beloved General Washington and went so far as to take a picture of Washington and put it in their outhouse. When Allen made no mention of the picture, the Englishmen asked him if he had seen it. Allen coolly responded, "ah yes and what an appropriate place for an Englishman to keep it, there is nothing that will make an Englishman sh★t so quick as the sight of General Washington."

Keep your wits about you, even when in a crisis—losing your cool will likely make things worse. In addition, your audience will probably view uncontrolled behavior as immature, unprofessional, and worse yet, unpersuasive. It gives the impression of desperation.

Clear and Concise

Lincoln did not always leave an audience agreeing with him. However, he very rarely left an audience not understanding him. The key to his clarity was the organization of his argument and the words he chose. As stated earlier, Lincoln used the "bottom line up front" method of organization, and he used words that even the simplest layman could comprehend.

If you cannot lay out a reasonable argument in a clear and concise manner, being logical is insufficient to win a case. Lincoln presented an additional benefit of being clear when he stated: "I am determined to be so clear that no honest man could misunderstand me, and no dishonest man could successfully misrepresent me." In essence, Lincoln is saying that if you are not careful in the use of your words, your opponents can twist your imprecision to their advantage.

⁊ ⁊ ⁊

Humor as a Weapon

As they are now, courtrooms during Lincoln's time were reverent places where people's lives or fortunes were at stake. Despite this, Lincoln was notorious for using humor in the courtroom to accentuate his position by showing how ridiculous an opponent's position was. He also used humor simply to be funny and gain popularity. His long-time friend Judge Davis remarked that Lincoln "never failed to produce joy and hilarity" while riding the circuit. So much was Lincoln the circuit comedian that the local populace eagerly awaited his arrival.

Lincoln's reputation as a jokester during trials was legendary. While on the circuit, Lincoln once faced John Scott, a youthful attorney who had the reputation of being a sore loser. Scott and Lincoln presented their cases to the jury and left for the day. The next morning, Lincoln met Scott at the courthouse and asked him how he thought his case was going. Scott, frustrated with the prior day's proceedings, responded with "it's gone to hell." Lincoln, without missing a beat, responded, "Oh well, then you'll see it again," and walked off.

This next story is a bit of Lincoln lore; it has been attributed many times as something he said during a trial, to his cabinet, and to visitors at the White House. The version of the story at trial goes like this: Lincoln looked over at his opposing counsel and said, "How many legs does a sheep have?" The attorney said: "four." Lincoln then said, "Now if I call a tail a leg, how many will it have?" The attorney said: "It will have five." After his humorous trap was set, Lincoln then turned to face the jury and said, "No it won't, it still will have four. Calling the tail a leg doesn't make it a leg." **This lesson illustrates how humor can make a convoluted legal point crystal clear.**

In the book *Lincoln the Lawyer*, Woldman gives several examples of Lincoln's using his humor as a tactical weapon to literally laugh cases out of court. Lincoln was defending a client, Colonel Dunlap, who had been charged with savagely assaulting a newspaper editor, Paul Selby, for writing what the colonel considered a defamatory article. The editor sued Dunlap for the huge sum of ten thousand dollars. Lincoln knew there was no viable defense for the assault, so he set his goal on reducing the damages. When he stood in front of the jury, he slowly picked up the victim's petition for assault and studied it with intensity. Then he unexpectedly broke out in a long, loud, and uncontrolled laugh. The effect of his laugh changed the entire atmosphere of the courtroom. The jury instantly became buoyant, and even the normally sterile Judge Woodson had a smile on his face—all of this before Lincoln had even said a word.

After he got control of himself he apologized to the court and explained that he had just noticed that in the victim's petition the original damages claimed was one thousand dollars, but later he added another zero changing it to ten thousand dollars. He remarked that he supposed the plaintiff Selby "had taken a second look at the Colonel's pile [bank account] and concluded that the wounds to his honor were worth an additional $9,000." The result of the merriment was exactly what Lincoln had hoped for. He lost the case, but was victorious in that the jury forgot the plea for punitive damages and set damages at a few hundred dollars.[45]

In another matter, Lincoln cross-examined J. Parker Green in a case where his client was accused of passing counterfeit money. Parker was a significant witness for the prosecution. When Lincoln stood up, he glared at Parker with a suspicious look, then casually asked his name, to which the witness responded by saying, "J. Parker Green." Lincoln did not stop there, he repeated J. Parker Green, J. Parker Green, J. Parker Green—as if he was searching his memory for something—and then asked what the "J" stood for. Green said "John." "Well," said Lincoln, "Why don't you call yourself John P. Green?"

> **Green:** "Well . . . ."
> **Lincoln:** "Most ordinary folks would call themselves John P. Green instead of J. Parker Green, wouldn't they?"
> **Green:** "Well . . . ."

Lincoln drilled the witness about his name for several minutes. To Lincoln it was a huge joke, but to the witness it was embarrassing, and he became confused and was moving uneasily in his chair. The jury could not understand why someone would be so nervous about questions over his name and determined that his unusual performance was due to his lying about something. His credibility was destroyed, and Lincoln's client was acquitted.[46]

Lincoln was funny inside and outside the courtroom. "It's not me who can't keep a secret—it's the people I tell that can't." "If I were two-faced, would I be wearing this one?"

Funny people are likeable; people will trust you and listen to you more intently when they like you and when your message is fun to listen to. Humor is an excellent way to prove a point, or, as seen above, to discredit someone. However, it must be noted that while humor is a useful tool, it is easily overdone. Specifically, a courtroom is a house of law—while humor is useful, it can often be seen as disrespectful or as not taking your case seriously.

Similarly, with other persuasive speaking, making a joke to break the ice can be to your advantage, but a constant stream of jokes will most likely be seen as flaky. Also, if you are spending all your time trying to be funny, you can miss opportunities to be persuasive.

ह‍ॐ ह‍ॐ ह‍ॐ

Committed to Fair Practice and the Pursuit of Justice

One of Lincoln's lasting legacies was his unwavering honesty and commitment to justice. Just as George Washington's cherry tree is cloaked in
myth, so are many of the Honest Abe stories. However, there is no doubt
that the very essence of Abraham Lincoln was his personal integrity.

In his twenty-three years of practice, he never deliberately misrepre-
sented the facts of a case for his client's advantage. Lincoln never surrendered his reputation, his conscience, or his ideals of justice for a private
profit. For, as Herndon pointed out, "justice and truth, rather than the
desire to win at all cost, were paramount with Lincoln the lawyer."

Honesty

Lincoln once said, "character is like a tree and reputation like its shadow.
The shadow is what we think of it; the tree is the real thing." Certainly,
Lincoln cared about his reputation (discussed later in the chapter), but the
root of Lincoln's honesty was self-edification. Lincoln believed that to be
legitimate as an officer of the court, one had to be ethically and intellectually honest. He was exasperated by the impression that to be successful as
a lawyer you had to be mendacious at times.

Because of his reputation as a genuinely honest lawyer, Lincoln was
often called upon to comment on attorney discipline issues. One such
incident occurred during a court sanctioning of a new attorney accused
of unethical conduct. Seeing Lincoln in the audience, the judge asked the
respected attorney if he had anything to add to the proceeding. Lincoln,
aware that the young attorney had just received heavy condemnation
from the court, did not want to add to his misery, but he felt a professional
and community obligation to address the attorney. Lincoln rose slowly,
expressing his sorrow in his very movement, and walked to the court's
well. There, in a soft and sad voice, he addressed the youth:

> Sir, . . . you have polluted the ermine of this court of justice, that should
> be as pure and spotless as the driven snow or the light of the brightest
> stars in the firmament. Justice is not a fiction; and though it is often held
> not to be a sentiment only, or a remote ideal, it is real, and it is bounded
> and guarded on all sides by the strongest powers of Divine and human
> law. The court will not pronounce your disbarment; you have done that
> yourself. The people will trust no one, without since reformation, who
> has been wrong and reckless, as you admit, in one of the most confiding
> relations that ever exists between men.

> A client is in court by his lawyer so often, and the custom so generally prevails that if he is not represented by honorable and trustworthy counsel, the right is of little value, and he is virtually denied the justice, to which our laws entitle him. The Wisest has said that "no man can serve two masters.". . . A lawyer who becomes by his admission to the bar of any of our courts part of the judicial establishment of the land, should have integrity beyond question or reproach. Courts of law as of equity can sustain no other without themselves becoming venal and corrupt. A tarnished lawyer is a homeless man. Therefore, seek until you find a real reformation in honest work, and the court will approve.[47]

The lawyer who knew him best, William Herndon, said of Lincoln's practice, "he had a keen sense of justice, and struggled for it, throwing aside forms, methods, and rules, until it appeared pure as a ray of light flashing through a fog-bank." Judge Davis said that "[t]he framework of his mental and moral being was honesty . . . ."

Because of Lincoln's honesty, he was exceptionally loyal to his client's interests, even when they were in conflict with his own. He once did some minor legal work for George Floyd; afterward Mr. Floyd sent Lincoln twenty-five dollars as payment for services rendered, Lincoln sent a note back saying, "you must think I am a high-priced man. You are too liberal with your money. Fifteen dollars is enough for the job. [Here is] a receipt for fifteen dollars, and . . . a ten-dollar bill." In this Lincoln put his client's interests above his own financial gain. While at first it appears that Lincoln's decision cost him ten dollars, in the end he probably made more money from this transaction. Who do you suppose Mr. Floyd contacted the next time he had a legal issue?

In addition to being honest with his clients, Lincoln was honest with the court and its participants. He viewed devious arguments as theft from his opponents—the moral equivalent of breaking into a man's house and robbing his goods. He was so earnest about his responsibility as an officer of the court that once when one of his own witnesses was elusive and shifty during cross-examination, Lincoln stood up and, with permission of the judge, overtly scolded the witness. The result was that the witness answered the remaining questions with candor. Lincoln's co-counsel for the case was Anthony Thornton, who later said of the incident: "it was a dangerous experiment which might have brought discredit on our most important witness."

However, to characterize him as merely honest is a disservice. As Woldman said, to "endow him with god-like qualities while performing the dry-as-dust functions of his profession, and depict him as a lawyer who would never take advantage of the technicalities, expediencies, limitations, and fine protective points of the law"[48] is to deny him greatness.

Though he was enthusiastic in implementing justice whenever possible, he was not a Don Quixote, traveling the road in search of the oppressed. Lincoln was a professional persuader, whose goal was the effective representation of his clients as an advocate. He was a general practitioner who took on almost all of the cases offered to him because it was his business, not because he wanted to implement a social agenda.

Reputation of Honesty as a Marketing Tool

Lincoln's honesty as an attorney made him more potent in the courtroom and in his political career. Lincoln's "very name had become a byword for integrity."[49] Because of this status, when he spoke, people believed him. Woldman said of this prominence that the jury knew Lincoln "never misconstrued the law nor perverted the evidence, [and thus they could] follow him and do no wrong. And, when a man brings that kind of a reputation on the hustings, his power with the people is almost omnipotent."[50]

Because his honesty was such a marketing asset in both his legal and political professions, any attack on this reputation was extremely upsetting to Lincoln—he saw it as both as an attack on his character and one on his ability to make a living. Lincoln was once charged with embezzlement of a client's funds. The accusation came from an involvement in his father-in-law, Robert S. Todd's, business. Specifically, it was alleged that he had collected funds ($472.54) for the business, but did not account for the funds. The claim came from other heirs to the Todd estate. Lincoln vehemently denied the charges and wrote a response letter to clear his name.[51] In his letter, Lincoln wrote: "I am here attending court a hundred and thirty miles from home, and where a copy of your letter . . . reached me. . . . I find it difficult to suppress my indignation towards those who have got up this claim against me."[52] In his letter, Lincoln systematically defended himself against the charges by first explaining that he did not collect $472.54 from anybody, but rather he collected $50.00 that Todd told him to retain. Despite being told to retain the money, he still reported the money for "adjustment of the estate."[53]

In response to Lincoln's letter, his accusers filed a bill of particulars that detailed the money they claimed Lincoln had collected.[54] Armed with this, Lincoln went to every person on the bill and secured sworn statements from each party in the bill refuting the plaintiff's charges.[55] The plaintiffs filed a motion to dismiss the case against Lincoln, and "[t]hus ended one of the most harassing and mortifying experiences in all of Lincoln's career."[56]

In the Peachy Harrison murder trial, which is discussed in detail below, Lincoln had effectively destroyed the prosecutor's case; the prosecutor desperately responded with a personal attack against Lincoln. Specifically, he accused Lincoln of putting on a show of candor and genuineness in an attempt to manipulate. He said:

> [Y]ou have heard Mr. Lincoln—"Honest Abe Lincoln," they call him, I believe. And I suppose you think you have heard his honest truth—or at least that Mr. Lincoln honestly believes what he has told you to be the truth. I tell you, he believes no such thing. That frank, ingenuous face of his, as you are weak enough to suppose, these looks and tones of such unsophisticated simplicity, those appeals to your minds and consciences as sworn jurors, are all assumed for the occasion, gentlemen—all a mask, gentlemen. You have been listening to an actor, who knows well how to play the role of honest seeming, for effect.[57]

This attack in open court was the most vicious in all of Lincoln's long years of practicing, and while it was being played out, he waited in silent indignation. He did not respond in anger. Rather, Lincoln stood up and looked at the state's attorney and with a reproachful tone said, "you have known me for years, and you know that not a word of that language can be truthfully applied to me."[58] The prosecutor, realizing he had gotten carried away in the moment, responded: "yes, Mr. Lincoln, I do know it, and I take it all back."[59] He then walked over to the future president and shook his hand. The jury also acquitted Lincoln's client.

You cannot buy respect and reputation; it is earned with hard work and lost on a whim.[60] **Guard your character with all your might—it is the most precious thing you have in business**. The reason this is such an issue in today's world is because so many people think it is acceptable to be crafty when persuading—this is just the opposite. Craftiness may get you one sale or win one case in one courtroom, but once you have the reputation of being wily and slick, it will spread. We all know of car dealerships that are untrustworthy, and we stay away from those. Similarly, judges know which lawyers are dishonest and treat them accordingly.

Justice

It is true that one of the reasons Lincoln became a lawyer was to facilitate his political desires, but it is also true that Lincoln saw lawyers as administers of justice—a thin line between civilized society and civil unrest. Lincoln appealed to the juror's morality and ability to distinguish right from wrong. It was Lincoln's concern for justice that gave him his motivation to act on behalf of his client.

To work in the justice system, a person must have respect for law and order. You cannot be a great lawyer or persuader if you do not respect the rules of the institution of justice. I have never known a great trial lawyer who felt that juries are stupid—yes, they get it wrong sometimes, but there has to be a respect for the institution. Said another way, it is almost impossible to be a great salesman if you do not respect your product.

Lincoln had a tremendous respect for the law of the land. "Let me not be understood as saying that there are no bad laws, nor that grievances may not arise for the redress of which no legal provisions have been made." Lincoln later further explained: "I do mean to say that although bad laws, if they exist, should be repealed as soon as possible, still, while they continue in force, for the sake of example they should be religiously observed."

Lincoln recognized that bad laws existed—slavery being the prime example—yet he was a firm believer that laws should be religiously observed while on the books. This was because he believed that "no grievance . . . is a fit object of redress by mob law."[61] Lincoln's commitment to justice in the courtroom followed him to his presidency. His main objection to the Southern rebellion was what he called an irreverence to law—the Constitution. Lincoln stated that the "national laws are now opposed and the execution thereof obstructed."

Some label Lincoln a hypocrite for his attitude toward *arma silent leges* (in war laws are silent) and, most notably, his disregard for the law of habeas corpus and other civil liberties. It is, however, important to note that every action Lincoln took while he was a wartime president was evaluated for its legal implications. True, there was debate over the legality of some of his actions, with some scholars believing those actions were unconstitutional and others believing he was within the bounds of a wartime president. But the notion that Lincoln was flagrantly abandoning the Constitution is untrue. Lincoln thought carefully about every action and acted in ways he thought were within the bounds of the law.

Lincoln cared deeply about the legality of his presidency and stated that "nearly all men can stand adversity, but if you want to test a man's character, give him power." When Lincoln had the opportunity to overtly abuse his power, he did not. Significantly, he did not suspend the congressional elections of 1862, just as he did not suspend his own presidential election in 1864, despite pressure from many to do so. To these critics he said, "if there is anything which it is the duty of the whole people to never entrust to any hands but their own, that thing is the preservation and perpetuity, of their own liberties, and institutions."

Work for something bigger than yourself. If you work for a sense of justice or the good of your fellow man, you will be more motivated, better prepared, and more persuasive. And you will handle your power more responsibly.

Refusal to Bring Unsupported or Frivolous Lawsuits

Part of being a good persuader is pushing the envelope. At the same time, part of being honest is not going too far. When practicing, Lincoln had no problem pushing the envelope on behalf of his client; however, he refused to act unethically or frivolously.

Lincoln refused to present a legal argument if he did not have a factual basis to rest it on. He flatly turned down clients when he thought their case was frivolous. On one such occasion, he wrote to a potential client: "I do not think there is the least use of doing anything more with your lawsuit. I not only do not think you are sure to gain it, but I do think you are sure to lose it." If Lincoln felt that the case was trivial, he would decline representation, even if he thought he could win.

One reason lawyers have a bad reputation in America today is because many push cases, not for the benefit of their client, but for the benefit of their wallets. What is amusing about this practice is that if these lawyers focused on their client's real needs, they would earn priceless goodwill and in the end probably make more money.

Willingness to Settle

One of the unnamed qualities of a great lawyer is the ability to compromise. A litigious lawyer, who wants to take every case to trial, even if he is a great trial attorney, will soon have a hard time finding clients. Lincoln understood, just as every persuader must, that clients want solutions to their problems in the most prompt and thrifty way possible. They go to lawyers or salesmen for help, not for a cookie-cutter solution of filing suit or buying the latest model refrigerator.

Lincoln sought to settle cases outside of court before he ever filed suit. His goal was to develop a compromise that benefited all interested parties. He often accomplished this by advising his clients to reach a settlement. A law clerk working in the Lincoln-Herndon law office heard Lincoln encourage clients to settle quarrels on numerous occasions. This attitude is further evidenced by the nearly one-third of his more than five thousand cases that were handled outside of the courtroom (this percentage is low for today's standards, but was high for Lincoln's time).

Lincoln's very first case as a lawyer, *Hawthorne v. Wooldridge*, was settled before trial. Lincoln's contemporary, Leonard Swett, commented that the parties in Lincoln's cases seemed to "always submit, they seem[ed] to think they [had] to submit, which is very little short of the power he exercised over a jury, before which these arbitrated disputes would otherwise come." Lincoln himself said that a lawyer is a peacemaker who has not only the opportunity, but the responsibility to settle cases. He further opined that by settling cases, a lawyer will actually increase his business, because a satisfied customer will bring business back to the lawyer who solves his problem in a quick and commercial manner.

Putting Out Fires

Before Lincoln was a lawyer, he was a citizen of his community. Therefore, even if a case had some merit, Lincoln often refused to become counsel if he felt the case would hurt the community or his personal friendships. During a law lecture, he once said to aspiring law students, "discourage litigation. Persuade your neighbors to compromise whenever you can. Point out to them how the nominal winner is often a real loser in fees, expenses and waste of time."

Other times, he would take volatile community cases if he felt he could be helpful at cooling the dissent. In one such case, Lincoln helped settle a case in which a Peter Spink filed suit against a Catholic Priest, Father Chiniquy, for slander. Specifically, in a sermon, Father Chiniquy had stated: "one among you has committed perjury; he went to Squire Smith's, and in a trial perjured himself." Apparently, it was common knowledge that Father Chiniquy was speaking of Spink.

Lincoln believed that because the trial would pit a church leader against one of his congregants, feelings would be so intense if the case went to trial that the community would be set aflame—ripping the church apart between the two parties. Lincoln detested such emotionally driven litigation, and he personally urged both parties to drop their claim for the good of the community, and he was successful. As Lincoln once said, "better give your path to a dog than be bitten by him in contesting for the right. Even killing the dog will not cure the bite."

In another instance, Lincoln turned down a winning case because of its moral questionability. He advised his client:

> Yes, we can doubtless gain your case for you. We can set a whole neighborhood at loggerheads. We can distress a widowed mother and her six fatherless children, and thereby get for you six hundred dollars to which you seem to have legal claim, but which rightfully belongs, it appears to me, as much to the woman and her children as it does to you. You must remember that some things legally right are not morally right. We shall not take your case, but will give you a little advice for which we will charge you nothing. You seem to be a sprightly, energetic man; we would advice you to try your hand at making six hundred dollars in some other way.[62]

Woldman said that Lincoln's office "assumed the appearance of a court of conciliation. The judicial spirit—the desire to act as peacemaker and leave the litigant friends—dominated whenever feasible."[63]

Leonard Swett, Lincoln's close friend and fellow attorney, gave first-hand testimony of how serious Lincoln was about his philosophy to settle; he observed that only one client had objected to Lincoln's "judgment" to settle, and threatened to take the case to trial. Lincoln looked at him and said: "Very well, Jim, I will take this case against you for nothing." The case settled.

People will do what you recommend if they have faith in you. And they will have faith in you if they find you competent and trustworthy.[64]

ࢌ ࢌ ࢌ

Compassion and Mercy

From justice and honesty comes compassion and mercy. Despite Lincoln's passionate belief in law and order, he was a tenderhearted man. His political rivals used this against him and tried to show him as weak. Others suggested that his tenderness was part of his shrewd political mind; mercy is sometimes a popular policy. However, Herndon observed that Lincoln showed mercy only in the presence of suffering. Speaker of the House Schuyler Colfax described Lincoln by saying, "no man clothed with such vast power ever wielded it more tenderly and forbearingly." Lincoln himself once said, "I have always found that mercy bears richer fruits than strict justice."

When dealing with the military courts, Lincoln was said to display "human sympathy, his lawyer-like caution, and his dislike of arbitrary rule that enabled him to exercise this unprecedented judicial power with a blending of merciful and practical considerations."[65] Every death warrant had to be signed by Lincoln—he was the court of last appeal for the deserting soldier. There was a constant stream of relatives of condemned soldiers seeking time to plead with the president. He was, in turns, stern and gentle with these individuals. To one soldier's mother who was sobbing on her knees, the mighty United States president said, "please go, your son will live; only go, if you don't want to have me sob."

In spite of draconian law, Lincoln often found a way to accept extenuating circumstances or extend special consideration. He was open with his reluctance to enforce the death penalty on scared young men fighting a horrible war. He candidly told a veterans group that capital punishment tore at his heart the most. On another occasion, when a general advised Lincoln that his merciful behavior was affecting military order and discipline, Lincoln bluntly replied: "General, there are too many weeping widows in the United States now. For God's sake, don't ask me to add to the number, for I tell you plainly I won't do it."

Though the court is a place of law and order, there is almost always a place for mercy and compassion even in the fiercest legal battles. Often the display of mercy will have other beneficial effects—people will see you as a moderate, and as someone willing to consider the facts of each case instead of making one blanket decision.

ào ào ào

Willing to Play the Game

Though Lincoln was intensely honest, he had tricks up his sleeve—for instance, the art of distraction. A story that teeters on myth but is noteworthy nonetheless involves his technique of distracting the jury with his chair-balancing act. As the story goes, when a particularly damaging portion of his case was being played out by his opponents either on direct, cross, or closing arguments, Lincoln would balance on the hind legs of his chair without touching anything else. Because of his unusual height this appeared very awkward and attracted much attention from the jurors, judge, and even his opponent's witnesses. The result was that the decision makers were focused on his balancing act, rather than his opponent's case.

While this particular decorum would be wholly unacceptable in today's courtrooms, it proves a point worth learning: **the magician's practice of distracting his audience with one hand while he hides the coin in the other works in both magic shows and persuasive speaking**. Again, this art form can easily turn from clever technique to deceitfulness—if ever you think an action could be viewed as dishonest, it will be by someone and should be abandoned. But this is another way to captivate your audience and control the narrative.

Most written pieces about Lincoln, at some point, describe his awkward looks and dress; this book is no exception. However, his appearance was, at least in part, a strategy. If you are selling yourself as a blue-collar salesman but you are wearing an Armani suit and driving a Porsche, you most likely missed your mark. Lincoln understood his reputation as a homegrown farmer and peoples' attorney, and he dressed with that in mind. At the same time, opponents who were not familiar with his skills were often disarmed by his apparent awkwardness, only to discover too late they had been "out-lawyered." Lincoln's friend Leonard Swett explained this phenomenon further by describing how an attorney would realize "too late and find himself beaten. He was wise as a serpent in the trial of a cause, but I have too many scars from his blows to certify that he was harmless as a dove." Swett went on to say that "any man that took Lincoln for a simple-minded man would very soon wake up with his back in a ditch."

Lincoln's most famous, most used, and most effective "trick" was his ploy to be seen as giving away his case by conceding all his points of law except one—the one point the case balanced on. Where most lawyers would object and blister away to save each point, Lincoln would say, "I reckon it would be fair to let this in." Other times when his opponent could not fully prove a point, but Lincoln knew it to be true, he would say, "I reckon that is the truth and fair to admit." Occasionally, when he would raise an objection and be overruled, he would respond with "well . . . I reckon I must be wrong then." Only when the entire case was over would Lincoln's opposition see that he had merely given up the points of law he could not keep. However, by giving away nine points but carrying the tenth, he carried the case—because it was the tenth point upon which Lincoln's entire case rested. On this strategy, Swett said that "if his adversary didn't understand him [he would learn] in a few minutes . . . that he had feared [the] Greeks too late and find himself beaten."

His clients often shuddered with what they viewed as a nonchalant approach to practicing law until the real issue of the case was before the court. Lincoln would stand firmly and say: "Here, gentlemen, is the real point in this case, and on it we rest our defense." At this point "with candor, clearness, and adroitness he would state what he regarded as the real issue, and finally 'now, this much we may ask, and when I state it, it will be a reasonable demand.'"[66]

Lincoln took the same approach in appellate cases. The Chief Justice of the Illinois Supreme Court said that if Lincoln "discovered a weak point in his cause, he frankly admitted it, and thereby prepared the mind to accept more readily his mode of avoiding it."

Do not argue the minor points that you cannot win: it tends to indicate that you are desperate and have a weak case, and it's a waste of time. You have only a limited amount of time to persuade your audience and close the deal, and wasting time on unwinnable points is bad strategy. Finally, arguing shady points hurts your credibility with the decision makers. They are likely to feel that you think them naïve and prone to believe foolish arguments. On the same point, some listeners will equate your stretched arguments to lying and disbelieve everything that comes out of your mouth from that point on.

🐦 🐦 🐦

Understanding Your Audience

A major advantage Lincoln had as an attorney was his understanding of the audiences he addressed. This understanding helps the persuader control the environment and better reach listeners.

Know Your People

To be able to understand an audience, you have to understand the people that comprise that audience—their desires, prejudices, needs, and everything that will help you to successfully persuade them. Lincoln was able to keep in touch with his audiences because he spent time with them. Traveling throughout the circuit six months of the year, he spent time with every type of citizen: powerful politicians, fellow attorneys, and ordinary farmers. With his remarkable ability to make a friend at the drop of a hat, Lincoln forged relationships with hundreds of his "road characters." With each encounter, he learned a little more about his potential jurors. He could talk about retail with county storekeepers, about crops with farmers, or about animals with drovers. What is more, he kept in contact with them via letters—discussing with them the political question of the day or current legal issues. It was on the trail that Lincoln built his foundation for a popularity that would ultimately lead him to the White House.[67]

This knowledge of the people put him at an advantage when selecting a jury. In the Almanac case discussed in Chapter 3, Lincoln took pains to select young men, for he believed that a young man would be able to relate to violence stemming from an argument. Lincoln kept the average age of the jury under 30 and got his client acquitted. **Stereotypes become stereotypes because there is usually an underlying truth to them**. Thus, with the caveat below, it is not unethical to use your audience's predispositions to your advantage—you are there to win for your client, not to attempt to make social change. The caveat is that, when picking a jury, there are legal and ethical bounds that have been established by the Supreme Court. For instance, a juror's race or sex should not be a factor when deciding if a juror will be stricken from the jury pool.[68]

Lincoln was also in touch with the average person's view on high society. As discussed, he dressed rather sloppily to display an image to his audience (this is not to suggest he was not boorish when it came to fashion—he was). In a case in which he was facing his old partner Logan, Logan was gaining the upper hand. Lincoln had studied Logan for a weakness but could not find one, until the older lawyer took off his jacket because of the day's especially hot and humid weather—it was there that

Lincoln saw his opening for attack. Interestingly, Lincoln did not launch a legal attack; rather, he played off the jury's distaste for "snooty" dressing. Lincoln noticed that Logan was wearing a shirt with buttons on the back, which was particularly unusual in the era. Lincoln stood to address the jury, and he started his summation with:

> Gentlemen, you must be careful and not permit yourselves to be over-come by the eloquence of counsel for the defense. Judge Logan, I know, is an effective lawyer. I have met him too often to doubt that; but shrewd and careful though he be, still he is sometimes wrong. Since this trial begun I have discovered that with all his caution and fastidious-ness, he hasn't knowledge enough to put his shirt on right.

It was then that the jury noticed Judge Logan's "pretentious" shirt and burst out with laughter—Lincoln won the case.

Lincoln knew that the farmers and laborers from Illinois made up his jury and they hated pomposity and haughtiness, especially in lawyers who did not have to perform physical labor. He handled a case in southern Illinois once in which he opposed a "college-bred" attorney. He described the attorney as extremely competent, noting that he impressed the court and the other attending attorneys—but all of this erudition was lost on the jurors, and theirs was the only opinion that mattered. Lincoln used this story to teach other attorneys that understanding the people in your audience is crucial in crafting an argument that will sway them. Talking over them may impress your peers, but it will not impress your client when you lose. **It is also important to know who your audience really is—in a trial, it is the jury, not fellow lawyers who come to observe.**

Lincoln's body language was choreographed to help reinforce his plea to his audience. Herndon described his posture in front of a jury as awkward, in that

> he used his head a great deal in speaking, throwing or jerking or mov-ing it now there, now in this position and now in that, in order to be more emphatic, to drive the idea home. Mr. Lincoln never beat the air, never sawed space with his hands, never acted for stage effect; as cool, careful, earnest, sincere, trustful, fair, self-processed, not insulting, not dictatorial; was pleasing, good-natured; had great strong naturalness of look, pose, and act.

Although the formal study of "body language" did not yet exist, Lincoln had a good understanding of it. During the Effie Afton case, discussed in Chapter 3, he sat calmly, whittling a piece of wood while his adversaries presented their case. Obviously this is not a strategy that is suggested today; however, **convey with your body language that**

you are unconcerned, lest you make your opponents and the jury believe that they are striking damaging blows.

When evaluating the people in your audience, you also need to understand their patience threshold. Lincoln understood that the jury had limited endurance for sitting and listening (this is even more critical today, as attention spans have grown ever shorter due to television, computers, and all means of high-tech instant gratification). Lincoln would rather discontinue his arguments early and not exhaust the jury's goodwill than cover a few more points and risk irritating them. He would usually let the jury know this to win their good graces by saying something like, "Gentlemen, I have not exhausted my stock of information and there are more things I could suggest regarding the case, but as I have doubtless used up my time, I presume I had better close."

Stop before you wear out your welcome. Attorneys tend to believe that the more they pontificate the smarter they sound, missing the point entirely—it's not about how smart you sound; its about how persuasive you are. People in your audience usually do not want to be there in the first place, especially jurors in a trial. Droning on and on will likely set their minds against you. As unjust as it is, jurors often make their decision based on which lawyer they like best—and that attorney is often the most concise one.

Respect Your Audience

Lincoln had immense respect for his audience and showed it by treating the "common folk" that sat on the jury with the same esteem that he gave his fellow lawyers or the judge. He spoke to jury members as peers and as individuals, taking each juror into his confidence and drawing them into his case. Lawyer Lincoln had the unique ability to suppress his "natural" role as partisan advocate and to effectively argue from within the jury. He influenced his audience to believe that they were the attorneys who were trying the case, and that they were not simply jurors. He avoided embodying the image of a lawyer voraciously fighting for his client's case because he wanted the jury to take that position for him.

If you do not respect your audience, they will feel it immediately, and you will pay the consequences for it when they make their decision. Too often attorneys fall into the trap of thinking that people on a jury are just citizens too stupid to get out of jury duty. As a collective body, the centuries have demonstrated that the jury is greater than the sum of its parts. On the whole, it is relatively free of corruption and is an accurate and just entity. **Respect the power and decision-making capabilities of your audience**. It will serve you and your client in the end.

Ability to Use Emotion When Necessary

Display personal emotion and passion to evoke similar feelings within the jury. For instance, if you tell a story of a man chasing a shopping cart downhill in a parking lot with a somber attitude, it's not very funny—your audience will feel sorry for the man. However, you can tell the same story with a jovial attitude, laughing as you tell it, and it will be perceived in a completely different way.

In the Peachy Harrison case, Lincoln demonstrated his abilities to effectively use emotion and become a lawyer with the tenacity of a pit bull. Lincoln was defending Peachy, who was accused of murdering his best friend, Greek Crafton. The victim and the defendant got into a fight that resulted in Crafton being stabbed and dying from his wounds three days later.

During the trial, the judge, E. J. Rice, made numerous rulings against the defense that seemed not only unmerited but also spiteful. This inequality fired Lincoln up to the point that he abandoned his normal humbleness and courtroom bearing. Lincoln left the courtroom the first day feeling that the case was almost lost; he told Herndon over dinner that night that: "I have determined to crowd the court to the wall and regain my position before night." The next morning, Lincoln stood and spoke with almost crazed zeal, in rapid succession hitting every point of the case. He pointed out the court's prior rulings, and with eloquence and a cutting tone made it known he thought they were not only absurd and contrary to law, but also dishonest.

It was not an uncontrolled tirade; he managed to keep his monologue just within the bounds of courtroom decorum, so as to not be held in contempt of court. Herndon said of the lecture, "figuratively speaking, he peeled the Court from head to foot." The prosecutor vigorously objected, but it was too late—Lincoln's "arraignment of law and facts had so effectively badgered the judge that, strange as it may seem, he pretended to see error in his former position, and finally reversed his decision in Lincoln's favor. The later saw his triumph, and surveyed a situation of which he was the master."[69]

After Lincoln's speech, the victim's grandfather took the stand. With sorrow in his voice, Lincoln asked the visibly upset grandfather, "How long have you known the prisoner?" He responded by saying, "I have know him since a babe. He laughed and cried on my knee." Lincoln then questioned him about his last visit to his dying grandson and what his final words were. The grandfather reported Crafton as saying, "I am dying; I will soon part with all I love on earth, and I want you to say to my slayer that I forgive him. I want to leave this earth with a forgiveness of all who have in any way injured me." The grandfather's testimony was deeply influential with the jury. By carefully bringing out the grandfather's emotion for his client's benefit, Lincoln was able to build sympathy for his client. This strategy worked, and Peachy was acquitted.[70]

There are several lessons within this story. (1) **Do not let a judge bully you**. Have deference for the court, but remember you serve justice and your client before you serve the court. (2) **It is always a good idea to put a human face on your client**, as Lincoln did by having Peachy described as a babe who laughed and cried on someone's knee. It is important for the jury to know that others love your client and would be adversely affected by his punishment. Having the jury hear that the victim forgave the defendant is using emotion at its best; any juror would think: "if the victim can forgive, so can I." (3) **If you can get the other side's witness to give positive testimony for your case, it will help far more than your own witnesses testifying for you**. A jury will think a witness called to testify on behalf of a party will be biased toward the calling party—when the same witness testifies for the other side, the witness gains considerable credibility. (4) **Showing passion in your argument shows a jury you are vested and believe in your argument**, and therefore your arguments carries more weight.

Another case where Lincoln brilliantly invoked emotion to win the jurors' hearts was *Case v. Snow Brothers*. There, Lincoln represented Mr. Case in an action against two young brothers who were claiming the defense of infancy in order to void a note for two hundred dollars they had signed to buy farm equipment.[71] The plaintiff, Mr. Case, an old farmer, had issued the note in an attempt to help the brothers get their farm started. The brothers had obtained three yoke of oxen with the money.

The defendants never denied that they signed the note; rather, they argued that they were not obliged to pay it since they were minors when it was signed. They further argued that the plaintiff knew they were minors when he issued the note.

The Minor Act was published to the jury, and Lincoln admitted it was applicable to the case at hand. Still, he pushed forward with his case. To one witness who knew of the brothers' farm operations, he asked this line of questions:

Q: Where is the prairie team now?
A: On the farm of the [Snow] Boys.
Q: Have you seen anyone breaking prairie with it lately?
A: Yes, the Snow boys were breaking up with it last week.
Q: How old are the boys now?
A: One is a little over twenty-one and the other near twenty-three.

Lincoln stopped his questioning there—it was all he needed for his emotional plea. Lincoln's argument was not based on law at all—instead, it was based on protecting the character of the Snow Brothers. He said to the jury:

> Are you willing to allow these boys to begin life with this shame and disgrace attached to their character? If you are, I am not. The best judge of human character that ever wrote has left these immortal words for all of us to ponder: Good name in man or woman, dear my Lord, Is the immediate jewel of their souls. Who steals my purse steals trash; 'tis something, nothing; 'Twas mine, 'tis his, and has been slave to thousands; But he that filches from me my good name robs me of that which not enriches him and make makes me poor indeed. . . . The judge will tell you what your own sense of justice has already told you, that these Snow boys, if they were mean enough to plead the baby act, when they came to be men should have taken the oxen and plow back. They cannot go back on their contract and also keep what the note was given for. And no Gentlemen, you have it in your power to set these boys right before the world.[72]

Lincoln never challenged the defense of infancy. He argued that while the black letter of the law was applicable, the spirit of the law was not—how could a law not only sanction but also encourage amoral business practices? Lincoln's argument was based solely on the idea of protecting the character of the two young men. It is noteworthy that he never even mentioned his client's name during his entire argument. The jury never left their seats to deliberate; they found for Lincoln's client despite the fact that the law seemingly dictated otherwise.

Not only did Lincoln win this case with the entire law against him, he won by arguing for his opponents instead of his client. **When the law is against you, you must think outside the box**; you should always think creatively, but especially when the law is not on your side. Here, Lincoln turned the entire argument around from his client being unwise by signing an unenforceable note to protecting the honor of two youths.

In the *Snow Brothers* case, the law was against Lincoln, but equity was not, and Lincoln used that to his advantage. He led the jury to understand that by following the black letter of the law, they would be perpetrating a fraud. In this way, he added the jury's honor to the equation by implying that they would help damage not only the character of the defendants, but also their own character, if they ruled for the defense.

Lincoln understood that an appeal to the heart was often more effective than an appeal to the brain—especially when dealing with nationalism. In Lincoln's time, patriotism ran deep, especially where connected to the Founding Fathers, the Revolutionary War, or the nation's founding documents. Lincoln used these sentiments to his advantage often. Lincoln once represented a Revolutionary War widow who had been swindled by a pension agent into giving an extensive portion of her pension to him as a commission in the case *Rebecca Thomas v. Erastus Wright*. In preparing for his case, Lincoln researched the Revolutionary War and made, as Herndon said, one of his most impassioned pleas to a jury. His argument laid out the suffering at Valley Forge and how his client's husband fought for the privileges and freedom that the jurors enjoyed. After he won the jury's sentiments, he systematically attacked the defendant and painted him as a scoundrel, taking advantage of a hero's wife, one who needed and deserved the most protection.

Not only did Lincoln win the case, but also he became the widow's surety, paying for her hotel bill and her way back home. When the judgment was received, he charged nothing for his services.

ꜱ̀ꜱ ꜱ̀ꜱ ꜱ̀ꜱ

Notes

1. Francis F. Browne, The Every-Day Life of Abraham Lincoln 162 (BiblioBazaar 2007) (quoting Lincoln's close friend Joshua Speed).

2. Brackenridge (1800–1862) practiced in Indiana and was celebrated for his rhetoric. It is rumored that he lent the young Lincoln books and that Lincoln would travel far to hear Brackenridge's closing arguments. Not much more is known about the accomplished attorney.

3. Albert A. Woldman, Lawyer Lincoln 12 (Carroll & Graf 2001) (1936).

4. See Douglas L. Wilson, Lincoln's Sword 4 (Alfred A. Knopf 2006) [hereinafter Wilson].

5. Id.

6. Carl Sandburg, Abraham Lincoln: The Prairie Years and the War Years 90–93 (Mariner Books 2002).

7. Isaac N. Arnold, Life of Abraham Lincoln 84, 4th ed. (Bisen Books 1994) [hereinafter Arnold].

8. Allen D. Spiegel, A. Lincoln, Esquire: A Shrewd, Sophisticated Lawyer in his Time 29 (Mercer Univ. Press 2002).

9. It should be noted that different sources have attributed this quote to different individuals to include Mark Twain and Samuel Johnson (a famous British author). Indeed, a similar adage dates back to the old testament: "Even a fool is thought wise if he keeps silent, and discerning if he holds his tongue." Proverbs 17:28. It is likely that many people throughout history have adapted this, including Lincoln.

10. Arnold, supra note, 7 at 84.

11. Wilson, supra note 4, at 6.

12. Id.

13. Id. at 7.

14. Id.

15. Id. at 246.

16. Id. at 248.

17. Id. at 248–49.

18. Id. at 249.

19. Id.

20. Woldman, supra note 3, at 271–73.

21. Id. at 275.

22. Id. at 282.

23. Id. at 288.

24. I must add a personal note here: more than any other quality Lincoln possessed, I admire this one the most.

25. Richard Carwardine, Lincoln: A Life of Purpose and Power 7 (Alfred A. Knopf 2006) [hereinafter Carwardine].

26. *Id.*

27. *Id.*

28. A personal favorite story of Lincoln leaving his ego at the door was when Lincoln sent someone (who happened to be an unnamed congressman) to retrieve something from the War Department building. When War Secretary Stanton refused to honor the presidential order, the congressman returned to the president and reported that Stanton not only countermanded the order, but called the president "a damn fool." Lincoln responded in a gentle tone: "Did Stanton say I was a damn fool?" The congressman confirmed: "he did Sir, and repeated it." Lincoln, with his typical cool demeanor, simply remarked, "if Stanton said I was a damn fool, then I must be one, for he is nearly always right and generally says what he means. I will step over and see him." This again is an example of Lincoln putting what was best for the country, Stanton as the War Secretary, ahead of his ego.

29. WOLDMAN, *supra* note 3, at 206.

30. *Id.* at 206–07.

31. *Id.* at 206.

32. CARWARDINE , supra note 25, at 50.

33. *Id.*

34. *Id.*

35. IDA M. TARBELL, THE LIFE OF ABRAHAM LINCOLN 49 (Bison Books 1997).

36. WOLDMAN, *supra* note 3, at 251.

37. *Id.* at. 101.

38. DORIS KEARNS GOODWIN, TEAM OF RIVALS: THE POLITICAL GENIUS OF ABRAHAM LINCOLN xvii (SIMON & SCHUSTER 2005).

39. Two versions of this story exist. One is that James B. Merwin on behalf of Mr. Corning, approached Lincoln. Another version is that Corning himself approached Lincoln.

40. WOLDMAN, *supra* note 3, at 284.

41. In my opinion, next to perseverance, the greatest attribute that Lincoln possessed, greater than his speech-making abilities, greater than his ability to talk to a jury and instantly become their friends, was his ability to learn.

42. JOE WHEELER, ABRAHAM LINCOLN, A MAN OF FAITH AND COURAGE 97 (Howard Books 2008).

43. BENJAMIN P. THOMAS, ABRAHAM LINCOLN: A BIOGRAPHY 99 (Barnes & Noble 1994) (1952).

44. WOLDMAN, *supra* note 3, at 248.

45. *Id.* at 128–29.

46. *Id.* at 129.

47. *Id.* at 197–98.

48. *Id.* at 199.

49. *Id.* at 214.

50. *Id.* at 223.

51. *Id.* at 213.

52. *Id.*

53. *Id.*

54. *Id.* at 214.

55. *Id.*

56. *Id.*

57. *Id.* at 217.

58. *Id.*

59. *Id.*

60. It is interesting to note that honesty in some ways is relative to time. For instance, consider the story of *People v. Goings*, where 70-year-old Melissa Goings was accused of murdering her 70-year-old husband, Roswell Goings, by hitting him on the head with a piece of stove wood during a drunken argument. As the story goes, Mr. Goings was strangling his wife when she struck him. Apparently aware of the discrimination that faced a wife accused of killing her husband, Lincoln advised her to flee the state. When accused by the court bailiff, Bob Cassell, of advising his client to leave the state to avoid prosecution, Lincoln casually responded: "Oh no Bob. I didn't run her off. She wanted to know where she could get a good drink of water, and I told her there was mighty good water in Tennessee." Today, an attorney could be disbarred for such behavior. Conversely, during Lincoln's time, this advice was within the bounds of creative lawyering.

61. This is in conflict with the view of Dr. Martin Luther King, Jr., who believed that unjust laws are not laws at all, but merely tools of oppression. As much esteem as I have for President Lincoln, I agree with Dr. King on this point.

62. WOLDMAN, *supra* note 3, at 155.

63. *Id.* at 153.

64. Again and again in the military, I have witnessed experienced warriors following 21-year-old lieutenants into battle with nothing more than faith in their training and leadership. I also have witnessed soldiers manipulate every order of a major with over twenty years of military service, when they had no respect for his decision-making abilities.

65. WOLDMAN, *supra* note 3, at 292.

66. *Id.* at 249.

67. *Id.* at 98.

68. *See* Batson v. Kentucky, 476 U.S. 79 (1986); *see also* J.E.B. v. Alabama *ex rel.* T.B., 511 U.S. 127 (1994).

69. WOLDMAN, *supra* note 3, at 118–19.

70. *Id.* at 119.

71. *Id.* at 208.

72. *Id.* at 208.

CHAPTER 6

EVEN THE GREAT MAKE MISTAKES

My father once told me that a stupid man never learns from his mistakes, an average man will learn from his mistakes, a smart man will learn from other people's mistakes, but a genius will anticipate a mistake before it happens and adapt to the situation. By examining and learning from Lincoln's professional blunders, we can all be smarter. After all, graceful handling of errors can be a mark of greatness.

꙰ ꙰ ꙰

The Ear Case

One of the hard rules to the art of cross-examination is never asking a question that you do not know the answer to. Despite this tenet, many trial attorneys will make this mistake. Lincoln, in all probability, made this mistake on more than on one occasion. The following is an example of a famous stumble.[1] A witness was testifying in a battery case where a man had been accused of biting off the ear of another man during a physical altercation; Lincoln was defending the accused.

> **Q:** You said in your direct testimony that you witnessed the altercation between plaintiff and my client.
> **A:** Yes.
> **Q:** You testified that you were concerned with your safety, and because of this you sought shelter.
> **A:** Yes, that is correct.
> **Q:** You further stated that while you were seeking shelter you turned your back to the fight.
> **A:** Yes I did.
> **Q:** So you were across the street when the incident took place?
> **A:** Yes.
> **Q:** Sir, is it not also true that you have worn glasses for myopia since you were eight years old?
> **A:** Yes, that is true.
> **Q:** And, is it not also true that your view of the incident was blocked by trees?
> **A:** Yes.
> **Q (haughtily):** Well, that begs the most interesting question, does it not—if you were seeking shelter and your back was to the fight, you were across the street with trees in your way and your eye sight suffers from myopia, how are you so sure it was in fact my client who bit off the plaintiff's ear?
> **A:** Well . . . I saw him spit it out.
> **Lincoln:** . . . No more questions your honor.

Lincoln expected the punch line from the witness to be something like: "because the plaintiff told me he did" or "I guess I am not sure." The answer was unpredictable, but at the same time made perfect sense, which is typically what will happen with an attorney who asks a question he does not know the answer to—a perfectly reasonable answer that is totally unpredictable.

The above examination also demonstrates another principle; law professor Irving Younger calls it the "question too far." Basically, this rule is broken when an attorney attempts to get the witness to provide the "punch line" instead of letting the last question be the one he can manipulate during his closing argument. Lincoln could have stopped his questioning as soon as he demonstrated that the witness had severe limitations on his ability to observe the fight. During his closing argument, Lincoln could have then extended the testimony by saying something like: "the witness sat on that stand and told you he had his back to the fight, he was across the street, he suffered from myopia, and there was a tree in his way—the truth is, gentlemen, that the witness never actually saw who bit the ear off the plaintiff." Lincoln knew that adding superfluous information or questions in a case will almost always serve to an attorney's detriment, but he fell into the trap anyway.[2]

Another hard-and-fast rule is to never ask a witness an open-ended question during cross-examination. During direct examination, the goal is to build rapport between the witness and the jury, so open-ended questions are a good tool. Cross-examination has a different goal—to box the witness in, corner him with your carefully constructed questions. Having a script for the examination is useful for staying on track; however, the script should be limited to an outline that allows you to bring the witness to your conclusions—the conclusions being ammunition you can use in your closing. Some accomplished attorneys would disagree with this point and advocate writing out each question to ask the hostile witness, but by using just an outline, you may be better able to move with and respond to the ebbs and flows of the testimony. Listening is imperative to good trial work and good salesmanship.

ॐ ॐ ॐ

Superstition

Despite all of Lincoln's logic, he was also superstitious. He avoided letting anyone with blue eyes or blond hair on the jury—he alleged they were overly and naturally anxious people who were difficult to influence, and were especially dangerous jurors in murder cases where they would naturally side with the state. Furthermore, he believed that men with high foreheads would make up their minds before the case started, in particular dark-haired men with high foreheads; he would only pick them if he felt they had already made up their minds in his favor. Lincoln's favorite juror was the overweight man. He believed stout men were jovial (maybe because of their similar looks to Santa Claus) and easily swayed.

Picking a jury is an art form, and specialists sometimes overanalyze potential jurors. There may be some logic in challenging jurors because of their appearance or demeanor, but this can easily be used to justify odious practices. One especially offensive practice is seen when prosecutors rid jury pools of black Americans in criminal cases because of a perceived propensity for them to side with the defendant. Many of us have a few superstitious quirks. However, if these quirks begin to interfere with your logical judgment and the representation of your client, or if they are unethical or prejudiced, they are a problem.

ৡ ৡ ৡ

Disorganized

Lincoln's reputation as being disorganized is legendary. An amusing yet disturbing tale is how he would put his important legal documents in his signature stovepipe hat. Once he had to write to a client and apologize for his failure to respond to his correspondence in a timely manner. When he finally found the letter he wrote to his client, "[f]irst, I have been busy in the United States Court, second, when I received the letter, I put it in my old hat and buying a new one the next day, the old one was set aside, and so the letter was lost sight of for a time." Another famous account of his disorganization concerns an envelope that stayed on Lincoln's desk with the words: "when you cannot find it anywhere else look in this," written on its front.

Disorganization results in hundreds of malpractice cases each year. If Lincoln were practicing today, he most likely would be a pauper because of lawsuits filed against him, or perhaps disbarred for his lack of due diligence. **When handling a client's case, you have a fiduciary duty to be assiduous not only when in court, but also with your organization.**

ঌ ঌ ঌ

Trash Talking

Lincoln learned a hard lesson in 1842 about professionalism. In the fall of that year, Lincoln wrote some newspaper articles that were critical of James Shields, the Illinois state auditor and a fellow attorney, under the pseudonym "Rebecca" (presumably a female name because it would be more damaging to Shields' ego). Shields was so enraged by the article that after Lincoln was identified as the author, he challenged Lincoln to a duel.

Lincoln was amazed that Shields would resort to violence, but because politicians could not refuse challenges (despite the fact that dueling was illegal in Illinois) or they would face accusations of cowardice in future political challenges, Lincoln accepted the duel. However, he had no intention of killing Shields or being killed, so taking advantage of the tradition that the one challenged had the privilege of choosing the time (September 22, 1842), location, and weapons for the duel, Lincoln set forth the most ridiculous set of conditions he could muster in an effort to turn Shields from the challenge, or at least give himself a decisive advantage. Lincoln picked an island for the duel that was claimed by Missouri—where dueling was still legal—and he picked cavalry broadswords[3] as the weapons to be used. Further, Lincoln stated he wanted the duel to take place in a pit ten feet wide by twelve feet long, with a wooden plank dividing the pit that neither man could cross. Lincoln believed that by making the conditions so advantageous to his six foot four inch frame and long reach (apparently Lincoln "towered" over Shields), Shields would see his folly and retract the challenge.

However, Shields was very stubborn, and he agreed to Lincoln's conditions with no negotiations. On the day of the duel, both Lincoln and Shields headed to the dueling site to face off. Both Lincoln's and Shields' friends (called "dueling seconds") were trying to negotiate a peaceful resolution to the conflict.[4]

On scene, Lincoln made some spectacle of chopping down high branches from a nearby tree; the branches were so high that Shields had no hope of performing the same feat. This demonstration was the final blow to Shields' delusions, and Shields agreed to settle the matter peacefully. Shields officially withdrew the challenge, and Lincoln stated that he did not intend to injure Shields' "personal or private character or standing as a man or gentleman."

Lincoln was embarrassed that he got himself mixed up in the whole affair. Interestingly, Shields and Lincoln had a cordial relationship after the event, and Lincoln personally appointed Shields as a brigadier general of the Union army.

Another trash-talking blunder that haunted Lincoln all the way into his presidency happened while he was a junior congressman. In a statement made criticizing President Polk over the Mexican War, Lincoln said that citizens "anywhere being inclined and having the power have the right to rise up and shake off the existing government, and form a new one that suits them better. This is a most valuable, a most *sacred right*—a right which we hope and believe is to liberate the world."

Lincoln inadvertently addressed this misstep in a letter he wrote to Usher E. Linder, stating that during a legal argument, "it is good policy never to plead what you need not, lest you oblige yourself to prove what you cannot." Lincoln made the argument about the war in a moment of passion; nonetheless, the statement was used later against Lincoln by the Confederates, who argued that their succession was a "sacred right." Simply put, **be precise in what you say**. Sweeping rhetoric and superfluous arguments can come back to haunt you . . . or kill you with a saber. . . a pistol. . . or maybe even "horse dung."

ૐ ૐ ૐ

Absolute Honesty

Can someone be honest to a fault? If your spouse asks you if her jeans make her look fat, and you say "yes," that's too much truth (and marital stupidity). Both his peers and historians have criticized Lincoln for being so honest that it worked to his detriment. He has also been accused of slacking on cases he didn't believe in. Both are traits we can learn from.

Honest to a Fault

The same integrity that marked Lincoln as a great man also limited him— not uncommon in greatness. This is true with artists whose instability is both the cause of their demise but also a link to their genius; Vincent van Gogh comes to mind, who shot himself in the head, but not before he cut off his ear lobe and gave it to a prostitute. Lincoln's strict principles often limited his usefulness to his clients when their scruples conflicted with his own. The pursuit of justice was his supreme objective, and he refused to proffer a fictitious argument for the sake of winning.

In *People v. Patterson*, Lincoln, with co-counsel Leonard Swett and Henry C. Whitney, was defending Patterson from a murder charge. After the State's witness decisively proved his client was guilty, Lincoln lost all enthusiasm. The court noticed his despondency, and after the court day ended, his friend Swett asked him about his lack of luster. Lincoln confessed that when he took the case, he thought his client was innocent, but now he was convinced otherwise. His conscience prevented him from tendering an untrue argument to free a criminal. He told Swett "the man is guilty. You defend him. I cannot." When Swett objected to this decision, Lincoln said, "I am satisfied that our client is guilty and that the witness for the state has told the truth. It is my opinion that the best thing we can do for our client is to have him plead guilty to the lowest punishment."

Despite his feelings, he did not abandon the case—realizing his Achilles' heel (having a guilty client), Lincoln helped in every way he felt comfortable with from the counsel table. However, because of Swett's and Whitney's persistence, Lincoln agreed to give the closing argument. Whitney opined that "[w]hile he made some good points, the honesty of his mental processes forced him into a line of argument and admission that was very damaging." The jury thought his closing was unconvincing as well and convicted Patterson.

Another of Lincoln's attorney friends, Samuel C. Parks, said that "above all things he must feel that he was right. . . . He was not only morally honest, but intellectually so. At the bar he was strong if convinced that he was in the right, but if he suspected that he might be wrong he was the weakest lawyer I ever saw." Lincoln was involved in a case with Parks defending a man charged with larceny. He told Parks, "if you can say anything for the man, do it. I can't." Again he sat by Parks and offered him advice, believing that if he argued the case the jury would see through him. Parks said, "for a man who was for a quarter of a century both a lawyer and a politician he was the most honest man I ever knew."

Lincoln summed up this refusal to mislead a jury with a statement to a potential client who had a winnable case based on a tricky reading of a technical rule: "all the time while standing talking to that jury I'd be thinking, 'Lincoln, you're a liar,' and I believe I should forget myself and say it out loud."

This attitude came to a head when Lincoln was trying a case to collect funds.[5] When the defendant produced a receipt showing that the account was paid in full, Lincoln gathered up his things and left the courthouse. The presiding judge sent for Lincoln, who was in his hotel room. When the messenger told Lincoln the judge requested his presence back at court, Lincoln refused, saying, "Tell the judge I can't come—my hands are dirty, and I came over here to clean them," referring to the proverb, "to receive equity one must do equity and come with clean hands."[6]

Lincoln's partner Herndon observed that Lincoln could "lose cases of the plainest justice, which the most inexperienced member of the bar would have gained without effort. Two things were essential to his success in managing a case. One was time; the other a feeling of confidence in the justice of the cause he represented."

It is easy to say every lawyer should fight with a "soldier of fortune attitude," with their client's best interests in mind and nothing else. This, however, is a large problem with the profession today. "I was just defending my client" is never an excuse to lie in court or in any other persuasive profession. Nevertheless, Lincoln's inability to zealously work on cases where he thought his client was guilty or at fault shows a limitation; for a sign of a great lawyer is his or her ability to suppress his feelings, charge ahead with a tenuous defense, and make it great.

Believe in Your Case

Anybody in the business of persuasion will eventually have a case, client, or account he doesn't believe in 100 percent. However, as long as the business is not unethical, you must serve the needs of your client or the cause for which you have agreed to advocate. This is particularly true for lawyers, who may get cases appointed to them from courts and are under certain rules of responsibility to represent clients despite personal feelings.

In addition to being weak when Lincoln felt the case was based on a lie, Lincoln was also weak when he did not believe in the cause of the case. For instance, in *Bailey v. Cromwell*, Lincoln was successful in appealing a circuit court's decision that allowed the selling of a slave girl by citing the Illinois Constitution that forbid slavery.[7] However, only five years later Lincoln represented Robert Matson, a Kentucky slave owner, in a habeas corpus action. Matson had brought the slaves from his Kentucky plantation to work on land he owned in Illinois. The slaves ran away during the move, believing they were free because the Northwest Ordinance forbade slavery in Illinois.

The Matson case was mentioned earlier as a case to learn from, in which Lincoln designed his entire argument avoiding the crux of the case—slavery—and his despicable client, who was a slaver. However, this case also is identified as a case where Lincoln lacked his usual keenness and enthusiasm. One biographer described his performance as "spiritless, half-hearted, and devoid of his usual wit, logic, and invective."[8]

You are going to get bad cases. It is your professional duty to do one of two things when this happens. First, if you can get out of it, do it— taking cases you do not believe in is a disservice to both your client and yourself. If that is not possible, suck it up and drive on. **The cornerstone of being a "professional" is doing the job at hand, even when you do not want to**—up to the moral or legal threshold. Believing in your client or case is great, but pushing forward when your client is a scoundrel is professional.

It is clear that Lincoln's career was not a perfect one. He made frequent mistakes and had numerous bad habits. However, he learned from his mistakes throughout his career, he learned from others and their mistakes and successes, and he often anticipated the mistakes that might be made and avoided them altogether.

༄ ༄ ༄
___

Notes

1. Because many of Lincoln's legal records have been destroyed, this story cannot be verified. What is verifiable is that many sources attribute this to him; this is a paraphrased transcript of the account.

2. I tried a case where an opposing witness was attesting to facts that had occurred more than forty years prior. After an hour of answering questions that generally supported the opposing case, she responded to one of my questions with: "you know, now that I think of it, I really don't remember; it was a long time ago. I don't even believe myself sometimes." I wanted so much to go through her earlier testimony again, pointing out that she in reality did not remember the facts she so insistently stated that she remembered. But instead, I closed my folder, disregarding the ten more minutes of questioning that I had and said "no more questions." The abrupt stop to the examination was an exclamation point on her last answer. We won the case.

3. There are different accounts about the weapons that were to be used at the duel. One account says that pistols were chosen, while another bizarrely states that the duel was to be "horse dung at five paces."

4. It should be noted that some versions of the story say that Shields' and Lincoln's friends hatched a plan to call off the duel. Shields' friends withdrew the challenge note (unknown to Shields himself). Upon notice that the challenge had been withdrawn, Lincoln's friends apologized on Lincoln's behalf (it is unknown whether Lincoln knew about the apology.) *See* ALLEN D. SPIEGEL, A. LINCOLN, ESQUIRE: A SHREWD, SOPHISTICATED LAWYER IN HIS TIME 226 (Mercer Univ. Press 2002).

5. JOHN GEORGE NICOLAY & JOHN HAY, ABRAHAM LINCOLN: A HISTORY, vol. I, 252 (BiblioLife 2008).

6. ALBERT A. WOLDMAN, LINCOLN LAWYER 201 (Carroll & Graf 1936).

7. AMERICA'S LAWYER-PRESIDENTS: FROM LAW OFFICE TO OVAL OFFICE 134 (Norman Gross ed., Northwestern Univ. Press 2004).

8. WOLDMAN, *supra* note 6, at 68.

THE GREATEST CLOSING ARGUMENT EVER MADE: THE GETTYSBURG ADDRESS

Seven score and nine years ago, a tired man stood upon a great battlefield and gave the speech of his life. The event was somber—a dedication. The first speaker, Edward Everett, was a famed orator. He used over two hours to paint a word picture of the event and its importance to the nation. To some in attendance, Lincoln's three-minute, 272-word dedication seemed terse and unfitting of the magnitude of the event. Yet it has become one of the most famous and best-loved speeches in the English language. This simple speech has become a founding "document" of the nation. On November 19, 1863, with fewer than three hundred people in attendance, Abraham Lincoln promised the country a "new birth of freedom" and delivered.

Before the Gettysburg address, Lincoln was looked upon as a simple man who won the presidency on a fluke. The world thought he was "vulgar, brutally boring, wholly ignorant of political science, of military affairs, of everything else which a statesmen should know," as reported in the *London Herald*. American newspapers were not much kinder to their president, as seen in the *Chicago Times*, when it stated, "the cheek of every American must tingle with shame as he reads the silly, flat, dishwatery utterances of the man who has to be pointed out to intelligent foreigners as the President of the United States." However, after the publication of the Gettysburg address, many started to see him as the remarkable man he was.

 è**è** è**è** è**è**

A New Birth

Even today, brevity in closing arguments isn't universally appreciated. If an attorney gave a three-minute closing argument, he may be sued for malpractice. Despite this, Lincoln used his skills as a persuasive litigator to breathe life into a cause that was costing so much human capital. The speech was more than simple dedicatory remarks for a memorial site. He set out a position that advocated why his position was correct, much as a lawyer does in making a closing argument, and he did it quickly and beautifully.

A closing argument is the chronological and psychological culmination of the legal battle. It is the last opportunity to directly campaign for your position before the jury retires to deliberate. The argument should be logically and forcefully presented using passion and emotion as tools. Most important, a good closing should have a clear theory or a theme, making it easy for the jury to come back with a favorable verdict because they accept that theme.

To capitalize on a good theme, the practitioner should tie his closing remarks into a theme he had "road mapped" in the opening statement. We see that Lincoln consistently did this. His co-counsel often gave the opening, and Lincoln would follow with the closing. In a sense, the "co-counsel" in the Gettysburg Address was none other than Thomas Jefferson. Jefferson's legal training and education in political philosophy led him to believe that England's taxing of the colonies was illegal, and that the colonial people had the right to dissolve the relationship with England. These ideas pushed Jefferson to become a revolutionist. He became the prime drafter of the Declaration of Independence (interestingly, he did so only after John Adams denied the opportunity—Adams viewed the charter as too taxing on his time). The Declaration has become one of the most influential documents in American history.

To fully understand the basis of Lincoln's "closing argument," it is essential that one fully understand the Declaration (the "opening argument") and its author. Jefferson was known more for his legal scholarship than as a dynamic presence in the courtroom. His practice—roughly nine hundred cases—focused on real estate law. However, his legal justification for the American Revolution made him famous. To his credit, Jefferson argued that the legal basis of the Declaration of Independence was rooted in English constitutional precedence, using England's own law against them.

Beyond Jefferson's real estate practice, he was also well known for being an expert on the law of slavery, partly because he owned more than two hundred slaves during his lifetime. His role in the slavery debate is not totally transparent. While it is clear he advocated the legal ownership of human chattel, he also supported a bill that gave slaves an avenue to freedom. That bill failed in the Virginia Assembly, thus, leaving the only legal assault on slavery in the Commonwealth of Virginia individual freedom suits. In addition, Jefferson was a member of a diminutive and unpopular group that would take pro bono freedom suits.

Jefferson was a model idealist; the Declaration and the Revolution were opportunities to change the condition of mankind on a global scale. To Lincoln, the Declaration was a promise to the nation. It was this promise that laid the foundation for his "new nation" and served as the base for his Gettysburg Address. When Jefferson said that all men were created equal, he meant it. However, excluded from Jefferson's definition of "men" were African Americans, other minorities, and women—basically anyone who was not a white male. Despite Jefferson's limited view on who should inherit the divine freedom that served as the underpinning of his Declaration, his words were bigger than himself, as evidenced by the fact that the country has expanded upon his unjust personal definitions.

Thanks in part to Lincoln, Americans have reshaped the words and thoughts of the Declaration of Independence into a true meaning of equality. Lincoln himself held the Declaration in the highest regard, saying once, "I have never had a feeling politically that did not spring from the sentiments embodied in the Declaration of Independence." When Lincoln said in the Gettysburg Address that "all men are created equal," he was in effect equating the bloodshed of the Civil War to the blood that was spilled during the nation's creation. In this reference to the Declaration of Independence, he boldly asserted that the Civil War was about equality, and the nation was hemorrhaging human life in order to uphold what the Declaration "really" stood for. In fact, in later writings and speeches, Lincoln referred to the Civil War and the lives lost fighting it as a quasi atonement for the nation's great sin of slavery. A good example of this can be seen in his second inaugural address, where he specifically stated:

> If we shall suppose that American Slavery is one of those offences which, in the providence of God, must needs come, but which, having continued through His appointed time, He now wills to remove, and that He gives to both North and South, this terrible war, as the woe due to those by whom the offence came, shall we discern therein any departure from those divine attributes which the believers in a Living God always

ascribe to Him? Fondly do we hope—fervently do we pray—that this mighty scourge of war may speedily pass away. Yet, if God wills that it continue, until all the wealth piled by the bond-man's two hundred and fifty years of unrequited toil shall be sunk, and until every drop of blood drawn with the lash, shall be paid by another drawn with the sword, as was said three thousand years ago, so still it must be said "the judgments of the Lord, are true and righteous altogether."

Here Lincoln analogized the enslavement of the nation of Israel, and to a larger extent, Christ's spilling of his blood as payment in full for man's sin, with the United States' shedding of human life as its own penitence. In his book, *Lincoln's Moral Vision: The Second Inaugural Address*, author James Tackach links the second inaugural to Christ's prayer in the Garden of Gethsemane, where Christ prays to have "this cup be taken from me" (Matthew 26:36–42.)[1] This parallel was not only used to demonstrate the cost that was paid and would continue to be paid, it was also used as an olive branch to the South. Lincoln also used Christ as a reference because of Christ's other title as the Prince of Peace. Indeed, in the same speech, Lincoln said "[w]ith malice toward none; with charity for all; with firmness in the right, as God gives us to see the right, . . . to bind up the nation's wounds . . . to do all which may achieve and cherish a just and lasting peace, among ourselves . . . ."

The second inaugural in effect echoed the Gettysburg Address. Lincoln had moved the war effort to a higher moral imperative, a second revolution to protect freedom.

On the day of the address, the members of his "jury" were those in attendance. In Garry Wills' book, *Lincoln at Gettysburg*, he wrote that everyone there was "intellectual[ly] pocket picked. The crowd departed with a new thing on its ideological luggage, that new constitution Lincoln had substituted for the one they brought there with them. They walked off, from [the battlefield] under a changed sky, into a different America."[2] The president had revolutionized the Revolutionary War, "giving people a new past to live with that would change their future indefinitely."[3]

The notion that the address was set at this historic backdrop is not a modern idea—from the moment the words exited Lincoln's mouth that day, the critics opened theirs. On November 23, 1863, just four days after the address, the *Chicago Times* lambasted Lincoln's attempt to redefine Jefferson's words by quoting a letter that stated:

It was to uphold this constitution, and the Union created by it, that our officers and soldiers gave their lives at Gettysburg. How dare he, then, standing on their graves, misstate the cause for which they died, and libel the statesman who founded the government? They were men possessing too much self-respect to declare that negroes were their equals, or were entitled to equal privileges.[4]

Despite the critic's view, his speech changed a nation, the words he delivered rose above the carnage and lifted the "battle to a level of abstraction that purges it of grosser matter—even 'earth' is mentioned as the thing from which the tested form of government shall not perish."[5]

ॐ ॐ ॐ

Mechanics

Modern studies indicate that listeners have much shorter attention spans than once thought—specifically, the average person has the capacity to effectively absorb and process information for about fifteen minutes. Moreover, it has been shown that the first one to three minutes are the most critical time for information absorption. This is precisely the reason many modern books on the art of legal advocating specifically state that the first one to two minutes of the closing are the most important, and in that time the theory of the case must be persuasively established with precision.

The brevity of Lincoln's speech surprised his audience. Different reports of the event varied. Some accounts state that onlookers were upset by the short speech; other, perhaps more reliable reports, indicate that most of the attendees were in awe of the spectacular performance. Because the speech was so manageable, each word was absorbed by the listeners and the readers in the next day's papers across the country.

An additional benefit to the manageable size of the address, one likely not foreseen by Lincoln, is the ease with which the words can be memorized. The address was absorbed and passed on by word of mouth, still a major media outlet in the 1800s. It is doubtful that most eighth graders in America would be required to memorize the address if it were thirty minutes long, as some expected it would be. Moreover, the almost poetic quality of the speech undoubtedly helped with memorization. The flow and length of the speech is the reason so many of us can rattle it off as a homegrown American mantra.

ð ð ð

The Rule of Three

As for the text of the address, few speeches have evoked such emotion with so few words. Lincoln constructed the speech using the rule of three, also called the triad. By using the triad, a persuasive speaker attempts to convey three brief messages instead of expounding minute details in a less organized fashion; and this is done in exactly three points, not two. Like many other famous speakers or writers of persuasive speeches and written words, Lincoln was a master of the rule of three. It is simply a way of delivering words persuasively, rhythmically, and memorably. This method of delivery is so effective because the brain is most proficient at processing, understanding, and recalling three items of information at a time.

Three is an important number throughout history. The ancient Greek philosopher Pythagoras, who is often described as the first pure mathematician, believed three was one of the most important numbers, even a divine number. This is supported by the Greek belief that three Gods created the world. The divinity of three is seen in other cultures as well. Three things prized above all in the ancient religion of Taoism are gentleness, frugality, and humility. The Hindu Trimurti, also called the Hindu trinity, consists of Brahma, Vishnu, and Shiva. The Christian belief in the Holy Trinity states that God exists in three separate but ultimately one person: the Father, Son, and the Holy Spirit. Our form of government is even broken into three equal branches: executive, legislative, and judicial.

History's most effective communicators were masters of the triad. Consider the Declaration of Independence: "We hold these truths to be self evident, that all men are created equal, that they are endowed by their creator with certain unalienable rights, that among these are **life, liberty** and **the pursuit of happiness**." In another example, Jefferson said in support of the Declaration that "[w]e mutually pledge to each other our **lives**, our **fortunes**, and our **sacred honor**." General Douglas MacArthur successfully used the triad when he said "**Duty—Honor—Country**, those three hallowed words reverently dictate what you ought **to be**, what you **can be**, and what you **will be**."

Three of the most successful individuals to use this tool in persuading speeches were Sir Winston Churchill, Dr. Martin Luther King, and most recently President Barack Obama. In one of his many speeches during World War II, Churchill stated that "[n]ever in the field of human conflict was **so** much owed by **so** many to **so** few." Even more famous was his address to the citizens of England during the Battle of Britain. On the radio, while the battle was waging, he stated, "[w]e shall fight them on the **beaches**, we shall fight them in the **streets**, we shall fight them in our **homes**, we shall **never, never, never** surrender." This address had the desired effect; the British steeled their backbones, prevailing through the battle and the war.

An especially persuasive written document was an April 16, 1963, letter written to fellow clergymen by Dr. King while he was in the Birmingham jail. There, Dr. King wrote that "[t]he Negro has many pent-up resentments and latent frustrations, and he must release them. So **let him** march; **let him** make prayer pilgrimages to the city hall; **let him** go on freedom rides and try to understand why he must do so." Even more celebrated is his "I Have a Dream" speech, given on August 28, 1963, appropriately on the steps of the Lincoln Memorial. There he delivered his most effective triad: "**Free at last!** **Free at last!** Thank God Almighty, we are **free at last!**"

President Obama used the triad to perfection in his 2008 campaign. Indeed, his campaign slogan was in and of itself a triad—"yes we can"— and he used this simple triad with mastery. On January 27, 2008, when he lost the New Hampshire primary, he gave the following speech:

> For when we have faced down impossible odds, when we've been told we're not ready or that we shouldn't try or that we can't, generations of Americans have responded with a simple creed that sums up the spirit of a people: **Yes, we can. Yes, we can. Yes, we can.**
>
> It was a creed written into the founding documents that declared the destiny of a nation: **Yes, we can.**
>
> It was whispered by slaves and abolitionists as they blazed a trail towards freedom through the darkest of nights: **Yes, we can.**
>
> It was sung by immigrants as they struck out from distant shores and pioneers who pushed westward against an unforgiving wilderness: **Yes, we can.**

The triad has not been used only for the good of mankind. Hitler too was a master of the rule. During a speech of note he made while he was in Munich on February 21, 1941, the Fuhrer, addressing the English and American hope of an internal German coup, stated:

> **Then they said**: "Winter, General Winter is coming, and he will force Germany to her knees." But, unfortunately, the German people are "winter-proof." German history has passed through I do not know how many tens of thousands of winters. We will get through this one, too.
>
> **Then they say**: "Starvation will come." We are prepared against this, too. We know the humanitarian sentiments of our British opponents and so have made our preparations. I believe that starvation will reach them before it reaches us.

Then they said: "Time is on our side." But time is only on the side of those who work. No one has been harder at work than we. Of that I can assure them. In fact, all these vague hopes which they are building up are absolutely childish and ridiculous.

Clearly, Lincoln did not invent the triad, but by centering his address around its principles, he perfected it. In the 272-word speech, Lincoln employed this tool three times in three paragraphs in three minutes.

The first instance of the triad came when he stated that:

"we can not dedicate"
"we can not consecrate"
"we can not hallow—this ground."

The second instance comes when he states that:

"It is rather for us to be here dedicated to the great task remaining before us—**that** from these honored dead we take increased devotion to that cause for which they gave the last full measure of devotion"

"**that** we here highly resolve that these dead shall not have died in vain"

"**that** this nation, under God shall have a new birth of freedom . . . ."

The third incidence in the speech of the triad is the most adroit usage, saying that the

"government of the **people**,"
"by the **people**,"
"for the **people**, shall not perish from the earth."

ॐ ॐ ॐ

Delivery Is Everything

It is common knowledge that a speaker can have the most stirring words and speak to the most attentive audience, but if the delivery is flat, the speech will be flat. There is no one method of delivery that is better than another, but audience engagement is always key. Hitler's almost psychotic style of speech was hypnotically effective for his particular audience. Many argue that Churchill's elegance has never been matched. Lincoln did not scream and pound his fists, nor did he dazzle his listeners with big words. His style was what some call "folksy," but was, at the same time, passionate.

In general, people like folksy speakers because they come across as one of their own. Having a folksy style has many advantages. By and large, people tend to believe speakers who use this style over a more formal orator. However, it is important not to overdo it. If you push the folksy style too far, you may come across not as the next-door neighbor, but as simple-minded, losing your persuasiveness. Lincoln achieved the right balance between combining a simple speaking style with a sophisticated message, giving him an exceptionally powerful delivery.

Lincoln also was fashionable in his speaking abilities. Wills sums this up in *Lincoln at Gettysburg*: "Lincoln's remarks anticipated the shift to vernacular rhythms that Mark Twain would complete twenty years later." Ernest Hemingway later said that every subsequent American novel can trace its ultimate roots to Huckleberry Finn.

Most impersonators of Lincoln, from Henry Fonda to the robot replica in Disneyland, give the president a deep baritone voice, which our culture considers more "presidential" and heroic. However, Lincoln's voice was in fact "high to the point of shrillness, and his Kentucky accent offended some Eastern sensibilities."[6] But while his voice was not majestic, it had the ability to carry over a distance, which was especially important in a time without microphones.

Beyond his precisely worded text, Lincoln's body language played a part in making the speech memorable. He arose from his seat and moved forward with solemn purpose, carrying only two sheets of paper. His demeanor conveyed the aura of a man who had something important to say, and the crowd recognized this. His short speech was interrupted with five rounds of applause.

A common myth is that the president was unhappy with the audience's response immediately following the speech, specifically "that he told the unreliable Lamon that his speech, like a bad plow, 'won't scour'—has no basis."[7] On the contrary, he had accomplished what he had set out to do, and as Wills states:

> Lincoln had far surpassed [the] hope for [his] words to disinfect the air of Gettysburg. The tragedy of macerated bodies, the many bloody and ignoble aspects of this inconclusive encounter, are transfigured in Lincoln's rhetoric, where the physical residue of battle is volatilized as the product of an experiment *testing* whether a government can maintain the *proposition* of equality.[8]

ː▲ ː▲ ː▲

_____

Preparation

By most accounts, the president was invited in late October to speak at the Gettysburg dedication. He officially told a correspondent on October 30, 1863, that he would be present, giving him roughly nineteen days to prepare for the speech.

The story that Lincoln wrote the speech in haste has many versions. The most familiar is that he wrote the speech on the back of an envelope or napkin. Other accounts have the president writing his remarks on a piece of cardboard on the trip to Gettysburg or quickly writing it while he stayed at David Wills' house the night before the dedication. Some stories go as far as to say that he wrote the speech as the first speaker, Everett, gave his oration.

Wills, in an attempt to clarify these recollections, explains that they are a result of "an understandable pride in participation at the historic occasion."[9] His theory is that those in attendance at Gettysburg wanted a more intimate experience with the marvelous speech, and by believing they were a part of its drafting, they were part of a magical moment in time or at the very least part of the inspiration that produced the speech.

There are numerous facts that disprove these accounts. Most important was the fact that the president was, by all accounts, busy from the time he got on the train until the time he gave the speech. There are also two individuals who attested that the speech was written in Washington long before the trip was made. The president's friend and bodyguard, Ward Lamon, was the first who claimed that Lincoln read him the speech "a day or two before the dedication." In addition, Noah Brooks, a journalist and friend of Lincoln's, said that the president told him about the speech. He said that the president had written and rewritten the speech two or three times.

Also calling into question the myths is the nature of the president himself; Lincoln was hesitant to give impromptu speeches. This is not to say he could not think quickly on his feet; rather, it was his belief that as president he had a duty to be thoughtful and deliberate with every word he delivered. Also making the myth seem unlikely was the amount of attention Lincoln paid to the dedication site. He called the cemetery's landscaper to a meeting in order to get a feel for the cemetery and how the surroundings would play into his speech, indicating he had premeditation and forethought to what he would say there. Lincoln personally got involved with the planning the trip, to the point of overriding a plan by Secretary of War Stanton to travel to Gettysburg the day of the speech, deciding instead to leave the day before. This shows his resolution to be certain of being at the event, and that it was not an unimportant occasion which could be missed if inconvenient. More evidence of his resolve to attend the dedication is seen with the president denying his wife's plea to stay in Washington, due to one of their children becoming ill.

ٿٹ ٿٹ ٿٹ

Lessons Learned

Before the Address, "the United States of America" was used to describe several sovereign states making up a loosely knitted country. Afterward, the term defined a young nation preparing to face the world as a unit.

Using History

Any law student or persuasive speaker could view the Gettysburg Address as a gold standard. From attorneys making their closings to pastors delivering their sermons, speakers can see how drawing from historical and societal values, such as the Declaration of Independence, can greatly empower an argument. The Declaration has an almost holy status in this country. By tying his speech to it, Lincoln forged a historical document that will remain in the country's memory forever.

People like to have the feeling that something has historic roots. It makes people more alert, more attentive, and more pliant to the speaker's words. Lincoln wove history into almost every legal argument, letter, and speech he made as president. He must have observed the success Thomas Jefferson had by using history and tradition in his writings. Jefferson used Greek, Roman, and English history in his work, and Lincoln did the same. We see this clearly in the Gettysburg Address—Wills argues that Lincoln mirrored the speech Pericles gave at an Athenian gravesite.[10] Pericles gave the Athenian funeral oratory speech over the graves of fallen Athenians who had died in battle after a year of war with the military city of Sparta. The great historian Thucydides added the speech to his volumes covering the Peloponnesian Wars. Lincoln knew that invoking certain historic themes could concisely identify and explain why something was important.

Subtly Selling a Big Idea

Lincoln took the opportunity of Gettysburg to subtly set and push an agenda. Certainly his intent was to honor the dead and the great sacrifice that they had made. However, his main agenda was to set forth the future of the nation. The word "Gettysburg" was never mentioned in the speech; "[t]he discussion is driven back and back, beyond the historical particulars, to great ideals that are made to grapple naked in an airy battle of the mind. Lincoln derives a new . . . significance from [the] bloody episode."[11] This significance was the new beginning of the country, which was his true agenda.

While the president unveiled his vision of a new country of true equality, he never actually used the buzzwords that would have distracted from his message, but the intent lingered just the same. If he had said "Negroes are equal," or "slavery is a great evil," the speech would have been labeled radical and forgotten. Lincoln realized that the War must be won in both military victories and ideological terms. By "sneaking" in his message and giving his detractors minimal ammunition, it became an easier pill to swallow, allowing him to achieve what he intended—to "not only . . . sweeten the air of Gettysburg, but to clear the infected atmosphere of American history itself, tainted with official sins and inherited guilt."[12] You must push your agenda at every possible moment, but do it in a way that offends the fewest people and gets them thinking about a cause with their souls and brains, not through anger or fear.

Infusing Passion and Emotion

By infusing passion and emotion into an argument, a speaker can burn the message into the listeners' minds and involve them in it by provoking their own emotions. Obviously there is a fine balance in this practice; one could easily overuse this tactic and leave the juror or listener feeling that they were psychologically victimized. Lincoln's ability to use words and symbolism to entice his listener to see a case or issue through his perspective was unmatched, and his main method of achieving this was by invoking the name of God.

Christians strive to be "Christ-like," and 1800s America was a strongly Christian society. Lincoln used this to his advantage; the deeply religious country made religion an obvious topic to link to his audience. Speaking to groups of soldiers, he would make religious parallels to recent victories to pull them in.

If God agrees with you, how can anybody disagree? In Lincoln's second inaugural, he demonstrated this technique; Lincoln said that both the North and the South "read the same Bible, and pray to the same God; and each invokes His aid against the other. It may seem strange that any [man] should dare to ask a just God's assistance in wringing their bread from the sweat of the other men's faces . . . ." This language is truly effective because it logically evaluates how God must look at prayers asking Him to smite your enemy—or even more profoundly, prayers to let your army win a battle so that you can keep others enslaved.

Every person has core values that act as triggers. Once these triggers are flipped, the listener is going to pay closer attention to the message and is likely to be more persuaded to the speaker's point of view.

Finally, one can learn from Lincoln's great poise as he delivered the speech, in addition to the words themselves. Lincoln was a student of the word; it was his "[e]conomy of words, grip, [and] precision"[13] that made the speech captivating. The "Gettysburg Address does not precede

THIS IS TRADITIONALLY CALLED THE LAST PHOTOGRAPH OF LINCOLN.

rhetoric, but burns its way through the lesser toward the higher eloquence, by a long discipline. Lincoln not only exemplifies this process,
but studied it, in himself and others."[14] In short, to become a master of
words, one must study and practice with words.

ﻷ ﻷ ﻷ

Notes

1. JAMES TACKACH, LINCOLN'S MORAL VISION: THE SECOND INAUGURAL ADDRESS 113 (Univ. Press of Mississippi 2002).

2. GARRY WILLS, LINCOLN AT GETTYSBURG: THE WORDS THAT REMADE AMERICA 38 (Touchstone Books 1992).

3. *Id.*

4. *Id.* at 38–39 (citing *The President at Gettysburg*, CHICAGO TIMES, Nov. 23, 1863).

5. *Id.* at 37.

6. *Id.* at 36.

7. *Id.*

8. *Id.* at 37.

9. *Id.* at 27.

10. *Id.* at 41 (citing James Hurt, *All the Living and the Dead: Lincoln's Imagery*, 52 AMERICAN LITERATURE 377 (1980)).

11. *Id.* at 37.

12. *Id.* at 38.

13. *Id.* at 149.

14. *Id.*

CONCLUSION

Americans today often perceive lawyers as individuals constantly in a state of pandemonium and strife. However, lawyers are the country's peacemakers who bring resolution to anguished parties, as President Lincoln did for a country in chaos.[1]

Lincoln was an anomaly; he came from virtually nothing and became the savior of our country. What is often overlooked is how he became, through the law, our great redeemer. It is odd that we as a nation, and particularly lawyers, do not spend more time thinking about what Abraham Lincoln can teach us.

In my attempt to show the lessons that Lincoln's career can teach our generation of persuasive speakers, I have saved the most critical lesson for last. If I were to sum up Lincoln's life in one word, it would be perseverance. Lincoln faced daunting obstacles in life, including severe poverty and chronic depression. Death haunted him; his baby brother died when Lincoln was 3 years old, his mother when he was 9, his sister when he was 18, and his first love, Ann Rutledge, several years later. Even more tragic for Lincoln were the deaths of his sons Eddie at the tender age of 4 and Willie at 12. Lincoln's youngest son Thomas (Tad—short for Tadpole because of his appearance as an infant) died at age 18, only six months after the assassination.

In spite of all this, Lincoln persevered, and summed up this attitude after a particularly devastating political defeat by saying: "[my] path had been worn pig-backed and was slippery. My foot slipped from under me, knocking the other out of the way; but I recovered and said to myself, it's a slip and not a fall." Many of his legal colleagues commented that he was a very good lawyer because of his perseverance. Leonard Swett, when commenting on Lincoln's ability to plug away at a case until he won, said that Lincoln "was hard to beat in a closely contested case as any lawyer I have ever met."

Lincoln was also a compassionate man, and his close friends saw how he used his human qualities to win a jury's favor. Some criticize Lincoln's legal abilities because he lacked a certain luster and control over legal mechanics; however, these critics fail to see that Lincoln made up for these shortcomings with a discriminating sense of humanity, which allowed him to argue from *within* the jury instead of *at* the jury. When speaking about his friend and mentor's legal abilities, William Herndon said:

> He had a keen sense of justice, and struggled for it, throwing aside forms, methods, and rules, until it appeared pure as a ray of light flashing through a fog-bank. . . . He was in every respect a case lawyer, never cramming himself on any question till he had a case in which the question was involved.

Lincoln brought his legal skills to his presidency and attacked the Confederacy as he would a defendant in a criminal case, with the crime being the exploitation of the Constitution. The Civil War was Lincoln's greatest trial; the people were his jury, and his army was his evidence.

Other commentators have noted that Lincoln, by his deeds, is not really any greater than our other Founding Fathers, yet we Americans have a quasi-spiritual connection with the awkward looking man.[2] Jacob Needleman, in his book *The American Soul*, tries to describe this cocktail of feelings:

> We were told about his great deeds—freeing the slaves, holding the nations together. We were given the Gettysburg Address to memorize and study. But it was not what he did or said that astonished me. It was what was in his face.
>
> We were told about his honesty, his humble beginnings, his simplicity—the whole legend of Lincoln. But the legend did not move me. It was his face. But I didn't know why. And of course I was not alone in this; I don't think any of us knew, even as we grew up, what it was about Lincoln—because none of us really understood what it was about man that was, or could be, great.[3]

From the story of his birth in a log cabin that we all hear in grammar school to his throne at the Lincoln Memorial in Washington, D.C., Americans hold a special place for Lincoln. It is my hope that we can look beyond his legend and learn the skills that made him great, so we can be great ourselves. It would likely be Lincoln's hope, as well.

☙ ☙ ☙

Notes

1. AMERICA'S LAWYER-PRESIDENTS: FROM LAW OFFICE TO OVAL OFFICE 137 (Norman Gross ed., Northwestern Univ. Press 2004).

2. I myself immediately feel a mixture of emotions every time I see a photo of Lincoln. It is the same feeling I have when the national anthem is played; I feel a sense of reverence for his position and accomplishments, and I feel compassion for the harsh life he lived and how it was taken from him.

3. JACOB NEEDLEMAN, THE AMERICAN SOUL: REDISCOVERING THE WISDOM OF THE FOUNDERS 173 (Tarcher & Putnam 2002).

APPENDIXES

The Gettysburg Address

Four score and seven years ago our fathers brought forth, upon this continent, a new nation, conceived in Liberty, and dedicated to the proposition that all men are created equal.

Now we are engaged in a great civil war, testing whether that nation, or any nation so conceived, and so dedicated, can long endure. We are met here on a great battlefield of that war. We have come to dedicate a portion of it as a final resting place for those who here gave their lives that that nation might live. It is altogether fitting and proper that we should do this.

But in a larger sense we can not dedicate—we can not consecrate—we can not hallow this ground. The brave men, living and dead, who struggled, here, have consecrated it far above our poor power to add or detract. The world will little note, nor long remember, what we say here, but can never forget what they did here.

It is for us, the living, rather to be dedicated here to the unfinished work which they have, thus far, so nobly carried on. It is rather for us to be here dedicated to the great task remaining before us—that from these honored dead we take increased devotion to that cause for which they here gave the last full measure of devotion— that we here highly resolve that these dead shall not have died in vain; that this nation shall have a new birth of freedom; and that this government of the people, by the people, for the people, shall not perish from the earth.

First Inaugural Address

Fellow-citizens of the United States: In compliance with a custom as old as the government itself, I appear before you to address you briefly, and to take, in your presence, the oath prescribed by the Constitution of the United States, to be taken by the President "before he enters on the execution of this office."

I do not consider it necessary at present for me to discuss those matters of administration about which there is no special anxiety or excitement.

Apprehension seems to exist among the people of the Southern States, that by the accession of a Republican Administration, their property, and their peace, and personal security, are to be endangered. There has never been any reasonable cause for such apprehension. Indeed, the most ample evidence to the contrary has all the while existed, and been open to their inspection. It is found in nearly all the published speeches of him who now addresses you. I do but quote from one of those speeches when I declare that "I have no purpose, directly or indirectly, to interfere with the institution of slavery in the States where it exists. I believe I have no lawful right to do so, and I have no inclination to do so." Those who nominated and elected me did so with full knowledge that I had made this, and many similar declarations, and had never recanted them. And more than this, they placed in the platform, for my acceptance, and as a law to themselves, and to me, the clear and emphatic resolution which I now read:

Resolved, That the maintenance inviolate of the rights of the States, and especially the right of each State to order and control its own domestic institutions according to its own judgment exclusively, is essential to that balance of power on which the perfection and endurance of our political fabric depend; and we denounce the lawless invasion by armed force of the soil of any State or Territory, no matter what pretext, as among the gravest of crimes."

I now reiterate these sentiments; and in doing so, I only press upon the public attention the most conclusive evidence of which the case is susceptible, that the property, peace and security of no section are to be in any wise endangered by the now incoming Administration. I add too, that all the protection which, consistently with the Constitution and the laws, can be given, will be cheerfully given to all the States when lawfully demanded, for whatever cause—as cheerfully to one section as to another.

There is much controversy about the delivering up of fugitives from service or labor. The clause I now read is as plainly written in the Constitution as any other of its provisions:

"No person held to service or labor in one State, under the laws thereof, escaping into another, shall, in consequence of any law or regulation therein, be discharged from such service or labor, but shall be delivered up on claim of the party to whom such service or labor may be due."

It is scarcely questioned that this provision was intended by those who made it, for the reclaiming of what we call fugitive slaves; and the intention of the law-giver is the law. All members of Congress swear their support to the whole Constitution—to this provision as much as to any other. To the proposition, then, that slaves whose cases come within the terms of this clause, "shall be delivered," their oaths are unanimous. Now, if they would make the effort in good temper, could they not, with nearly equal unanimity, frame and pass a law, by means of which to keep good that unanimous oath?

There is some difference of opinion whether this clause should be enforced by national or by state authority; but surely that difference is not a very material one. If the slave is to be surrendered, it can be of but little consequence to him, or to others, by which authority it is done. And should any one, in any case, be content that his oath shall go unkept, on a merely unsubstantial controversy as to how it shall be kept?

Again, in any law upon this subject, ought not all the safeguards of liberty known in civilized and humane jurisprudence to be introduced, so that a free man be not, in any case, surrendered as a slave? And might it not be well, at the same time to provide by law for the enforcement of that clause in the Constitution which guarantees that "the citizens of each State shall be entitled to all privileges and immunities of citizens in the several States"?

I take the official oath to-day, with no mental reservations, and with no purpose to construe the Constitution or laws, by any hypercritical rules. And while I do not choose now to specify particular acts of Congress as proper to be enforced, I do suggest that it will be much safer for all, both in official and private stations, to conform to, and abide by, all those acts which stand unrepealed, than to violate any of them, trusting to find impunity in having them held to be unconstitutional.

It is seventy-two years since the first inauguration of a President under our national Constitution. During that period fifteen different and greatly distinguished citizens, have, in succession, administered the executive branch of the government. They have conducted it through many perils; and, generally, with great success. Yet, with all this scope for [of] precedent, I now enter upon the same task for the brief constitutional term of four years, under great and peculiar difficulty. A disruption of the Federal Union, heretofore only menaced, is now formidably attempted.

I hold, that in contemplation of universal law, and of the Constitution, the Union of these States is perpetual. Perpetuity is implied, if not expressed, in the fundamental law of all national governments. It is safe to assert that no government proper, ever had a provision in its organic law for its own termination. Continue to execute all the express provisions of our national Constitution, and the Union will endure forever—it being impossible to destroy it, except by some action not provided for in the instrument itself.

Again, if the United States be not a government proper, but an association of States in the nature of contract merely, can it, as a contract, be peaceably unmade, by less than all the parties who made it? One party to a contract may violate it— break it, so to speak; but does it not require all to lawfully rescind it?

Descending from these general principles, we find the proposition that, in legal contemplation, the Union is perpetual, confirmed by the history of the Union itself. The Union is much older than the Constitution. It was formed in fact, by the Articles of Association in 1774. It was matured and continued by the Declaration of Independence in 1776. It was further matured and the faith of all the then thirteen States expressly plighted and engaged that it should be perpetual, by the Articles of Confederation in 1778. And finally, in 1787, one of the declared objects for ordaining and establishing the Constitution, was "to form a more perfect Union." But if [the] destruction of the Union, by one, or by a part only, of the

States, be lawfully possible, the Union is less perfect than before the Constitution, having lost the vital element of perpetuity.

It follows from these views that no State, upon its own mere motion, can lawfully get out of the Union,—that resolves and ordinances to that effect are legally void, and that acts of violence, within any State or States, against the authority of the United States, are insurrectionary or revolutionary, according to circumstances.

I therefore consider that in view of the Constitution and the laws, the Union is unbroken; and to the extent of my ability I shall take care, as the Constitution itself expressly enjoins upon me, that the laws of the Union be faithfully executed in all the States. Doing this I deem to be only a simple duty on my part; and I shall perform it, so far as practicable, unless my rightful masters, the American people, shall withhold the requisite means, or in some authoritative manner, direct the contrary. I trust this will not be regarded as a menace, but only as the declared purpose of the Union that will constitutionally defend and maintain itself.

In doing this there needs to be no bloodshed or violence; and there shall be none, unless it be forced upon the national authority. The power confided to me will be used to hold, occupy, and possess the property and places belonging to the government, and to collect the duties and imposts; but beyond what may be necessary for these objects, there will be no invasion—no using of force against or among the people anywhere. Where hostility to the United States in any interior locality, shall be so great and so universal, as to prevent competent resident citizens from holding the Federal offices, there will be no attempt to force obnoxious strangers among the people for that object. While the strict legal right may exist in the government to enforce the exercise of these offices, the attempt to do so would be so irritating, and so nearly impracticable with all, that I deem it better to forego, for the time, the uses of such offices.

The mails, unless repelled, will continue to be furnished in all parts of the Union. So far as possible, the people everywhere shall have that sense of perfect security which is most favorable to calm thought and reflection. The course here indicated will be followed, unless current events and experience shall show a modification or change to be proper; and in every case and exigency my best discretion will be exercised according to circumstances actually existing, and with a view and a hope of a peaceful solution of the national troubles, and the restoration of fraternal sympathies and affections.

That there are persons in one section or another who seek to destroy the Union at all events, and are glad of any pretext to do it, I will neither affirm nor deny; but if there be such, I need address no word to them. To those, however, who really love the Union may I not speak?

Before entering upon so grave a matter as the destruction of our national fabric, with all its benefits, its memories, and its hopes, would it not be wise to ascertain precisely why we do it? Will you hazard so desperate a step, while there is any possibility that any portion of the ills you fly from have no real existence? Will you, while the certain ills you fly to, are greater than all the real ones you fly from? Will you risk the commission of so fearful a mistake?

All profess to be content in the Union, if all constitutional rights can be maintained. Is it true, then, that any right, plainly written in the Constitution, has been denied? I think not. Happily the human mind is so constituted, that no party can reach to the audacity of doing this. Think, if you can, of a single instance in which a plainly written provision of the Constitution has ever been denied. If by the mere force of numbers, a majority should deprive a minority of any clearly written constitutional right, it might, in a moral point of view, justify revolution—certainly would, if such right were a vital one. But such is not our case. All the vital rights of minorities, and of individuals, are so plainly assured to them, by affirmations and negations, guaranties and prohibitions, in the Constitution, that controversies never arise concerning them. But no organic law can ever be framed with a provision specifically applicable to every question which may occur in practical administration. No foresight can anticipate, nor any document of reasonable length contain express provisions for all possible questions. Shall fugitives from labor be surrendered by national or by State authority? The Constitution does not expressly say. May Congress prohibit slavery in the territories? The Constitution does not expressly say. Must Congress protect slavery in the territories? The Constitution does not expressly say.

From questions of this class spring all our constitutional controversies, and we divide upon them into majorities and minorities. If the minority will not acquiesce, the majority must, or the government must cease. There is no other alternative; for continuing the government, is acquiescence on one side or the other. If a minority, in such case, will secede rather than acquiesce, they make a precedent which, in turn, will divide and ruin them; for a minority of their own will secede from them whenever a majority refuses to be controlled by such minority. For instance, why may not any portion of a new confederacy, a year or two hence, arbitrarily secede again, precisely as portions of the present Union now claim to secede from it? All who cherish disunion sentiments, are now being educated to the exact temper of doing this.

Is there such perfect identity of interests among the States to compose a new Union, as to produce harmony only, and prevent renewed secession?

Plainly, the central idea of secession, is the essence of anarchy. A majority, held in restraint by constitutional checks and limitations, and always changing easily with deliberate changes of popular opinions and sentiments, is the only true sovereign of a free people. Whoever rejects it, does, of necessity, fly to anarchy or to despotism. Unanimity is impossible; the rule of a minority, as a permanent arrangement, is wholly inadmissible; so that, rejecting the majority principle, anarchy or despotism in some form is all that is left.

I do not forget the position assumed by some, that constitutional questions are to be decided by the Supreme Court; nor do I deny that such decisions must be binding in any case, upon the parties to a suit; as to the object of that suit, while they are also entitled to very high respect and consideration in all parallel cases by all other departments of the government. And while it is obviously possible that such decision may be erroneous in any given case, still the evil effect following it, being limited to that particular case, with the chance that it may be over-ruled, and never become a precedent for other cases, can better be borne than could the evils of a different practice. At the same time, the candid citizen must confess that if the policy of the government upon vital questions, affecting the whole people, is to be irrevocably fixed by decisions of the Supreme Court, the instant they are made, in ordinary litigation between parties, in personal actions, the people will have ceased to be their own rulers, having to that extent practically resigned their government into the hands of that eminent tribunal. Nor is there in this view any assault upon the court or the judges. It is a duty from which they may not shrink, to decide cases properly brought before them; and it is no fault of theirs if others seek to turn their decisions to political purposes.

One section of our country believes slavery is right, and ought to be extended, while the other believes it is wrong, and ought not to be extended. This is the only substantial dispute. The fugitive slave clause of the Constitution, and the law for the suppression of the foreign slave trade, are each as well enforced, perhaps, as any law can ever be in a community where the moral sense of the people imperfectly supports the law itself. The great body of the people abide by the dry legal obligation in both cases, and a few break over in each. This, I think, cannot be perfectly cured, and it would be worse in both cases after the separation of the sections, than before. The foreign slave trade, now imperfectly suppressed, would be ultimately revived without restriction, in one section; while fugitive slaves, now only partially surrendered, would not be surrendered at all, by the other.

Physically speaking, we cannot separate. We can not remove our respective sections from each other, nor build an impassable wall between them. A husband and wife may be divorced, and go out of the presence, and beyond the reach of each other; but the different parts of our country cannot do this. They cannot but remain face to face; and intercourse, either amicable or hostile, must continue between them. Is it possible, then, to make that intercourse more advantageous or more satisfactory, after separation than before? Can aliens make treaties easier than friends can make laws? Can treaties be more faithfully enforced between aliens than laws can among friends? Suppose you go to war, you cannot fight always; and when, after much loss on both sides, and no gain on either, you cease fighting, the identical old questions, as to terms of intercourse, are again upon you.

This country, with its institutions, belongs to the people who inhabit it. Whenever they shall grow weary of the existing Government, they can exercise their constitutional right of amending it, or their revolutionary right to dismember or overthrow it. I cannot be ignorant of the fact that many worthy and patriotic citizens are desirous of having the national Constitution amended. While I make no recommendation of amendments, I fully recognize the rightful authority of the people over the whole subject to be exercised in either of the modes prescribed in the instrument itself; and I should, under existing circumstances, favor rather than oppose a fair opportunity being afforded the people to act upon it.

I will venture to add that to me the Convention mode seems preferable, in that it allows amendments to originate with the people themselves, instead of only permitting them to take or reject propositions, originated by others, not especially chosen for the purpose, and which might not be precisely such as they would wish to either accept or refuse. I understand a proposed amendment to the Constitution, which amendment, however, I have not seen, has passed Congress, to the effect that the federal government shall never interfere with the domestic institutions of the States, including that of persons held to service. To avoid misconstruction of what I have said, I depart from my purpose not to speak of particular amendments, so far as to say that holding such a provision to now be implied constitutional law, I have no objection to its being made express and irrevocable.

The Chief Magistrate derives all his authority from the people, and they have referred none upon him to fix terms for the separation of the States. The people themselves can do this if also they choose; but the executive, as such, has nothing to do with it. His duty is to administer the present government, as it came to his hands, and to transmit it, unimpaired by him, to his successor.

Why should there not be a patient confidence in the ultimate justice of the people? Is there any better or equal hope, in the world? In our present differences, is either party without faith of being in the right? If the Almighty Ruler of nations, with his eternal truth and justice, be on your side of the North, or on yours of the South, that truth, and that justice, will surely prevail, by the judgment of this great tribunal of the American people.

By the frame of the government under which we live, this same people have wisely given their public servants but little power for mischief; and have, with equal wisdom, provided for the return of that little to their own hands at very short intervals.

While the people retain their virtue and vigilance, no administration, by any extreme of wickedness or folly, can very seriously injure the government in the short space of four years.

My countrymen, one and all, think calmly and well, upon this whole subject. Nothing valuable can be lost by taking time. If there be an object to hurry any of you, in hot haste, to a step which you would never take deliberately, that object will be frustrated by taking time; but no good object can be frustrated by it. Such of you as are now dissatisfied still have the old Constitution unimpaired, and, on the sensitive point, the laws of your own framing under it; while the new administration will have no immediate power, if it would, to change either. If it were admitted that you who are dissatisfied, hold the right side in the dispute, there still is no single good reason for precipitate action. Intelligence, patriotism, Christianity, and a firm reliance on Him, who has never yet forsaken this favored land, are still competent to adjust, in the best way, all our present difficulty.

In your hands, my dissatisfied fellow countrymen, and not in mine, is the momentous issue of civil war. The government will not assail you. You can have no conflict without being yourselves the aggressors. You have no oath registered in Heaven to destroy the government, while I shall have the most solemn one to "preserve, protect, and defend it."

I am loath to close. We are not enemies, but friends. We must not be enemies. Though passion may have strained, it must not break our bonds of affection. The mystic chords of memory, stretching from every battle-field, and patriot grave, to every living heart and hearth-stone, all over this broad land, will yet swell the chorus of the Union, when again touched, as surely they will be, by the better angels of our nature.

Second Inaugural Address

At this second appearing to take the oath of the presidential office, there is less occasion for an extended address than there was at the first. Then a statement, somewhat in detail, of a course to be pursued, seemed fitting and proper. Now, at the expiration of four years, during which public declarations have been constantly called forth on every point and phase of the great contest which still absorbs the attention, and engrosses the energies of the nation, little that is new could be presented. The progress of our arms, upon which all else chiefly depends, is as well known to the public as to myself; and it is, I trust, reasonably satisfactory and encouraging to all. With high hope for the future, no prediction in regard to it is ventured.

On the occasion corresponding to this four years ago, all thoughts were anxiously directed to an impending civil war. All dreaded it—all sought to avert it. While the inaugeral [sic] address was being delivered from this place, devoted altogether to saving the Union without war, insurgent agents were in the city seeking to destroy it without war—seeking to dissole [sic] the Union, and divide effects, by negotiation. Both parties deprecated war; but one of them would make war rather than let the nation survive; and the other would accept war rather than let it perish. And the war came.

One eighth of the whole population were colored slaves, not distributed generally over the Union, but localized in the Southern part of it. These slaves constituted a peculiar and powerful interest. All knew that this interest was, somehow, the cause of the war. To strengthen, perpetuate, and extend this interest was the object for which the insurgents would rend the Union, even by war; while the government claimed no right to do more than to restrict the territorial enlargement of it. Neither party expected for the war, the magnitude, or the duration, which it has already attained. Neither anticipated that the cause of the conflict might cease with, or even before, the conflict itself should cease. Each looked for an easier triumph, and a result less fundamental and astounding. Both read the same Bible, and pray to the same God; and each invokes His aid against the other. It may seem strange that any men should dare to ask a just God's assistance in wringing their bread from the sweat of other men's faces; but let us judge not that we be not judged. The prayers of both could not be answered; that of neither has been answered fully. The Almighty has his own purposes. "Woe unto the world because of offences! for it must needs be that offences come; but woe to that man by whom the offence cometh!" If we shall suppose that American Slavery is one of those offences which, in the providence of God, must needs come, but which, having continued through His appointed time, He now wills to remove, and that He gives to both North and South, this terrible war, as the woe due to those by whom the offence came, shall we discern therein any departure from those divine attributes which the believers in a Living God always ascribe to Him? Fondly do we hope—fervently do we pray—that this mighty scourge of war may speedily pass away. Yet, if God wills that it continue, until all the wealth piled by the bond-man's two hundred and fifty years of unrequited toil shall be sunk, and until every drop of blood drawn with the lash, shall be paid by another drawn with the sword, as was said three thousand years ago, so still it must be said "the judgments of the Lord, are true and righteous altogether."

With malice toward none; with charity for all; with firmness in the right, as God gives us to see the right, let us strive on to finish the work we are in; to bind up the nation's wounds; to care for him who shall have borne the battle, and for his widow, and his orphan—to do all which may achieve and cherish a just and lasting peace, among ourselves, and with all nations.

Cooper Union Speech

Mr. President and fellow citizens of New York:

The facts with which I shall deal this evening are mainly old and familiar; nor is there anything new in the general use I shall make of them. If there shall be any novelty, it will be in the mode of presenting the facts, and the inferences and observations following that presentation.

In his speech last autumn, at Columbus, Ohio, as reported in The New York Times, Senator Douglas said:

"Our fathers, when they framed the Government under which we live, understood this question just as well, and even better, than we do now."

I fully indorse this, and I adopt it as a text for this discourse. I so adopt it because it furnishes a precise and an agreed starting point for a discussion between Republicans and that wing of the Democracy headed by Senator Douglas. It simply leaves the inquiry: "What was the understanding those fathers had of the question mentioned?"

What is the frame of government under which we live?

The answer must be: "The Constitution of the United States." That Constitution consists of the original, framed in 1787, (and under which the present government first went into operation,) and twelve subsequently framed amendments, the first ten of which were framed in 1789.

Who were our fathers that framed the Constitution? I suppose the "thirty-nine" who signed the original instrument may be fairly called our fathers who framed that part of the present Government. It is almost exactly true to say they framed it, and it is altogether true to say they fairly represented the opinion and sentiment of the whole nation at that time. Their names, being familiar to nearly all, and accessible to quite all, need not now be repeated.

I take these "thirty-nine," for the present, as being "our fathers who framed the Government under which we live."

What is the question which, according to the text, those fathers understood "just as well, and even better than we do now?"

It is this: Does the proper division of local from federal authority, or anything in the Constitution, forbid our Federal Government to control as to slavery in our Federal Territories?

Upon this, Senator Douglas holds the affirmative, and Republicans the negative. This affirmation and denial form an issue; and this issue—this question—is precisely what the text declares our fathers understood "better than we."

Let us now inquire whether the "thirty-nine," or any of them, ever acted upon this question; and if they did, how they acted upon it—how they expressed that better understanding?

In 1784, three years before the Constitution—the United States then owning the Northwestern Territory, and no other, the Congress of the Confederation had before them the question of prohibiting slavery in that Territory; and four of the "thirty-nine" who afterward framed the Constitution, were in that Congress, and voted on that question. Of these, Roger Sherman, Thomas Mifflin, and Hugh Williamson voted for the prohibition, thus showing that, in their understanding, no line dividing local from federal authority, nor anything else, properly forbade the Federal Government to control as to slavery in federal territory. The other of the four—James M'Henry—voted against the prohibition, showing that, for some cause, he thought it improper to vote for it.

In 1787, still before the Constitution, but while the Convention was in session framing it, and while the Northwestern Territory still was the only territory owned by the United States, the same question of prohibiting slavery in the territory again came before the Congress of the Confederation; and two more of the "thirty-nine" who afterward signed the Constitution, were in that Congress, and voted on the question. They were William Blount and William Few; and they both voted for the prohibition—thus showing that, in their understanding, no line dividing local from federal authority, nor anything else, properly forbids the Federal Government to control as to slavery in Federal territory. This time the prohibition became a law, being part of what is now well known as the Ordinance of '87.

The question of federal control of slavery in the territories, seems not to have been directly before the Convention which framed the original Constitution; and hence it is not recorded that the "thirty-nine," or any of them, while engaged on that instrument, expressed any opinion on that precise question.

In 1789, by the first Congress which sat under the Constitution, an act was passed to enforce the Ordinance of '87, including the prohibition of slavery in the Northwestern Territory. The bill for this act was reported by one of the "thirty-nine," Thomas Fitzsimmons, then a member of the House of Representatives from Pennsylvania. It went through all its stages without a word of opposition, and finally passed both branches without yeas and nays, which is equivalent to a unanimous passage. In this Congress there were sixteen of the thirty-nine fathers who framed the original Constitution. They were John Langdon, Nicholas Gilman, Wm. S. Johnson, Roger Sherman, Robert Morris, Thos. Fitzsimmons, William Few, Abraham Baldwin, Rufus King, William Paterson, George Clymer, Richard Bassett, George Read, Pierce Butler, Daniel Carroll, James Madison.

This shows that, in their understanding, no line dividing local from federal authority, nor anything in the Constitution, properly forbade Congress to prohibit slavery in the federal territory; else both their fidelity to correct principle, and their oath to support the Constitution, would have constrained them to oppose the prohibition.

Again, George Washington, another of the "thirty-nine," was then President of the United States, and, as such approved and signed the bill; thus completing its validity as a law, and thus showing that, in his understanding, no line dividing local from federal authority, nor anything in the Constitution, forbade the Federal Government, to control as to slavery in federal territory.

No great while after the adoption of the original Constitution, North Carolina ceded to the Federal Government the country now constituting the State of Tennessee; and a few years later Georgia ceded that which now constitutes the States of Mississippi and Alabama. In both deeds of cession it was made a condition by the ceding States that the Federal Government should not prohibit slavery in the ceded territory. Besides this, slavery was then actually in the ceded country. Under these circumstances, Congress, on taking charge of these countries, did not absolutely prohibit slavery within them. But they did interfere with it—take control of it—even there, to a certain extent. In 1798, Congress organized the Territory of Mississippi. In the act of organization, they prohibited the bringing of slaves into the Territory, from any place without the United States, by fine, and giving freedom to slaves so bought. This act passed both branches of Congress without yeas and nays. In that Congress were three of the "thirty-nine" who framed the original Constitution. They were John Langdon, George Read and Abraham Baldwin. They all, probably, voted for it. Certainly they would have placed their opposition to it upon record, if, in their understanding, any line dividing local from federal authority, or anything in the Constitution, properly forbade the Federal Government to control as to slavery in federal territory.

In 1803, the Federal Government purchased the Louisiana country. Our former territorial acquisitions came from certain of our own States; but this Louisiana country was acquired from a foreign nation. In 1804, Congress gave a territorial organization to that part of it which now constitutes the State of Louisiana. New Orleans, lying within that part, was an old and comparatively large city. There were other considerable towns and settlements, and slavery was extensively and thoroughly intermingled with the people. Congress did not, in the Territorial Act, prohibit slavery; but they did interfere with it—take control of it—in a more marked and extensive way than they did in the case of Mississippi. The substance of the provision therein made, in relation to slaves, was:

First. That no slave should be imported into the territory from foreign parts.

Second. That no slave should be carried into it who had been imported into the United States since the first day of May, 1798.

Third. That no slave should be carried into it, except by the owner, and for his own use as a settler; the penalty in all the cases being a fine upon the violator of the law, and freedom to the slave.

This act also was passed without yeas and nays. In the Congress which passed it, there were two of the "thirty-nine." They were Abraham Baldwin and Jonathan Dayton. As stated in the case of Mississippi, it is probable they both voted for it. They would not have allowed it to pass without recording their opposition to it, if, in their understanding, it violated either the line properly dividing local from federal authority, or any provision of the Constitution.

In 1819–20, came and passed the Missouri question. Many votes were taken, by yeas and nays, in both branches of Congress, upon the various phases of the general question. Two of the "thirty-nine"—Rufus King and Charles Pinckney— were members of that Congress. Mr. King steadily voted for slavery prohibition and against all compromises, while Mr. Pinckney as steadily voted against slavery prohibition and against all compromises. By this, Mr. King showed that, in his understanding, no line dividing local from federal authority, nor anything in the Constitution, was violated by Congress prohibiting slavery in federal territory; while Mr. Pinckney, by his votes, showed that, in his understanding, there was some sufficient reason for opposing such prohibition in that case.

The cases I have mentioned are the only acts of the "thirty-nine," or of any of them, upon the direct issue, which I have been able to discover.

To enumerate the persons who thus acted, as being four in 1784, two in 1787, seventeen in 1789, three in 1798, two in 1804, and two in 1819–20—there would be thirty of them. But this would be counting John Langdon, Roger Sherman, William Few, Rufus King, and George Read each twice, and Abraham Baldwin, three times. The true number of those of the "thirty-nine" whom I have shown to have acted upon the question, which, by the text, they understood better than we, is twenty-three, leaving sixteen not shown to have acted upon it in any way.

Here, then, we have twenty-three out of our thirty-nine fathers "who framed the government under which we live," who have, upon their official responsibility and their corporal oaths, acted upon the very question which the text affirms they "understood just as well, and even better than we do now;" and twenty-one of them—a clear majority of the whole "thirty-nine"—so acting upon it as to make them guilty of gross political impropriety and willful perjury, if, in their understanding, any proper division between local and federal authority, or anything in the Constitution they had made themselves, and sworn to support, forbade the Federal Government to control as to slavery in the federal territories. Thus the twenty-one acted; and, as actions speak louder than words, so actions, under such responsibility, speak still louder.

Two of the twenty-three voted against Congressional prohibition of slavery in the federal territories, in the instances in which they acted upon the question. But for what reasons they so voted is not known. They may have done so because they thought a proper division of local from federal authority, or some provision or principle of the Constitution, stood in the way; or they may, without any such question, have voted against the prohibition, on what appeared to them to be sufficient grounds of expediency. No one who has sworn to support the Constitution can conscientiously vote for what he understands to be an unconstitutional measure, however expedient he may think it; but one may and ought to vote against a measure which he deems constitutional, if, at the same time, he deems it inexpedient. It, therefore, would be unsafe to set down even the two who voted against the prohibition, as having done so because, in their understanding, any proper division of local from federal authority, or anything in the Constitution, forbade the Federal Government to control as to slavery in federal territory.

The remaining sixteen of the "thirty-nine," so far as I have discovered, have left no record of their understanding upon the direct question of federal control of slavery in the federal territories. But there is much reason to believe that their understanding upon that question would not have appeared different from that of their twenty-three compeers, had it been manifested at all.

For the purpose of adhering rigidly to the text, I have purposely omitted whatever understanding may have been manifested by any person, however distinguished, other than the thirty-nine fathers who framed the original Constitution; and, for the same reason, I have also omitted whatever understanding may have been manifested by any of the "thirty-nine" even, on any other phase of the general question of slavery. If we should look into their acts and declarations on those other phases, as the foreign slave trade, and the morality and policy of slavery generally, it would appear to us that on the direct question of federal control of slavery in federal territories, the sixteen, if they had acted at all, would probably have acted just as the twenty-three did. Among that sixteen were several of the most noted anti-slavery men of those times—as Dr. Franklin, Alexander Hamilton and Gouverneur Morris—while there was not one now known to have been otherwise, unless it may be John Rutledge, of South Carolina.

The sum of the whole is, that of our thirty-nine fathers who framed the original Constitution, twenty-one—a clear majority of the whole—certainly understood that no proper division of local from federal authority, nor any part of the Constitution, forbade the Federal Government to control slavery in the federal territories; while all the rest probably had the same understanding. Such, unquestionably, was the understanding of our fathers who framed the original Constitution; and the text affirms that they understood the question "better than we."

But, so far, I have been considering the understanding of the question manifested by the framers of the original Constitution. In and by the original instrument, a mode was provided for amending it; and, as I have already stated, the present frame of "the Government under which we live" consists of that original, and twelve amendatory articles framed and adopted since. Those who now insist that federal control of slavery in federal territories violates the Constitution, point us to the provisions which they suppose it thus violates; and, as I understand, that all fix upon provisions in these amendatory articles, and not in the original instrument. The Supreme Court, in the Dred Scott case, plant themselves upon the fifth amendment, which provides that no person shall be deprived of "life, liberty or property without due process of law;" while Senator Douglas and his peculiar adherents plant themselves upon the tenth amendment, providing that "the powers not delegated to the United States by the Constitution" "are reserved to the States respectively, or to the people."

Now, it so happens that these amendments were framed by the first Congress which sat under the Constitution—the identical Congress which passed the act already mentioned, enforcing the prohibition of slavery in the Northwestern Territory. Not only was it the same Congress, but they were the identical, same individual men who, at the same session, and at the same time within the session, had under consideration, and in progress toward maturity, these Constitutional amendments, and this act prohibiting slavery in all the territory the nation then owned. The Constitutional amendments were introduced before, and passed after the act enforcing the Ordinance of '87; so that, during the whole pendency of the act to enforce the Ordinance, the Constitutional amendments were also pending.

The seventy-six members of that Congress, including sixteen of the framers of the original Constitution, as before stated, were pre-eminently our fathers who framed that part of "the Government under which we live," which is now claimed as forbidding the Federal Government to control slavery in the federal territories.

Is it not a little presumptuous in any one at this day to affirm that the two things which that Congress deliberately framed, and carried to maturity at the same time, are absolutely inconsistent with each other? And does not such affirmation become impudently absurd when coupled with the other affirmation from the same mouth, that those who did the two things, alleged to be inconsistent, understood whether they really were inconsistent better than we—better than he who affirms that they are inconsistent?

It is surely safe to assume that the thirty-nine framers of the original Constitution, and the seventy-six members of the Congress which framed the amendments thereto, taken together, do certainly include those who may be fairly called "our fathers who framed the Government under which we live." And so assuming, I defy any man to show that any one of them ever, in his whole life, declared that, in his understanding, any proper division of local from federal authority, or any part of the Constitution, forbade the Federal Government to control as to slavery in the federal territories. I go a step further. I defy any one to show that any living man in the whole world ever did, prior to the beginning of the present century, (and I might almost say prior to the beginning of the last half of the present century,) declare that, in his understanding, any proper division of local from federal authority, or any part of the Constitution, forbade the Federal Government to control as to slavery in the federal territories. To those who now so declare, I give, not only "our fathers who framed the Government under which we live," but with them all other living men within the century in which it was framed, among whom to search, and they shall not be able to find the evidence of a single man agreeing with them.

Now, and here, let me guard a little against being misunderstood. I do not mean to say we are bound to follow implicitly in whatever our fathers did. To do so, would be to discard all the lights of current experience—to reject all progress—all improvement. What I do say is, that if we would supplant the opinions and policy of our fathers in any case, we should do so upon evidence so conclusive, and argument so clear, that even their great authority, fairly considered and weighed, cannot stand; and most surely not in a case whereof we ourselves declare they understood the question better than we.

If any man at this day sincerely believes that a proper division of local from federal authority, or any part of the Constitution, forbids the Federal Government to control as to slavery in the federal territories, he is right to say so, and to enforce his position by all truthful evidence and fair argument which he can. But he has no right to mislead others, who have less access to history, and less leisure to study it, into the false belief that "our fathers who framed the Government under which we live" were of the same opinion—thus substituting falsehood and deception for truthful evidence and fair argument. If any man at this day sincerely believes "our fathers who framed the Government under which we live," used and applied principles, in other cases, which ought to have led them to understand that a proper division of local from federal authority or some part of the Constitution, forbids the Federal Government to control as to slavery in the federal territories, he is right to say so. But he should, at the same time, brave the responsibility of declaring that, in his opinion, he understands their principles better than they did themselves; and especially should he not shirk that responsibility by asserting that they "understood the question just as well, and even better, than we do now."

But enough! Let all who believe that "our fathers, who framed the Government under which we live, understood this question just as well, and even better, than we do now," speak as they spoke, and act as they acted upon it. This is all Republicans ask—all Republicans desire—in relation to slavery. As those fathers marked it, so let it be again marked, as an evil not to be extended, but to be tolerated and protected only because of and so far as its actual presence among us makes that toleration and protection a necessity. Let all the guarantees those fathers gave it, be, not grudgingly, but fully and fairly, maintained. For this Republicans contend, and with this, so far as I know or believe, they will be content.

And now, if they would listen—as I suppose they will not—I would address a few words to the Southern people.

I would say to them: You consider yourselves a reasonable and a just people; and I consider that in the general qualities of reason and justice you are not inferior to any other people. Still, when you speak of us Republicans, you do so only to denounce us as reptiles, or, at the best, as no better than outlaws. You will grant a hearing to pirates or murderers, but nothing like it to "Black Republicans." In all your contentions with one another, each of you deems an unconditional condemnation of "Black Republicanism" as the first thing to be attended to. Indeed, such condemnation of us seems to be an indispensable prerequisite—license, so to speak—among you to be admitted or permitted to speak at all. Now, can you, or not, be prevailed upon to pause and to consider whether this is quite just to us, or even to yourselves? Bring forward your charges and specifications, and then be patient long enough to hear us deny or justify.

You say we are sectional. We deny it. That makes an issue; and the burden of proof is upon you. You produce your proof; and what is it? Why, that our party has no existence in your section—gets no votes in your section. The fact is substantially true; but does it prove the issue? If it does, then in case we should, without change of principle, begin to get votes in your section, we should thereby cease to be sectional. You cannot escape this conclusion; and yet, are you willing to abide by it? If you are, you will probably soon find that we have ceased to be sectional, for we shall get votes in your section this very year. You will then begin to discover, as the truth plainly is, that your proof does not touch the issue. The fact that we get no votes in your section, is a fact of your making, and not of ours. And if there be fault in that fact, that fault is primarily yours, and remains until you show that we repel you by some wrong principle or practice. If we do repel you by any wrong principle or practice, the fault is ours; but this brings you to where you ought to have started—to a discussion of the right or wrong of our principle. If our principle, put in practice, would wrong your section for the benefit of ours, or for any other object, then our principle, and we with it, are sectional, and are justly opposed and denounced as such. Meet us, then, on the question of whether our principle, put in practice, would wrong your section; and so meet it as if it were possible that something may be said on our side. Do you accept the challenge? No! Then you really believe that the principle which "our fathers who framed the Government under which we live" thought so clearly right as to adopt it, and indorse it again and again, upon their official oaths, is in fact so clearly wrong as to demand your condemnation without a moment's consideration.

Some of you delight to flaunt in our faces the warning against sectional parties given by Washington in his Farewell Address. Less than eight years before Washington gave that warning, he had, as President of the United States, approved and signed an act of Congress, enforcing the prohibition of slavery in the Northwestern

Territory, which act embodied the policy of the Government upon that subject up to and at the very moment he penned that warning; and about one year after he penned it, he wrote LaFayette that he considered that prohibition a wise measure, expressing in the same connection his hope that we should at some time have a confederacy of free States.

Bearing this in mind, and seeing that sectionalism has since arisen upon this same subject, is that warning a weapon in your hands against us, or in our hands against you? Could Washington himself speak, would he cast the blame of that sectionalism upon us, who sustain his policy, or upon you who repudiate it? We respect that warning of Washington, and we commend it to you, together with his example pointing to the right application of it.

But you say you are conservative—eminently conservative—while we are revolutionary, destructive, or something of the sort. What is conservatism? Is it not adherence to the old and tried, against the new and untried? We stick to, contend for, the identical old policy on the point in controversy which was adopted by "our fathers who framed the Government under which we live;" while you with one accord reject, and scout, and spit upon that old policy, and insist upon substituting something new. True, you disagree among yourselves as to what that substitute shall be. You are divided on new propositions and plans, but you are unanimous in rejecting and denouncing the old policy of the fathers. Some of you are for reviving the foreign slave trade; some for a Congressional Slave-Code for the Territories; some for Congress forbidding the Territories to prohibit Slavery within their limits; some for maintaining Slavery in the Territories through the judiciary; some for the "gur-reat pur-rinciple" that "if one man would enslave another, no third man should object," fantastically called "Popular Sovereignty;" but never a man among you is in favor of federal prohibition of slavery in federal territories, according to the practice of "our fathers who framed the Government under which we live." Not one of all your various plans can show a precedent or an advocate in the century within which our Government originated. Consider, then, whether your claim of conservatism for yourselves, and your charge or destructiveness against us, are based on the most clear and stable foundations.

Again, you say we have made the slavery question more prominent than it formerly was. We deny it. We admit that it is more prominent, but we deny that we made it so. It was not we, but you, who discarded the old policy of the fathers. We resisted, and still resist, your innovation; and thence comes the greater prominence of the question. Would you have that question reduced to its former proportions? Go back to that old policy. What has been will be again, under the same conditions. If you would have the peace of the old times, readopt the precepts and policy of the old times.

You charge that we stir up insurrections among your slaves. We deny it; and what is your proof? Harper's Ferry! John Brown!! John Brown was no Republican; and you have failed to implicate a single Republican in his Harper's Ferry enterprise. If any member of our party is guilty in that matter, you know it or you do not know it. If you do know it, you are inexcusable for not designating the man and proving the fact. If you do not know it, you are inexcusable for asserting it, and especially for persisting in the assertion after you have tried and failed to make the proof. You need to be told that persisting in a charge which one does not know to be true, is simply malicious slander.

Some of you admit that no Republican designedly aided or encouraged the Harper's Ferry affair, but still insist that our doctrines and declarations necessarily lead to such results. We do not believe it. We know we hold to no doctrine, and make no declaration, which were not held to and made by "our fathers who framed the Government under which we live." You never dealt fairly by us in relation to this affair. When it occurred, some important State elections were near at hand, and you were in evident glee with the belief that, by charging the blame upon us, you could get an advantage of us in those elections. The elections came, and your expectations were not quite fulfilled. Every Republican man knew that, as to himself at least, your charge was a slander, and he was not much inclined by it to cast his vote in your favor. Republican doctrines and declarations are accompanied with a continual protest against any interference whatever with your slaves, or with you about your slaves. Surely, this does not encourage them to revolt. True, we do, in common with "our fathers, who framed the Government under which we live," declare our belief that slavery is wrong; but the slaves do not hear us declare even this. For anything we say or do, the slaves would scarcely know there is a Republican party. I believe they would not, in fact, generally know it but for your misrepresentations of us, in their hearing. In your political contests among yourselves, each faction charges the other with sympathy with Black Republicanism; and then, to give point to the charge, defines Black Republicanism to simply be insurrection, blood and thunder among the slaves.

Slave insurrections are no more common now than they were before the Republican party was organized. What induced the Southampton insurrection, twenty-eight years ago, in which, at least three times as many lives were lost as at Harper's Ferry? You can scarcely stretch your very elastic fancy to the conclusion that Southampton was "got up by Black Republicanism." In the present state of things in the United States, I do not think a general, or even a very extensive slave insurrection is possible. The indispensable concert of action cannot be attained. The slaves have no means of rapid communication; nor can incendiary freemen, black or white, supply it. The explosive materials are everywhere in parcels; but there neither are, nor can be supplied, the indispensable connecting trains.

Much is said by Southern people about the affection of slaves for their masters and mistresses; and a part of it, at least, is true. A plot for an uprising could scarcely be devised and communicated to twenty individuals before some one of them, to save the life of a favorite master or mistress, would divulge it. This is the rule; and the slave revolution in Hayti [sic] was not an exception to it, but a case occurring under peculiar circumstances. The gunpowder plot of British history, though not connected with slaves, was more in point. In that case, only about twenty were admitted to the secret; and yet one of them, in his anxiety to save a friend, betrayed the plot to that friend, and, by consequence, averted the calamity. Occasional poisonings from the kitchen, and open or stealthy assassinations in the field, and local revolts extending to a score or so, will continue to occur as the natural results of slavery; but no general insurrection of slaves, as I think, can happen in this country for a long time. Whoever much fears, or much hopes for such an event, will be alike disappointed.

In the language of Mr. Jefferson, uttered many years ago, "It is still in our power to direct the process of emancipation, and deportation, peaceably, and in such slow degrees, as that the evil will wear off insensibly; and their places be, pari passu, filled up by free white laborers. If, on the contrary, it is left to force itself on, human nature must shudder at the prospect held up."

Mr. Jefferson did not mean to say, nor do I, that the power of emancipation is in the Federal Government. He spoke of Virginia; and, as to the power of emancipation, I speak of the slaveholding States only. The Federal Government, however, as we insist, has the power of restraining the extension of the institution—the power to insure that a slave insurrection shall never occur on any American soil which is now free from slavery.

John Brown's effort was peculiar. It was not a slave insurrection. It was an attempt by white men to get up a revolt among slaves, in which the slaves refused to participate. In fact, it was so absurd that the slaves, with all their ignorance, saw plainly enough it could not succeed. That affair, in its philosophy, corresponds with the many attempts, related in history, at the assassination of kings and emperors. An enthusiast broods over the oppression of a people till he fancies himself commissioned by Heaven to liberate them. He ventures the attempt, which ends in little else than his own execution. Orsini's attempt on Louis Napoleon, and John Brown's attempt at Harper's Ferry were, in their philosophy, precisely the same. The eagerness to cast blame on old England in the one case, and on New England in the other, does not disprove the sameness of the two things.

And how much would it avail you, if you could, by the use of John Brown, Helper's Book, and the like, break up the Republican organization? Human action can be modified to some extent, but human nature cannot be changed. There is a judgment and a feeling against slavery in this nation, which cast at least a million and a half of votes. You cannot destroy that judgment and feeling—that senti-ment—by breaking up the political organization which rallies around it. You can scarcely scatter and disperse an army which has been formed into order in the face of your heaviest fire; but if you could, how much would you gain by forcing the sentiment which created it out of the peaceful channel of the ballot-box, into some other channel? What would that other channel probably be? Would the number of John Browns be lessened or enlarged by the operation?

But you will break up the Union rather than submit to a denial of your Consti-tutional rights.

That has a somewhat reckless sound; but it would be palliated, if not fully justi-fied, were we proposing, by the mere force of numbers, to deprive you of some right, plainly written down in the Constitution. But we are proposing no such thing.

When you make these declarations, you have a specific and well-understood allu-sion to an assumed Constitutional right of yours, to take slaves into the federal ter-ritories, and to hold them there as property. But no such right is specifically written in the Constitution. That instrument is literally silent about any such right. We, on the contrary, deny that such a right has any existence in the Constitution, even by implication.

Your purpose, then, plainly stated, is that you will destroy the Government, unless you be allowed to construe and enforce the Constitution as you please, on all points in dispute between you and us. You will rule or ruin in all events.

This, plainly stated, is your language. Perhaps you will say the Supreme Court has decided the disputed Constitutional question in your favor. Not quite so. But waiving the lawyer's distinction between dictum and decision, the Court have decided the question for you in a sort of way. The Court have substantially said, it is your Constitutional right to take slaves into the federal territories, and to hold them there as property. When I say the decision was made in a sort of way, I mean it was made in a divided Court, by a bare majority of the Judges, and they not quite agreeing with one another in the reasons for making it; that it is so made as that its avowed supporters disagree with one another about its meaning, and that it was mainly based upon a mistaken statement of fact—the statement in the opinion that "the right of property in a slave is distinctly and expressly affirmed in the Constitution."

An inspection of the Constitution will show that the right of property in a slave is not "distinctly and expressly affirmed" in it. Bear in mind, the Judges do not pledge their judicial opinion that such right is impliedly affirmed in the Constitution; but they pledge their veracity that it is "distinctly and expressly" affirmed there—"distinctly," that is, not mingled with anything else—"expressly," that is, in words meaning just that, without the aid of any inference, and susceptible of no other meaning.

If they had only pledged their judicial opinion that such right is affirmed in the instrument by implication, it would be open to others to show that neither the word "slave" nor "slavery" is to be found in the Constitution, nor the word "property" even, in any connection with language alluding to the things slave, or slavery; and that wherever in that instrument the slave is alluded to, he is called a "person;"— and wherever his master's legal right in relation to him is alluded to, it is spoken of as "service or labor which may be due,"—as a debt payable in service or labor. Also, it would be open to show, by contemporaneous history, that this mode of alluding to slaves and slavery, instead of speaking of them, was employed on purpose to exclude from the Constitution the idea that there could be property in man.

To show all this, is easy and certain.

When this obvious mistake of the Judges shall be brought to their notice, is it not reasonable to expect that they will withdraw the mistaken statement, and reconsider the conclusion based upon it?

And then it is to be remembered that "our fathers, who framed the Government under which we live"—the men who made the Constitution—decided this same Constitutional question in our favor, long ago—decided it without division among themselves, when making the decision; without division among themselves about the meaning of it after it was made, and, so far as any evidence is left, without basing it upon any mistaken statement of facts.

Under all these circumstances, do you really feel yourselves justified to break up this Government unless such a court decision as yours is, shall be at once submitted to as a conclusive and final rule of political action? But you will not abide the election of a Republican president! In that supposed event, you say, you will destroy the Union; and then, you say, the great crime of having destroyed it will be upon us! That is cool. A highwayman holds a pistol to my ear, and mutters through his teeth, "Stand and deliver, or I shall kill you, and then you will be a murderer!"

To be sure, what the robber demanded of me—my money—was my own; and I had a clear right to keep it; but it was no more my own than my vote is my own; and the threat of death to me, to extort my money, and the threat of destruction to the Union, to extort my vote, can scarcely be distinguished in principle.

A few words now to Republicans. It is exceedingly desirable that all parts of this great Confederacy shall be at peace, and in harmony, one with another. Let us Republicans do our part to have it so. Even though much provoked, let us do nothing through passion and ill temper. Even though the southern people will not so much as listen to us, let us calmly consider their demands, and yield to them if, in our deliberate view of our duty, we possibly can. Judging by all they say and do, and by the subject and nature of their controversy with us, let us determine, if we can, what will satisfy them.

Will they be satisfied if the Territories be unconditionally surrendered to them? We know they will not. In all their present complaints against us, the Territories are scarcely mentioned. Invasions and insurrections are the rage now. Will it satisfy them, if, in the future, we have nothing to do with invasions and insurrections? We know it will not. We so know, because we know we never had anything to do with invasions and insurrections; and yet this total abstaining does not exempt us from the charge and the denunciation.

The question recurs, what will satisfy them? Simply this: We must not only let them alone, but we must somehow, convince them that we do let them alone. This, we know by experience, is no easy task. We have been so trying to convince them from the very beginning of our organization, but with no success. In all our platforms and speeches we have constantly protested our purpose to let them alone; but this has had no tendency to convince them. Alike unavailing to convince them, is the fact that they have never detected a man of us in any attempt to disturb them.

These natural, and apparently adequate means all failing, what will convince them? This, and this only: cease to call slavery wrong, and join them in calling it right. And this must be done thoroughly—done in acts as well as in words. Silence will not be tolerated—we must place ourselves avowedly with them. Senator Douglas' new sedition law must be enacted and enforced, suppressing all declarations that slavery is wrong, whether made in politics, in presses, in pulpits, or in private. We must arrest and return their fugitive slaves with greedy pleasure. We must pull down our Free State constitutions. The whole atmosphere must be disinfected from all taint of opposition to slavery, before they will cease to believe that all their troubles proceed from us.

I am quite aware they do not state their case precisely in this way. Most of them would probably say to us, "Let us alone, do nothing to us, and say what you please about slavery." But we do let them alone—have never disturbed them—so that, after all, it is what we say, which dissatisfies them. They will continue to accuse us of doing, until we cease saying.

I am also aware they have not, as yet, in terms, demanded the overthrow of our Free-State Constitutions. Yet those Constitutions declare the wrong of slavery, with more solemn emphasis, than do all other sayings against it; and when all these other sayings shall have been silenced, the overthrow of these Constitutions will be demanded, and nothing be left to resist the demand. It is nothing to the contrary, that they do not demand the whole of this just now. Demanding what they do, and for the reason they do, they can voluntarily stop nowhere short of this consummation. Holding, as they do, that slavery is morally right, and socially elevating, they cannot cease to demand a full national recognition of it, as a legal right, and a social blessing.

Nor can we justifiably withhold this, on any ground save our conviction that slavery is wrong. If slavery is right, all words, acts, laws, and constitutions against it, are themselves wrong, and should be silenced, and swept away. If it is right, we cannot justly object to its nationality—its universality; if it is wrong, they cannot justly insist upon its extension—its enlargement. All they ask, we could readily grant, if we thought slavery right; all we ask, they could as readily grant, if they thought it wrong. Their thinking it right, and our thinking it wrong, is the precise fact upon which depends the whole controversy. Thinking it right, as they do, they are not to blame for desiring its full recognition, as being right; but, thinking it wrong, as we do, can we yield to them? Can we cast our votes with their view, and against our own? In view of our moral, social, and political responsibilities, can we do this?

Wrong as we think slavery is, we can yet afford to let it alone where it is, because that much is due to the necessity arising from its actual presence in the nation; but can we, while our votes will prevent it, allow it to spread into the National Territories, and to overrun us here in these Free States? If our sense of duty forbids this, then let us stand by our duty, fearlessly and effectively. Let us be diverted by none of those sophistical contrivances wherewith we are so industriously plied and belabored—contrivances such as groping for some middle ground between the right and the wrong, vain as the search for a man who should be neither a living man nor a dead man—such as a policy of "don't care" on a question about which all true men do care—such as Union appeals beseeching true Union men to yield to Disunionists, reversing the divine rule, and calling, not the sinners, but the righteous to repentance—such as invocations to Washington, imploring men to unsay what Washington said, and undo what Washington did.

Neither let us be slandered from our duty by false accusations against us, nor frightened from it by menaces of destruction to the Government nor of dungeons to ourselves. LET US HAVE FAITH THAT RIGHT MAKES MIGHT, AND IN THAT FAITH, LET US, TO THE END, DARE TO DO OUR DUTY AS WE UNDERSTAND IT.

Emancipation Proclamation

By the President of the United States of America:

A Proclamation.

Whereas, on the twenty-second day of September, in the year of our Lord one thousand eight hundred and sixty-two, a proclamation was issued by the President of the United States, containing, among other things, the following, to wit:

"That on the first day of January, in the year of our Lord one thousand eight hundred and sixty-three, all persons held as slaves within any State or designated part of a State, the people whereof shall then be in rebellion against the United States, shall be then, thenceforward, and forever free; and the Executive Government of the United States, including the military and naval authority thereof, will recognize and maintain the freedom of such persons, and will do no act or acts to repress such persons, or any of them, in any efforts they may make for their actual freedom.

"That the Executive will, on the first day of January aforesaid, by proclamation, designate the States and parts of States, if any, in which the people thereof, respectively, shall then be in rebellion against the United States; and the fact that any State, or the people thereof, shall on that day be, in good faith, represented in the Congress of the United States by members chosen thereto at elections wherein a majority of the qualified voters of such State shall have participated, shall, in the absence of strong countervailing testimony, be deemed conclusive evidence that such State, and the people thereof, are not then in rebellion against the United States."

Now, therefore I, Abraham Lincoln, President of the United States, by virtue of the power in me vested as Commander-in-Chief, of the Army and Navy of the United States in time of actual armed rebellion against the authority and government of the United States, and as a fit and necessary war measure for suppressing said rebellion, do, on this first day of January, in the year of our Lord one thousand eight hundred and sixty-three, and in accordance with my purpose so to do publicly proclaimed for the full period of one hundred days, from the day first above mentioned, order and designate as the States and parts of States wherein the people thereof respectively, are this day in rebellion against the United States, the following, to wit:

Arkansas, Texas, Louisiana, (except the Parishes of St. Bernard, Plaquemines, Jefferson, St. John, St. Charles, St. James Ascension, Assumption, Terrebonne, Lafourche, St. Mary, St. Martin, and Orleans, including the City of New Orleans) Mississippi, Alabama, Florida, Georgia, South Carolina, North Carolina, and Virginia, (except the forty-eight counties designated as West Virginia, and also the counties of Berkley, Accomac, Northampton, Elizabeth City, York, Princess Ann, and Norfolk, including the cities of Norfolk and Portsmouth), and which excepted parts, are for the present, left precisely as if this proclamation were not issued.

And by virtue of the power, and for the purpose aforesaid, I do order and declare that all persons held as slaves within said designated States, and parts of States, are, and henceforward shall be free; and that the Executive government of the United States, including the military and naval authorities thereof, will recognize and maintain the freedom of said persons.

And I hereby enjoin upon the people so declared to be free to abstain from all violence, unless in necessary self-defence; and I recommend to them that, in all cases when allowed, they labor faithfully for reasonable wages.

And I further declare and make known, that such persons of suitable condition, will be received into the armed service of the United States to garrison forts, positions, stations, and other places, and to man vessels of all sorts in said service.

And upon this act, sincerely believed to be an act of justice, warranted by the Constitution, upon military necessity, I invoke the considerate judgment of mankind, and the gracious favor of Almighty God.

In witness whereof, I have hereunto set my hand and caused the seal of the United States to be affixed.

Done at the City of Washington, this first day of January, in the year of our Lord one thousand eight hundred and sixty three, and of the Independence of the United States of America the eighty-seventh.

By the President: ABRAHAM LINCOLN

WILLIAM H. SEWARD, Secretary of State.

The Hodges Letter

Executive Mansion, Washington, April 4, 1864.

A.G. Hodges, Esq Frankfort, Ky.

My dear Sir: You ask me to put in writing the substance of what I verbally said the other day, in your presence, to Governor Bramlette and Senator Dixon. It was about as follows:

"I am naturally anti-slavery. If slavery is not wrong, nothing is wrong. I can not remember when I did not so think, and feel. And yet I have never understood that the Presidency conferred upon me an unrestricted right to act officially upon this judgment and feeling. It was in the oath I took that I would, to the best of my ability, preserve, protect, and defend the Constitution of the United States. I could not take the office without taking the oath. Nor was it my view that I might take an oath to get power, and break the oath in using the power. I understood, too, that in ordinary civil administration this oath even forbade me to practically indulge my primary abstract judgment on the moral question of slavery. I had publicly declared this many times, and in many ways. And I aver that, to this day, I have done no official act in mere deference to my abstract judgment and feeling on slavery. I did understand however, that my oath to preserve the constitution to the best of my ability, imposed upon me the duty of preserving, by every indispensable means, that government—that nation—of which that constitution was the organic law. Was it possible to lose the nation, and yet preserve the constitution? By general law life and limb must be protected; yet often a limb must be amputated to save a life; but a life is never wisely given to save a limb. I felt that measures, otherwise unconstitutional, might become lawful, by becoming

indispensable to the preservation of the constitution, through the preservation of the nation. Right or wrong, I assumed this ground, and now avow it. I could not feel that, to the best of my ability, I had even tried to preserve the constitution, if, to save slavery, or any minor matter, I should permit the wreck of government, country, and Constitution all together. When, early in the war, Gen. Fremont attempted military emancipation, I forbade it, because I did not then think it an indispensable necessity. When a little later, Gen. Cameron, then Secretary of War, suggested the arming of the blacks, I objected, because I did not yet think it an indispensable necessity. When, still later, Gen. Hunter attempted military emancipation, I again forbade it, because I did not yet think the indispensable necessity had come. When, in March, and May, and July 1862 I made earnest, and successive appeals to the border states to favor compensated emancipation, I believed the indispensable necessity for military emancipation, and arming the blacks would come, unless averted by that measure. They declined the proposition; and I was, in my best judgment, driven to the alternative of either surrendering the Union, and with it, the Constitution, or of laying strong hand upon the colored element. I chose the latter. In choosing it, I hoped for greater gain than loss; but of this, I was not entirely confident. More than a year of trial now shows no loss by it in our foreign relations, none in our home popular sentiment, none in our white military force,—no loss by it any how or any where. On the contrary, it shows a gain of quite a hundred and thirty thousand soldiers, seamen, and laborers. These are palpable facts, about which, as facts, there can be no caviling. We have the men; and we could not have had them without the measure.

["]And now let any Union man who complains of the measure, test himself by writing down in one line that he is for subduing the rebellion by force of arms; and in the next, that he is for taking these hundred and thirty thousand men from the Union side, and placing them where they would be but for the measure he condemns. If he can not face his case so stated, it is only because he can not face the truth.["]

I add a word which was not in the verbal conversation. In telling this tale I attempt no compliment to my own sagacity. I claim not to have controlled events, but confess plainly that events have controlled me. Now, at the end of three years struggle the nation's condition is not what either party, or any man devised, or expected. God alone can claim it. Whither it is tending seems plain. If God now wills the removal of a great wrong, and wills also that we of the North as well as you of the South, shall pay fairly for our complicity in that wrong, impartial history will find therein new cause to attest and revere the justice and goodness of God. Yours truly,

A. Lincoln

Index

233

ABOUT THE AUTHOR

Arthur Rizer holds a J.D. from Gonzaga University, where he graduated Magna Cum Laude, and an LL.M. from Georgetown University Law Center with distinction. He lives with his family in Northern Virginia and works as an Adjunct Professor of Law at Georgetown University's Law Center. Professor Rizer also works as a trial attorney with the U.S. Department of Justice, Criminal Division. Other positions held in the Department include: trial attorney on DOJ's Guantanamo Bay Litigation Team, Federal Prosecutor in the Southern District of California (SAUSA), trial attorney with the Office of Immigration Litigation-District Court Section, and Attorney Advisor with the Board of Immigration Appeals. Professor Rizer started his legal career as a federal judicial law clerk in the Middle District of Pennsylvania. Before attending law school he served in the U.S. Army as an Armor and Military Police officer, where he is currently serving in the Army Reserves. As a soldier, Professor Rizer deployed to Fallujah, Iraq, and helped train the Iraqi Army to fight the insurgency. Before law school, he worked as a police officer for the city of Cheney, Washington. The views in this book are not those of the Department of Justice, the Georgetown Law Center, or the U.S. Army.

Professor Rizer has several publications: *The Gulf Spill and 9/11: The National Security Threat of Energy Dependence: A Call for a Nuclear Renaissance, Harvard National Security Journal; Dog Fight: Did the International Battle Over Airline Passenger Name Records Enable the Christmas Day Bomber?, Catholic Law Review; The*

National Security Implications of Human Trafficking, Widener Law Review; The Filibuster of Judicial Nominations: Constitutional Crisis or Politics as Usual?, Pepperdine Law Review; Mandatory Arrest: Do We Need to Take a Closer Look?, Univ. of West Las Angles Law Review; Prosecutors: The "Other" Defenders of the Constitution, The Prosecutor Magazine; Does True Conservatism Equal Anti-Death Penalty?, Howard Scroll Social Justice Law Review; Gun Control: Targeting Rationality in a Loaded Debate, Kansas Journal of Law and Public Policy; and *The Race Effect on Wrongful Convictions, William Mitchell Law Review.*